Between Care and Criminality

The Politics of Marriage and Gender:
Global Issues in Local Contexts

Series Editor: Péter Berta

The Politics of Marriage and Gender: Global Issues in Local Context series from Rutgers University Press fills a gap in research by examining the politics of marriage and related practices, ideologies, and interpretations, and addresses the key question of how the politics of marriage has affected social, cultural, and political processes, relations, and boundaries. The series looks at the complex relationships between the politics of marriage and gender, ethnic, national, religious, racial, and class identities, and analyzes how these relationships contribute to the development and management of social and political differences, inequalities, and conflicts.

For a list of all the titles in the series, please see the last page of the book.

Between Care and Criminality

Marriage, Citizenship, and Family in Australian Social Welfare

HELENA ZEWERI

RUTGERS UNIVERSITY PRESS

NEW BRUNSWICK, CAMDEN, AND NEWARK, NEW JERSEY

LONDON AND OXFORD

Rutgers University Press is a department of Rutgers, The State University of New Jersey, one of the leading public research universities in the nation. By publishing worldwide, it furthers the University's mission of dedication to excellence in teaching, scholarship, research, and clinical care.

LIBRARY OF CONGRESS CATALOGING-IN-PUBLICATION DATA

Names: Zeweri, Helena, author.
Title: Between care and criminality : marriage, citizenship, and family in Australian social welfare / Helena Zeweri.
Description: New Brunswick : Rutgers University Press, [2023] | Series: Politics of marriage and gender: global issues in local contexts | Includes bibliographical references and index.
Identifiers: LCCN 2023016203 | ISBN 9781978829022 (paperback) | ISBN 9781978829039 (hardcover) | ISBN 9781978829046 (epub) | ISBN 9781978829053 (pdf)
Subjects: LCSH: Forced marriage—Australia. | Islamic marriage customs and rites—Australia | Muslims—Australia—Social conditions. | Citizenship—Australia.
Classification: LCC HQ706 .Z49 2023 | DDC 306.840994—dc23/eng/20230421
LC record available at https://lccn.loc.gov/2023016203

A British Cataloging-in-Publication record for this book is available from the British Library.

Copyright © 2024 by Helena Zeweri

All rights reserved

No part of this book may be reproduced or utilized in any form or by any means, electronic or mechanical, or by any information storage and retrieval system, without written permission from the publisher. Please contact Rutgers University Press, 106 Somerset Street, New Brunswick, NJ 08901. The only exception to this prohibition is "fair use" as defined by U.S. copyright law.

References to internet websites (URLs) were accurate at the time of writing. Neither the author nor Rutgers University Press is responsible for URLs that may have expired or changed since the manuscript was prepared.

⊚ The paper used in this publication meets the requirements of the American National Standard for Information Sciences—Permanence of Paper for Printed Library Materials, ANSI Z39.48-1992.

rutgersuniversitypress.org

To Samia

CONTENTS

Series Foreword by Péter Berta   ix

	Introduction: An Emergent Regime of Truth	1
1	A Genealogy of Forced Marriage Prevention	36
2	The Threat of Suffering: Configuring Victimhood in Forced Marriage Scenario Planning	65
3	Reluctant Disclosure: Epistemic Doubt and Ethical Dilemmas in Prevention Work	89
4	Phantom Figures: The Erasures of Biopolitical Narratives	102
5	Beyond Criminality: Narratives of Familial Duress in Times of Displacement	124
	Conclusion: Reflections on the Coercive State	153

Acknowledgments   165
Notes   171
References   183
Index   205

SERIES FOREWORD

The politics of marriage (and divorce) is an often-used strategic tool in various social, cultural, economic, and political identity projects as well as in symbolic conflicts between ethnic, national, or religious communities. Despite having multiple strategic applicabilities, pervasiveness in everyday life, and huge significance in performing and managing identities, the politics of marriage is surprisingly underrepresented both in the international book publishing market and the social sciences.

The Politics of Marriage and Gender: Global Issues in Local Contexts is a series from Rutgers University Press examining the politics of marriage as a phenomenon embedded into and intensely interacting with much broader social, cultural, economic, and political processes and practices such as globalization; transnationalization; international migration; human trafficking; vertical social mobility; the creation of symbolic boundaries between ethnic populations, nations, religious denominations, or classes; family formation; or struggles for women's and children's rights. The series primarily aims to analyze practices, ideologies, and interpretations related to the politics of marriage, and to outline the dynamics and diversity of relatedness—interplay and interdependence, for instance—between the politics of marriage and the broader processes and practices mentioned above. In other words, most books in the series devote special attention to how the politics of marriage and these processes and practices mutually shape and explain each other.

The series concentrates on, among other things, the complex relationships between the politics of marriage and gender, ethnic, national, religious, racial, and class identities globally, and examines how these relationships contribute to the development and management of social, cultural, and political differences, inequalities, and conflicts.

The series seeks to publish single-authored books and edited volumes that develop a gap-filling and thought-provoking critical perspective, that are well balanced between a high degree of theoretical sophistication and empirical richness, and that cross or rethink disciplinary, methodological, or theoretical boundaries. The thematic scope of the series is intentionally left broad to encourage creative submissions that fit within the perspectives outlined above.

Among the potential topics closely connected with the problem sensitivity of the series are "honor"-based violence; arranged (forced, child, etc.) marriage;

transnational marriage markets, migration, and brokerage; intersections of marriage and religion/class/race; the politics of agency and power within marriage; reconfiguration of family: same-sex marriage/union; the politics of love, intimacy, and desire; marriage and multicultural families; the (religious, legal, etc.) politics of divorce; the causes, forms, and consequences of polygamy in contemporary societies; sport marriage; refusing marriage; and so forth.

Based on fourteen months of anthropological fieldwork in Melbourne, Australia, *Between Care and Criminality: Marriage, Citizenship, and Family in Australian Social Welfare* documents and analyzes the formation and implementation of a 2013 law that federally criminalized the practice of forced marriage—interpreting it as dangerous and harmful to immigrant communities and as a national moral crisis. In this thought-provoking ethnographic study, Zeweri insightfully demonstrates how ideologies and strategies of institutionalized care and criminalization can be subtly intertwined in the contexts of the social welfare system and legislation in Australia. *Between Care and Criminality* shows, in a nuanced way, why and how public and professional discourses on marital practices of Muslim immigrants became a highly contested field where ideas of care, well-being, good citizenship, and cultural sensitivity, as well as Islamophobia and the racialized nature of the Australian criminal justice system shape each other. Zeweri not only highlights the reasons and motivations behind the formation of the law, but she investigates, in an exemplary way, the complex system of its impacts (and of the related national prevention strategy) on family life and relations in Muslim communities, on the activity of immigrant community leaders, and on the social welfare system and practitioners in Australia.

> Péter Berta
> University College London,
> School of Slavonic and
> East European Studies /
> Budapest Business School,
> Department of
> Communication

Between Care and Criminality

Introduction

An Emergent Regime of Truth

Configuring Violence

This book is about how violence is made an object of knowledge. More specifically, it is about how violence is identified, thought about, and explained by those who work in social welfare and the people they help. The questions that guide this book are: How and why do social policies seek to intervene in violence? What other kinds of violence do they ignore and produce in the process? How do social welfare practitioners come to know the people they are trying to help and the problem they are trying to solve? What does it mean to undertake this responsibility in a settler colonial society that has long used care, concern, and even empowerment as pretenses for policing and criminalization?

THE PARTICIPANTS LOOKED AT EACH OTHER in awkward silence as they sat around conjoined desks in a classroom in Dandenong, a suburb forty minutes southeast of Melbourne, Australia. The community workers had just begun their training on preventing forced marriage.[1]

As part of the training, the workers had read a scenario about a father who had given his daughter an ultimatum that if she did not marry the spouse he had found for her, he would pull her out of secondary school.[2] The parents were Afghan, and they had recently resettled in Australia as refugees. The daughter was an Australian-born citizen. The community workers expressed their disapproval of the father's actions. One noted that the parents were being manipulative. A participant interjected that the father's intentions were selfish in that he was orchestrating the marriage to be relieved of pressure from his friends and family. Another added that the parents' approach was a result of their lack of education, unlike the community workers at the training. A third person noted that in certain culturally sanctioned belief systems, girls are seen as familial burdens who need to be married off. Lori, the training facilitator, began to look uneasy.[3] There was something unsettling about the rapidity with which a moral consensus was forming around the scenario. Explanations for the parents' motivations were sedimenting one on top of the other, quickly being converted into moral judgments about the family. Lori had long been struggling with how to ensure that communities were not demonized within forced marriage prevention training material. In our previous conversations, Lori had often wondered how prevention trainings could rehumanize parents who tended to be depicted as villains and unfit parents, while also acknowledging the power and control to which they subjected their children. Lori took a deep breath and perched her head down. With a sense of skeptical anticipation, she looked up and made the following statement, highly aware of its weight and the moral dilemmas it might evoke for the participants: "From the perspective of this project, let's come from the point of view that the parent could be given the benefit of the doubt as a way of engaging with them, and not pushing them away. We should not excuse the violence. But when we work with the person, can we think the best of them? We don't ignore violence, *but we get closer to it.*"

Get closer to the violence. This phrase gave me pause and has come to haunt my thinking about forced marriage prevention work. It is the phrase around which this book is organized. I realized that Lori's call to *get closer to the violence* was a response to two things. First, in the context of the training, it was a call to avoid profiling parents who coerced their children into marriage as socially deviant. Lori's call to the audience also reflected a question she had been contemplating for a long time: was government policy really committed to understanding how and why forced marriage occurred as it tried to develop more culturally sensitive prevention approaches vis-à-vis Muslim migrant communities, whom the state deemed most at risk of this practice? In previous conversations, Lori had expressed that the Australian government's approach to forced marriage prevention was overly shaped by a criminal justice response focused more on defining criminality and identifying perpetrators than understanding the many structural factors that made marriage an option for parents in the first place. Secondly then, for Lori, *getting closer to the violence* would mean understanding the conditions under which parents and extended kin considered these decisions prudent. It would mean entertaining the possibility that they were not the byproduct of any essential notion of migrant culture, but were produced by the ongoing consequences of war, displacement, and resettlement in a new country, including economic precarity, fragmented kin relations, and a lack of belonging. As I spent more time with Lori and the forced marriage prevention sector, including a select number of victims and survivors, I realized that, for me, as an anthropologist, *getting closer to the violence* meant the following: a) ceasing to make rapid moral judgments that treat forced marriage as a cultural practice that migrants import from their home countries; and b) seriously considering the role of structural violence in producing situations of forced marriage. This book is a study of how social welfare attempts to do both, how and why it falls short, and what lessons this offers for undertaking migrant-targeted care with more understanding and empathy.

By ethnographically examining a social policy designed to prevent forced marriage, this book shows how an epistemology of violence is created in Australia, a place that prides itself on culturally sensitive social welfare but is haunted by ongoing anxieties about the importation of "strange" migrant cultural practices. More specifically, the book explores the work of those tasked with identifying, assessing, and making recognizable a category of violence known today in global human rights discourse and domestic policy as "forced marriage." In doing so, the book not only attends to victim/survivor experiences of violence but also focuses on practitioner experiences of generating a system of knowledge about violence prevention.[4] Doing so shows how differently situated people come to know violence differently and that cultural sensitivity and community-led work do not, on their own, offer easy or foolproof frameworks to address violence.

Since 2013, when the law making forced marriage a federal crime passed in Australia, forced marriage prevention has disproportionately targeted recently resettled Muslim migrant communities. Housed under the Australian Criminal Code's "Slavery and Slavery-Like Practices" section, the law stated: "A marriage is a forced marriage if one party to the marriage (the victim) entered into the marriage without freely and fully consenting: (a) because of the use of coercion, threat, or deception; or (b) because the party was incapable of understanding the nature and effect of the marriage ceremony" (Crimes Legislation Amendment 2013, sec. 270.7A). The law caused shockwaves across migrant communities primarily because of its harsh prison sentences. It carried a maximum penalty of nine years imprisonment and twenty-five years for an aggravated offense (which meant taking an individual under the age of eighteen overseas for the marriage). For the social welfare sector, forced marriage was a fairly new term. Those who were familiar with it had previously heard it referenced in the context of human rights abuses in the global South and developing countries. A common refrain I heard in prevention sector meetings was, "I can't believe something like forced marriage could happen in Australia." Thus, forced marriage entered the public consciousness as a long-established category of violence associated with the "developing" or "underdeveloped" world that was foreign to Australia but somehow found its way into its borders.[5]

I define forced marriage prevention, in the Australian context, as a set of interlocking social welfare, policing, and advocacy practices which continue to be contested and reimagined. In other words, practitioners are still in the process of figuring out what makes someone at risk, how to know when coercion into marriage has occurred, and what care for victims/survivors looks like within and outside a criminal justice framework. Forced marriage is a category of violence born out of global feminist and human rights movements that, historically, are connected to the global violence against women movement and the movement to protect children's rights. However, the term "forced marriage" is highly critiqued because it relies on a consent/coercion binary that assumes that all people either freely choose who and how they marry or that their choices are fully determined for them, which fails to consider how people's choices are shaped by many variables in a given situation. In addition, it tends to be discussed within global human rights discourse in relation to postcolonial and racialized societies in South Asia, the Middle East, and parts of East Africa. As many scholars have written, the term tends to function less to denote the complexities of specific situations of violence, and more as a catch-all phrase to diagnose a range of interpersonal relations and structural vulnerabilities. In doing so, the term has historically created false distinctions between the global South as a site of constraint, individual subjugation, and social coercion, and the global North as a bastion of freedom, personal autonomy, and consent (Pardy 2012; Patton 2018; Razack 2004). At the same time, it is important to acknowledge that the term is used by advocates from migrant communities when referring to situations of marriage that reflect undeniably coercive situations.

Rather than dispense with the term all together, in this book, I use the term "forced marriage" primarily when explaining its history and when referring to it as an object of policy and advocacy discussions. I use the phrase "coercion into marriage" when analyzing the different layers of pressure felt by the people I interviewed regarding marriage-related decisions. While "coercion" is not an ideal alternative to "forced marriage," the word is flexible enough to encompass a range of pressures and forms of duress that cut across interpersonal relations and structural factors. By refusing the self-evident nature of forced marriage, I treat it as an "engaged universalism," to borrow a concept from cultural anthropologist Anna Tsing (2005). An engaged universalism is a concept that is ubiquitously used, which gives the impression that its definition is universally agreed upon. However, in different contexts (especially policy contexts) the same concept can mean different things to different stakeholders who engage with and are impacted by it in different ways. This is certainly the case with forced marriage. As my fieldwork illustrated, not only do different societies define it differently, but even within a given society, what kinds of power relations count as a forced marriage is an object of debate among practitioners.[6] Additionally, the scales at which forced marriage operates as a threat are different for policymakers who see it as a threat to the nation versus for victims and survivors who experience the violence at a deeply intimate level.

Another term I use in this book is "violence." There is a difference between the usage of this term within the forced marriage prevention sector and the way I use it in my analysis. I use violence to describe the state's treatment of migrants which, as I will demonstrate in the next chapter, is tied to technologies of state-sanctioned violence against Indigenous communities. I also use violence to describe situations of coercion that individuals have experienced at the hands of their family members through speaking with those individuals themselves, rather than through secondary accounts, such as advocacy and policy reports. Cultural Anthropology allows me to understand the different scales at which violence operates in these situations, whereas secondary reports published by state-funded organizations (local and federal) already have clear cut demarcations on why a familial interaction is violent. These demarcations tend to remain in the personal and intimate domains and rarely consider public and structural factors. In this way, I seek to open up what is considered violent about situations of forced marriage that include, but go beyond, interpersonal relations and any static notion of culture. Veena Das (2008, 284) discusses the importance of not policing the definition of violence, but to look at how *it* is being policed: "Sometimes one feels that there is a kind of definitional vertigo in the deployment of the term violence, yet there is merit in the idea that the contests around the question of what can be named as violence are themselves a sign of something important at stake." Similarly, I ask: how do different stakeholders try to define coercion into marriage as violent and what is at stake for the Australian state to create a whole apparatus dedicated to this effort? As I illustrate in this book, while coercive relations within families reflect interpersonal violence, they also reflect structural violence—the enduring effects of war, displacement, and building a new life in Australia.

In this book, I ethnographically examine forced marriage prevention in Australia from 2015 to 2017. I begin from the premise that forced marriage prevention is a biopolitical project in that it is presented to the public as rooted in a concern for the well-being of not only victims (potential and actual) but also of the general Australian population. In other words, forced marriage is not only presented in policy language as harmful to those who would be married but as a threat to Australian national security as well as social and cultural values. Prevention efforts tend to focus on a specific sector of society—recently arrived migrants who have fled ongoing war and civil conflict in the Middle East and South Asia and who identify as Muslim. I examine how this biopolitical project is constituted by historical forms of policing, long-held colonial social welfare practices, and cultural competency frameworks, which themselves are paradoxically shaped by deeply othering attitudes toward migrants from the Muslim world. While most practitioners I interacted with genuinely attempted to develop a multi-scalar and holistic understanding of the life stories of victims/survivors, much of the training, conclusions, and premises the prevention sector works with produces partial truths (Clifford 1986), figurations, and essentialisms about such individuals.[7] In taking Lori's call *to get closer to the violence* seriously, this book attends to how those tasked with carrying out emergent violence prevention social policy produce "truths" about the people they are helping. It examines the ethical dilemmas they confront in doing so, and the possibilities and limitations of contesting those truths. Finally, the book examines how migrant women themselves explain violence in their families in ways that include, but also go well beyond, the events and interactions that surround a marital event.

The overarching argument of this book is twofold. First, forced marriage prevention is a migrant-targeted biopolitical project that is shaped by the state's concerns around the consequences of Muslim migration on Australian "social values," which itself is a fiction premised on colonial imaginaries of the consenting subject. While prevention involves the criminal justice and immigration systems, the social welfare system is a particularly critical node in producing knowledge about the kinds of intimate interactions and power relations that signal an imminent forced marriage. The epistemology of violence it produces unfolds in the classrooms of training workshops and in everyday conversations between practitioners, and it is one that increasingly sees coercive family relationships as a threat to Australian borders. Second, practitioners and Muslim migrant women contest such epistemologies in ways that both identify the neo-coloniality of the policy while also uncovering the multiple layers of violence that shape their lived experiences.

The first layer of this book's argument explores the epistemic assumptions of forced marriage as a biopolitical project—namely, how it renders migrant lives knowable. In that sense, forced marriage prevention is a truth regime in the making. Michel Foucault's (1976, 112–113) definition of a "truth regime" reflects how I position the forced marriage prevention apparatus—not only as a form of intervention into people's lives through the social welfare-juridical system, but also as a knowledge-building apparatus. According to Foucault, a truth regime connotes: "(1) The types of discourse [society] harbours and causes to function as true; (2) the mechanisms and instances which enable one to distinguish true from false statements; (3) the way in which each is sanctioned; (4) the techniques and procedures which are valorised for obtaining truth; and (5) the status of those who are charged with saying what counts as true. . . . Truth is a system of ordered procedures for the production, regulation, distribution, circulation and functioning of statements."

I posit that during the period of my fieldwork, forced marriage prevention was an emergent truth regime because: there were contestations and debates between caseworkers, migrant community leaders, and victims/survivors within the realms of discourse, evidence, and verity (how to know that the problem at stake was pervasive enough to require government intervention); how to know when coercion happened; what motivated families to organize such marriages; when was there enough evidence for state and federal police to investigate a report of forced marriage; what aspects of victim/survivor experiences different practitioners should have access to; and to what extent one case would be reflective of a larger, society-wide problem. I found that forced marriage prevention combines practices in family violence and human trafficking prevention with the praxis of cultural competence to construct a corpus of knowledge about Muslim migrants' intimate kin relations in the name of "wanting to know migrant communities better." Such knowledge, however, is not invested in understanding the everyday lives of migrants, but in creating profiles of risk and potential criminality. Foucault's idea of *dispositif* (1977b) is a helpful concept in explaining how such knowledge-gathering practices bring together the criminal justice system's and social welfare's seemingly disconnected logics of risk assessment, disclosure, and evidence-gathering. The tactics by which this prevention *dispositif* identifies the individual's risk of coercion within a broader cultural milieu reflects what anthropologist Reva Jaffe-Walter (2015, 7) calls contemporary "technologies of concern" around Muslim migrant communities. Technologies of concern differ from overt uses of state power because they are "anonymous, multiple, pale, colorless," and harder to identify. However, it is precisely within technologies of concern that we can locate how communities are constructed by the state and social welfare as "problems to manage." In the prevention sector, social welfare practitioners are not simply messengers of state policy. While their specific initiatives are funded by a range of federal government departments and state departments, such as the Victoria Department of Health and Human Services, case workers and case managers (who are part of the direct service sector) often have a certain level of autonomy in how they interpret the guidelines of such government-funded programs. With a policy as new as the forced marriage one, direct service providers found themselves with an unusual amount of flexibility in terms of how they developed risk assessment profiles and scenario trainings. By "studying up" (Nader 1972; Gusterson 1997) and focusing on the everyday experiences of practitioners, this book offers a sense of the ethical and political complexities of different domains of expertise and institutions (Cabot 2019) in the prevention sector, as well as the effects they may have on the marginalized (Green 1972). Anthropological analyses can see how policies are "fluid sites of political contestation" and "the power relations and interactions of parties to a policy process" (Wedel et al. 2005, 1).

The second layer of this book's argument explores how practitioners and migrant women grapple with and contest the policy's epistemic assumptions by offering alternative ways of thinking about intervention and reframing narratives of violence. More specifically, practitioners do not easily accept the assumptions the policy asks them to make about the kinds of familial interactions that make someone at risk, especially in school settings—key frontiers for prevention work. They actively discuss when cultural sensitivity becomes cultural essentialization and profiling. Migrant women also contest the ways in which social welfare deploys cultural essentialism to withhold or undertake interventions that render victims/survivors as passive and unable to reconstruct their familial relations in ways they feel genuinely support the collective and individual futures they want to create.

Australian Anxieties around Migration

As I will lay out in greater detail in the next chapter, state anxieties around forced marriage have their origins in settler colonial forms of social engineering. However, over the last twenty years and in the wake of the Global War on Terror and the mass displacement it has caused, forced marriage has come to be seen by the state as a problem caused by the mass importation of "strange" cultural practices by refugees. It has been mobilized as one of many reasons the state should adopt more punitive and deterrence-based immigration policies. This section provides a sense of how Australia's approaches to refugee acceptance in recent decades have become increasingly punitive since the War on Terror, especially in relation to maritime (or "boat") arrivals seeking asylum. Boat arrivals, which primarily reflect asylum seekers from Afghanistan, Iran, Sri Lanka, and Iraq, are key targets of Australia's deterrence and punitive border policies because they have been constructed as "national security" threats and "non-vetted" migrants.

Australia has been a site of war-related migration since the beginning of World War I (1914). However, its concern with maritime arrivals became intensified at the end of the Vietnam War (1975). From 1975 to 2015, Australia resettled 276,739 refugees through its offshore program (refugees who were registered with the United Nations High Commissioner for Refugees, or UNHCR; Karlsen 2016).[8] However, Australia's intake of globally displaced peoples is low compared to other countries. According to the *UNHCR Global Trends: Forced Displacement in 2021* (2022) report, 27.1 million people have been externally displaced and are under UNHCR's mandate and 4.6 million people are seeking asylum. The top ten hosting countries for both registered refugees and people displaced across borders does not include Australia or any countries in the global North. As of the 2021 statistics, Australia has also not made the top ten countries that resettle the greatest number of refugees. In 2021, Australia ranked fifteenth among countries that resettle refugees compared to their populations (Refugee Council of Australia 2022a). Australia's intake of refugees through its offshore humanitarian program (refugees registered with the UNHCR) and onshore humanitarian program (migrants already in Australia seeking asylum) has maintained an average of about 12,000 refugees per year since the mid-1980s, compared to about 28,000 for Canada and 23,000 in the United States in 2018 (Radford and Connor 2019).

Australia's policies toward asylum seekers attempting to enter Australia via boat took a dramatic shift at the start of the Global War on Terror (GWOT). The GWOT has resulted in the displacement of thirty-seven million people since it began in 2001 (Vine et al. 2020). While the number of asylum seekers attempting to arrive in Australia via boat was already on the decline in the early 2000s at the start of the war, Australia's immigration policies became increasingly militarized and focused on deterrence. Since 2001, maritime boat arrivals have totaled 2,357 compared to 3,054 from 1980–2000 (Refugee Council of Australia 2022c). However, in a post-9/11 global landscape with Islamophobia and xenophobia on the rise, Australia began to increasingly militarize its borders and attempt to deter migration. From 2012 to 2019, maritime arrivals were put in offshore detention centers on the islands of Manus in Papua New Guinea and the Republic of Nauru. In addition, approximately 283,230 refugees were resettled in Australia during this period (Refugee Council of Australia 2022b). Many of the migrant community leaders and women I spoke with had immediate and extended family who were detained for years in offshore detention, making this period a particularly difficult one when it came to the preservation of family relations. Upon return, young people were reunited with their fathers (as mostly single men were detained on

Manus), and sometimes the pressure they felt to say yes to their marriage proposals resulted from years of separation. Saying yes to marriage was a way to communicate that one supported one's parent and to avoid further estrangement. It was in this global and national context of global displacement, detention, and familial fragmentation that the forced marriage policy came into being.

Local Demographics

In this book, I focus on social welfare providers and the communities they service in the state of Victoria, in the context of Melbourne and its suburbs, including Dandenong, Narre Warren, Roxburgh Park, Morwell, Shepparton, and Noble Park. These suburbs have become key spots of resettlement for refugees from the Middle East and South Asia over the past two decades. While this book is not about the everyday lives of recently resettled Afghan refugees in Australia, many of the individual community members I spoke with fled Afghanistan as refugees in the late 1990s, during the reign of the Taliban, and between 2001 and 2013, during the first half of the U.S./NATO-led military intervention. Thus, many though not all of the stories featured in this book reflect a historically distinct experience of displacement borne out of multiple civil and global wars. However, Afghan migration in the twentieth century goes back to the 1980s when a small number of Afghans were resettled in Australia following the beginning of the Afghan-Soviet War (1979–1989), and estimates put it at 1,000 people during the early 1990s (Victoria Museum of Immigration 2017). According to the 2016 census (Victoria State Government 2016), 87 percent of the Afghan population has arrived in Australia since 1996 following the rise of the Taliban and the subsequent U.S./NATO intervention (most of this group migrated in the ten-year period between 2006 and 2015; Evason 2023). According to the 2016 census, there are approximately 46,800 people who were born in Afghanistan living in Australia. However, this number is poised to increase with the August 2021 displacement of people after the second Taliban takeover. From 2011 to 2016, the Afghan-born population in the state of Victoria also increased from 9,945 to 18,124. More specifically, Narre Warren, Dandenong, and Noble Park are ranked as part of the top two areas where the Afghan-born population lives in Victoria as of 2016 and increasingly comprises Afghans from the Hazara ethnic background, a minoritized group which has experienced a long history of persecution in Afghanistan and has created a culturally and politically active presence in Australia. Shepparton, Sunshine West, and Roxburgh Park were also places where much educational work was occurring and are ranked at three, five, and six for this community (Victoria State Government 2016). These cities constitute where a majority of my conversations with the women in chapter 5 took place, and where policing and educational resources were focused since 2013. These suburbs are places where people build community and find social acceptance but also spaces that are highly policed and surveilled. For example, they have been sites of new initiatives around Countering Religious Extremism, community policing initiatives between Islamic religious leadership and state police, and the emergence of Multicultural Liaison Officers (MCLOs). MCLOs are tasked with working to address family violence and forced marriage through a culturally appropriate framework which includes speaking the same language and observing certain social etiquettes and customs when interacting with families from different regions. One MCLO I interviewed, who had recently quit his job in Broadmeadows, noted that MCLOs could try and de-escalate domestic violence and family violence situations because families were more willing to welcome them into the home. However, there is an ongoing conversation within community organizations serving migrant and refugee populations about how much MCLOs can really do to support communities outside of the juridical domain, namely families who did not want to pursue a criminal justice or civil approach to family or domestic violence besides providing alternative resources.

Logics of Domestic and Transnational Border Control

While forced marriage prevention was implemented at the local level, it was aimed toward transnational concerns. At the local level, the law sought to intervene in marriages conducted within Australia in which young adult women and, in some cases, people under eighteen were being married through religious ceremonies within people's homes. Parents and extended kin were depicted by policymakers and media reports as bad citizens, unwilling to assimilate to Australian culture or values around personal autonomy, choice, and marriage as consensual. The 2013 law was founded on the idea that it would prompt migrant communities to become more law-abiding. Studies have shown how laws and policies function to declare what counts as "antisocial" immigrant behavior in the name of preserving state interests, thereby defining what counts as "illegal" and "criminal" behavior (Coutin 2000; De Genova 2002; Harrison and Lloyd 2012; Inda and Dowling 2013; Menjívar and Kanstroom 2013). Such definitions function to naturalize migrants as existing in a state of criminality and illegality, rather than seriously considering the many variables that drive their choices. This book builds on this literature, showing how migrant-targeted social welfare becomes the new frontier where migrant criminality is produced. In contrast to contemporary border policies which associate illegality with crossing borders, social welfare approaches associate illegality with how migrants conduct their intimate familial relationships both within and beyond Australia's borders.

At the transnational level, the 2013 law also sought to intervene in situations in which an Australian-born adult woman (typically) would be taken by her parents overseas to their home country to be married through a religious ceremony. Upon return to Australia, she would be asked to sponsor the person's application for a spousal visa to migrate to Australia. The goal with such cases on the part of the Australian Federal Police (AFP) and the Department of Foreign Affairs and Trade (DFAT) was to both ensure the victim would be returned to Australia and

FORCED MARRIAGE

Forced Marriage: SAFETY PLAN

What is forced marriage?

Making someone get married when they don't want to is never acceptable and is a crime in Australia. A 'forced marriage' happens when somebody gets married without freely and fully consenting, because they have been coerced, threatened or deceived, or when they aren't able to understand the meaning and consequences of getting married. Anybody can be a victim of a forced marriage, regardless of their age, gender, sexual orientation or religious or cultural background. You can find more information about forced marriage online at <www.ag.gov.au/forcedmarriage> or at <www.mybluesky.org.au>.

What does freely and fully consenting mean?

Freely and fully consenting means that a person wants to get married and is able to choose if, who and when they marry. The table below explains what free and full consent means.

Free and full consent is:	Free and full consent is not:
• choosing to marry because you feel you are ready to marry	• agreeing to marry because of the threat or use of force or coercion against yourself or others, including physical or sexual violence
• choosing to marry because you wish to marry	• agreeing to marry because you are being unlawfully detained or held against your will
• choosing to marry because you want to marry your potential spouse	• agreeing to marry because of emotional or psychological pressure, including not wanting to cause shame to your family
• choosing to marry because you *understand* what getting married means and how it will affect your life	• agreeing to marry out of obedience to somebody in a position of trust or authority such as your parents or grandparents
• being able to choose not to marry without fear of the consequences for yourself, and	• agreeing to marry because that is what other people in your culture or community expect
• being able to choose not to marry without fear of the consequences to others.	• agreeing to marry because you are being financially abused (for example, your wages, money for everyday things like food, or other forms of support are being withheld)
	• agreeing to marry because of other forms of coercion, including blackmail or somebody withholding important documentation from you, such as your passport, or
	• agreeing to marry when you have been tricked or deceived about the proposed marriage.

Free and full consent cannot be given by somebody who is unable to understand what they are consenting to. This means that some people cannot give valid consent to marriage because of their age or intellectual capacity.

FIGURE 1 Forced Marriage information sheet circulated to direct service providers following the law's passage that distinguishes between a consensual and coerced marriage (Australian Attorney-General's Department).

that any spousal visa application would be canceled. Ultimately, social welfare's role was to produce knowledge about how to spot someone at risk of being taken overseas, to report such cases, and to encourage other public servants like educators to learn about the signs and report them to the federal authorities. The state's anxieties over not only overseas marriages but also the transnational relationships that recent migrant communities maintain with their countries of origin thus became objects of knowledge and concern.[9] Much literature has examined how migrant transnational mobility between the global North and the Middle East and South Asia have become visible national security problems that require more militarized, surveillance-heavy forms of border control, especially after 9/11 (Andersson 2018; 2014; Bermant 2017; De Genova 2017; Gerard and Pickering 2014; Kampmark 2017; Mountz 2011; 2015; Scheel 2017; 2018). This book focuses on how migrants' intimate familial relations portend forms of transnational mobility that may result in unwanted migrants entering the borders of the nation-state. In that sense, social welfare is an importation domain to examine how transnational connections between migrants become objects of risk assessment and profiling.[10]

Preventing a "Hidden" Problem

The justification for the 2013 Amendment to Australia's *1995 Criminal Code*, which made forced marriage a federal crime, was primarily based on anecdotal evidence consisting of news stories of young Muslim Australian citizen girls being forcibly taken abroad to their parents' home countries to marry cousins or older male family members. According to the National Children's Youth Law Centre's (NCYLC; 2013) report on Forced Marriage in Australia, between 2011 and 2013, eight cases were identified by criminal investigators out of 103 referrals made to the AFP as forced marriages.[11] According to advocate Laura Vidal (2018, 4), anecdotal reports from direct service organizations show that reported cases tend to involve females between sixteen and twenty-one as the main demographic bracket.[12] However, overall there were a lack of comprehensive statistics when the amendment was first proposed, resulting in Parliamentarians citing select news stories which emphasized that the practice was happening in the borders of Australia.[13]

Despite the lack of robust data on the problem's social prevalence (especially given the fact that not all referrals were investigated), policymakers insisted that the lack of disclosures themselves was an indication of a problem that required criminal intervention. For example, Nicola Roxon, the Member of Parliament (MP) who proposed the forced marriage amendment, noted that the lack of clarity around forced marriage was, in fact, more reason for the law to be implemented. She noted, "It's already underground. It's not common in Australia, but the long-term consequences are devastating" (*Parliamentary Debates* 2012). For Roxon, a small number of cases marked the beginning of the erosion of Australian social values. In 2014, Victoria Police Superintendent Rod Journing also noted in an *ABC*

News article, "We know it's grossly under-reported." Several reports advocating for either criminal or civil protections related to forced marriage written from 2012 to today continue to point to the nonexistence of comprehensive statistics on the prevalence of the practice (Australian Red Cross 2019; Burn 2013; Centre for Multicultural Youth 2016; Vidal 2016; Wilton 2015).[14] A recent paper on forced marriage has noted: "In 2019, the Australian Institute of Criminology published a small study on forced marriage, noting that data is difficult to obtain for reasons that include the hesitation of victims to report to police, and the hidden nature of forced marriage, which requires someone in the marriage or situation, or someone close to them, to be able to identify that consent to marry is not present" (Vidal 2020). While studies have shown the ways in which statistics are employed as mechanisms of governmentality and population control (Foucault 1977b; Rose 1998; Stevenson 2014), less has been written about how the nonexistence of statistics also function to make policy efficacious. In the case of Australian forced marriage prevention, it is the nonexistence of statistics and demographic data that make forced marriage even more real as a social problem to be managed. In forced marriage network meetings, a key debate between community leaders and social welfare practitioners was whether communities knew the practice was wrong, which often turned into a conversation about the extent to which it was reported. Practitioners would often say that communities know it is happening. Community leaders would respond that this may be so, but communities do not know that it is unlawful. Rendering it unlawful was seen as a means to make the practice more visible to migrant communities and to activate behavioral reforms among them.

As a biopolitical project, forced marriage is unique in that it has been deemed a hidden problem, yet the magnitude of this problem at the population level remains unclear. While there are statistics around the number of reported and investigated cases, there remain zero prosecutions. While people have reported coercion into marriage, this does not reflect the actual number of legitimate cases. What does it mean to create a federal law and a policy based on little empirically verifiable data? For policymakers, forced marriage exists but constantly must be rendered knowable in the absence of both statistical data and prosecutions. In making a problem around which there is little empirical and statistical data or legal precedents visible through emphasizing its "hiddenness," social welfare functions to activate a set of anxieties among frontline workers about Muslim migrants as threatening subjects. This "hiddenness," however, is not experienced as an empty signifier. For practitioners, calling the problem "hidden" activates in their audiences a range of racialized and gendered tropes about migrants from the Muslim world as deviant figures who engage in non-normative forms of domestic familial relations. To call the problem of forced marriage "hidden" is to activate latent affective responses among frontline workers that render migrants' intimate familial relations as excessively coercive and transnational, and which could ultimately result in undesirable patterns of migration to the nation-state. Examining the prevention education phase of this policy shows how the "truth" of migrant illegality is cemented at the point where longstanding imaginaries of Muslim migrants meet newly securitized configurations of social welfare.

In that sense, the law itself, which made it a crime to both coerce someone into a marriage and to be party to a forced marriage aimed to deter a public and social threat whose full contours had not yet been identified, but were, in its isolated occurrences, sufficient to warrant an expansive legal and policy response. This prompts the question: what is the work of understanding and identifying "a hidden crisis"? Forced marriage prevention and criminalization, then, is a window into understanding how a social problem is pre-emptively identified and constructed at the same time.

In the contemporary world, pre-emptive logics are present within the domains of war, border security, and biosecurity interventions (Collier and Lakoff 2008a; Massumi 2016).[15] The logic of pre-emption finds iterations within contemporary border regimes and domestic forms of policing, as documented and analyzed by Harsha Walia. Walia (2021, 56) discusses interdiction as a form of pre-emptive apprehension of migrants in both the Australian and European contexts. She also notes that the pre-emptive logics of the Global War on Terror find expression as "permanent and omni-present structures of control" that reinforce the same racial logics within the U.S. nation-state. For example, the Counterintelligence Program (COINTELPRO) also gets reconfigured as a counterterrorism body that pre-emptively focuses on Black and Brown communities now reframed not only as anti-American but potential terror threats. Analogous programs in Australia include Countering Violent Extremism, which have disproportionately focused on scrutinizing the teachings and behaviors of teachers, faith leaders, social workers, and family members from a Muslim background. Other examples of pre-emptive biopolitical projects include airport security apparatuses, surveillance mechanisms at airports, scenario planning in military exercises, and biosecurity interventions.

Pre-emptive biopolitical projects base their object of intervention and social control not on the past but on projections of the plausible future, where the fear of the "exceptional event" organizes action moving forward (Adey 2009; Amoore 2006; Dillon and Lobo-Guerrero 2008; Massumi 2016). As Mary Douglas and Aaron Wildavsky (1982) have written in characterizing contemporary liberal democracies' strategies for managing different "risks" to the population, the hierarchy of potential threats or dangers in the "risk portfolio" of individuals, groups, or cultures at a given moment is rarely related to their actual probabilities of inflicting injury. The work of risk assessment is a technology of knowledge which seeks to identify the plausibility of a narrative by constructing a profile of the potentially threatening subject (Spene and Murray 1999, 488) and the harm they may inflict. Colleen Bell (2006, 160) writes that in biopolitical projects centered around security, subjects are "accounted for on the basis of behavioural potentialities, rather than on the basis of how they have actually acted." Profiling, then, is pre-emptive in that it calls into being and attempts to avert imaginaries of a possible future whose plausibility is not based on documented past occurrences or events; rather, it is based on the future, in which the exceptional event becomes feared as the norm. Thus, non-pre-emptive biopolitical projects take their cues from past events and occurrences the state does not want reproduced, whereas pre-emptive biopolitical projects produce the specificities of the future occurrences they seek to prevent as identifiable.

In this book, I seek to understand how pre-emptive logics operate in the more benign and oft-overlooked space of social welfare that is tasked with identifying a phenomenon that has not yet been established as a social problem. However, I ask: what kind of knowledge is created in a space where there is a consensus that forced marriage is a hidden social problem? This question is a window into a broader anthropological concern of this analysis: how social policy produces knowledge about its objects of intervention in real time and how it creates the substance of a category of violence after it has declared its existence as a social problem and attempts to prevent it.

Muslim Women and the Logic of Rescue

The idea of the suffering Muslim woman in the global South who needs to be saved by the global North through militarized humanitarianism is a legacy of longstanding colonial technologies of power and colonial forms of knowledge. These were resuscitated with new life after 9/11 in the United States, Australia, and other places in the West seeking to execute a range of imperial projects in Afghanistan in 2001 and Iraq in 2003 (Abu-Lughod 2013; cooke 2007; Grewal 2013; Khan 1998; Mohanty 1988; Naber 2012). When it comes to Muslim women immigrants in the global North, as literature in feminist and gender studies as well as global studies have shown, immigration and border policies have functioned to extend longstanding savior narratives about such women. These include systems that expect Muslim women to perform their identities as subjugated by their cultures in order to access asylum and visas (Razack 1995; 2008; Ticktin 2008; 2011) as well as government-run assimilation programs that center proper comportment as a precondition for full inclusion into the nation-state (Bloemraad et al. 2008; Carpi 2017; Jaffe-Walter 2015; Korteweg and Triadafilopoulos 2013). They also include laws that ban forms of dress such as the hijab in public in the name of the host country's commitment to liberty and freedom (Eid 2015; Fernando 2014; Laborde 2008; Winter 2008). Other pieces have examined how assimilationist programs function to govern Muslim women's dress and comportment in the work place (Aziz 2014; 2015) and within social welfare (Ahmad and Sheriff 2001; Husain and O'Brien 1999), as well as in programs geared toward economic inclusion (Fozdar 2014). Other literature has shown that Muslim women are often hailed by religious deradicalization programs as allies in the domestic arms of the Global War on Terror in terms of helping Muslim men move away from religious extremism (Barlas 2002; Scott 2010; Shehabuddin 2014; Terrio 2010; Tohidi 2007). As noted by Australian scholars Nahid Kabir

(2015) and Sameena Yasmeen (2007), Islamophobic discourse has been distinctly racialized and gendered in how it frames the victims of Islamic misogyny and who is responsible for Islamic society's reformation.

In this book, by turning attention to the everyday implementation of an emergent social policy targeted toward Muslim migrant women, I show how their private relationships are rendered not only things to be saved but things that can predict the nation-state's permeability to future Muslim migrants. While forced marriage prevention certainly seeks to "save" Muslim migrant women from their "oppressive" family members (as shown in chapters 3 and 4), during the period in which I examined this emerging policy, another key focus for prevention was Muslim migrant women's familial relationships in terms of what they signal about the vulnerability of Australian borders and, by extension, social values. Literature has shown how Muslim women's oppression becomes the point of departure for states to stoke public fears about the emergence of parallel migrant interior societies in which "alien" ways of life exist, where concepts like consent, freedom, and women's rights are not respected (El-Tayeb 2013; Lenneis and Agergaard 2018; Yurdakul and Korteweg 2013). I seek to bring attention to how the fear of an emergence of a parallel society is thought about in everyday policy conversations. I conclude that forced marriage prevention portrays Muslim women as "in need of saving" because they are seen as subjects who are prone to "hidden" and "underground" forms of violence, one of which is coercion into marriage, which is seen as signaling a whole host of other "hidden violences" that threaten the Australian social fabric. The state's anxiety around this "hiddenness" finds expression in the call to have prevention work develop standardized and portable forms of knowledge that focus on "knowing migrant women better" which is framed as culturally competent but often becomes culturally essentialist.

The Politics of Cultural Relativism

To conduct an ethnography of forced marriage that decenters a cultural explanation is not to refuse a moral stance on certain configurations of coercion into marriage. As the book shows, the everyday work of prevention is not as focused on extreme stories of young girls being taken overseas to be married to older people, extended family or not. However, these are the stories that tended to stir up moral outrage about the practice. It is clear that such stories are tragic and the committal of such acts morally wrong and require a robust and holistic support apparatus for victims/survivors. One can say this and claim, as I do, that current approaches, including the foundational logics that construct migrants as social problems, require critical reflection. In saying this, we can also question the logic of carceral feminism that views accountability for victims/survivors of gender-based violence as rooted in a criminal justice response that ignores the violences produced within such carceral systems which interlock with other systems of oppression, including sexual violence, racialized discrimination, and deportation (Bernstein 2010; Goodmark 2023; Kim 2018; Taylor 2018).

Here, I am inspired by Maree Pardy's (2012, 142–143) analysis of feminism as marked by both critique and responsibility. Pardy writes: "Notwithstanding the convincing critique of the ethnocentric nature of judgements by feminists around forced marriage, it remains untenable for feminists to refuse to judge; feminism, by definition, is a project that demands political judgement. Is it possible to respond to violence against women without sliding into arguments about forced marriage as evidence of cultural backwardness? How do we develop critical judging practices through a frame of feminist responsibility?" For Pardy, one can critically reflect on forced marriage as a set of violences while being critical of contemporary frameworks used to analyze such violence. Pardy (2012, 154) continues that: "Responsibility calls for judgement and decision, but it is always experimental and provisional. There is no end to it." For Pardy, acting responsibly is not the same as taking responsibility for another, and thus is not invested in removing the subject's agency. To act responsibly is to refuse biopolitical demands for quick, definitive, and final solutions that can be scaled up or standardized. As such, it also refuses a quick diagnosis of the forms of injustice that are at stake for feminist practice and thought. I take Pardy's approach seriously and believe that analyzing prevention work around gender-based violence must be iterative—it is constantly being worked out by those most affected by it and those who seek to support them in some way. This book is one part of this ongoing process of trying to make sense of what we cannot deny and attempts to address it. At the same time, it is not a definitive study of what the problem of coercion into marriage is and what is to be done. This analysis is situated in a particular moment in time and may run its course in terms of utility or explanation after a certain period of time. Like most social science analyses, it is not a temporally or spatially transcendent form of knowledge. Rather, this book seeks to provide some insight which may be of interest to social welfare practitioners who are open to reflecting critically on their work around gender-based violence with migrant communities and scholars who are open to thinking about issues of borders, migration, and cultural competence through an anthropological framework that takes the violence of coercion into marriage seriously.

Here, it is important to note how my own positionality plays a role in this analysis. The anthropologist is, like anyone, an intersectional subject and their analysis is refracted through their life experiences. What social dynamics they pay attention to over others, the questions they ask, and how they interpret their findings are not only shaped by the scholarship they read, but also by the systems, environments, and structures (including the moral frameworks) they have lived within. Growing up in a close-knit Afghan Muslim diasporic community in New York, I have witnessed people coerced in explicit and subtle ways into marriages at a variety of ages, from adolescence to adulthood. I am comfortable saying that, in many instances, this was morally wrong and unjust in that it deprived individuals (mostly women but also men) from exploring the capacity of their human potential and their ability to carve out their own sense of purpose. In addition to the impact on individual identity, such marriages disrupted people's relationships with their family members and communities, making it difficult to feel a part of a larger community which in other instances and moments were sources of joy, empowerment, care, and love. Family members became estranged, grew apart, and resentment sedimented over time. Yet, looking back, I would not explain these instances simply as situations in which morally depraved people who were "stuck" within rigid cultural frameworks inflicted harm that was worthy of a carceral response.

An anthropological perspective has afforded me the ability to explain such decisions that I witnessed in my own community through a much more nuanced and layered framework. It is anthropology's dedication to understanding the everyday as well as its interaction with feminist theory and migration studies that affords new ways to explain these decisions. Anthropology also affords me the ability to see coercion into marriage as a problem that, viewed from the perspective of structural violence, does not only affect Muslim migrant communities. If we think about coercion into long-term relationships (of the life-long kind) as tied to considerations of economic security or citizenship, then who else in our lives are pulled into relationships in which the weight of the future is always a concern? Here, I do not mean to imply that all relationships organized around insecurities of different kinds are qualitatively the same. Lifelong intimate and partner-based relationships are of a particular kind, but such relationship configurations often do not hinge on pure choice, pure love, or pure desire. I invite the reader to be open to unsettling the common sense that coercion can be reduced to a set of orders, demands, and expectations orchestrated by one's family in any linear fashion. Rather, I seek to show that coercion operates at multiple scales that work simultaneously to make marriage an option in select situations, which produces additional violences.

Humanitarian Reason: The Suffering Subject as a Threat to the Nation

Humanitarian reason is a form of governance and, thus, an intervention into human suffering based on the deployment of moral sentiment (Fassin 2012, 1). Humanitarian reason is not simply a mode of intervening into spaces in which lives are literally on the line; it is also a mode of distinguishing what counts as suffering that is worthy of intervention.[16] While much literature has examined how humanitarian reason constructs victimhood (Chouliaraki and Zaborowski 2017; De La Concha 2017; Fassin and Rechtman 2009), less has explored how projects of humanitarian governance view threat in relation to victimhood. If humanitarian reason constructs how particular lives matter to the state and what they represent, then what do victims represent to the state? In this book, I will show (particularly through chapter 2), how representations (specifically, scenarios that develop profiles of a typical or hypothetical victim) in forced marriage prevention construct the suffering subject as the threatening subject simultaneously. I show that the potential victim of forced marriage is viewed as an embodiment of an imminent threat to national sovereignty—namely the state's jurisdiction over acceptable forms of entry into and familial relations within the nation-state. In doing so, I posit that humanitarian reason's "politics of precarious lives" (Fassin 2012, 4) is not only interested in determining suffering but also in determining threats to the polity more broadly. According to Robert Samet (2019), conceptualizations of the suffering subject in Anthropology have not been exhausted, contrary to claims otherwise (Robbins 2013). A question that still needs research regarding the suffering subject in regimes of care is: to what extent is humanitarian government as much about a politics of suffering lives as it is a politics of threatening lives?

Contesting Social Policy

This book also intervenes in anthropological studies of social policy and begins with the question: what is the work of creating knowledge about the problem a policy seeks to intervene in? It begins from the premise that policy is not apolitical and neutral. Policies, despite claiming rationality and neutrality, should be understood as shaped by structures of power which can be rooted in political and ideological agendas. Within biopolitical regimes, policy is invested in the ongoing classification of human beings and human behavior as normative and nonnormative which function to regulate what kinds of behavior require what modes of power, control, and discipline (Wedel et al. 2005, 37). As Wedel et al. write, "It is not that policy dictates the behavior of its target population but rather that it imposes an ideal type of what a 'normal' citizen should be." While state-sanctioned policies define norms, they are not always neatly executed.

By focusing on the work of executing policy rather than primarily on its social impact, I will show how the problems policies intervene in are being defined in real time rather than examine how effectively the interventions that are crafted around them function, especially in contexts that take a more pre-emptive stance toward governing migrant populations.[17] In highlighting the productive power of policy, this book shows how policy produces the contours of the problem that it aims to intervene in (Shore and Wright 2003). As Junaid Rana (2011, 1) writes, "A policy finds expression through a sequence of events; it creates new social and semantic spaces, new sets of relations, new political subjects, and new webs of meaning."

This book also shows how policy processes exceed the intentions of those who execute them. As Wedel and others (2005, 2) have written, "by focusing on players . . . and on the interactions in which parties to the policy process engage, anthropological analysis can disentangle the outcomes that can help explain how and why they often contradict the stated intentions of policymakers." In this book,

I focus less on the outcomes and more on how people participate in a policy process whose premises are still being worked out. For example, in chapter 3, I show how practitioners are questioning and grappling with each other's views on culture and minoritization as well as with the state-sanctioned policies they are acting in the name of. Doing so offers a zoomed-in view of how policy production occurs in less strategic and consensual ways than we might imagine (Lea 2020, 85).

Culturally Competent Social Welfare

Understanding how policies are formed in real time is urgent in a context where sensibilities to culture not only shape the tools of response but also play a role in defining the causes of family violence itself. Cultural competence, despite originally being designed to better accommodate and serve Indigenous communities, has ended up essentializing and homogenizing their ways of life, reproducing binaries that further "other" Indigenous communities in relation to White Anglo communities (Hollinsworth 2012, 33). Other scholars of social work and medicine have argued that cultural competence frameworks do not actually consider how individuals interact and engage with their cultural communities but rather treat cultural knowledge as a static body of information (Dreher and MacNaughton 2002; Jenks 2011; Johnson and Munch 2009; Laird and Tedam 2019; Santiago-Irizarry 2001; Shaw 2005). In Australia, the question of what it means to enact culturally competent social welfare remains contested. This book examines how culture is used to make sense of, explain, and put into focus the moment, nature, and cause of coercion into marriage. It explores how coercion is rendered knowable through a cultural explanation and how such a mode of knowing is routinely contested and, in some cases, rejected.

For over thirty years, hundreds of social service organizations have emerged with the sole purpose of providing culturally sensitive services to victims of family violence in the name of holistic and tailored support. Cultural competence has many definitions, but one that is particularly applicable in this context is proposed by Tom Calma, who, in 2006, was the national race discrimination commissioner and Aboriginal and Torres Strait Islander social justice commissioner in Australia:

> Cultural competence is defined as a set of congruent behaviours, attitudes, and policies that come together in a system, agency, or among professionals and enables that system, agency, or those professionals to work effectively in cross–cultural situations. Further, cultural competence is the willingness and ability of a system to value the importance of culture in the delivery of services to all segments of the population. It is the use of a systems perspective which values differences and is responsive to diversity at all levels of an organization, i.e., policy, governance, administrative, workforce, provider, and consumer / client (Calma 2006).

According to Calma, cultural competence is a potential antidote to the indirect forms of discrimination a range of communities including Indigenous, migrant, and newly arrived refugees could confront that are not currently addressed as unlawful in Australia's Racial Discrimination Act of 1975. This landmark piece of legislation prohibits: "a person to do any act involving a distinction, exclusion, restriction or preference based on race, colour, descent or national or ethnic origin which has the purpose or effect of nullifying or impairing the recognition, enjoyment, or exercise, on an equal footing, of any human right or fundamental freedom in the political, economic, social, cultural, or any other field of public life" (Racial Discrimination Act 1975). Calma argues that the section, "purpose or effect of nullifying" allows institutions to undertake cultural competency measures to account for the many indirect ways that people could be discriminated against. This includes dismissing their cultural identities, which Calma does not explicitly define, but it is usually limited to language, social etiquette in client interactions, and understanding a community's relationship to social institutions historically. In refugee and migrant-targeted social welfare literature, culturally competent approaches were developed to comply with the Anti-Discrimination Act (1977) in the wake of the codification of multiculturalism as a guide for social welfare work in the 1970s. Culture in these spaces is not defined universally with each agency having its own specific definition. In one framework proposed by the Service for the Treatment and Rehabilitation of Torture and Trauma Survivors (STARTTS), the definition of culture includes the following components: language (verbal and nonverbal); classifications based on age and gender; family and kin relations through marriage; conceptions of sexuality and its regulation; rituals; morality and ethics; and power and hierarchy (STARTTS 2015).[18] However, such definitions of culture are not particularly effective at accounting for cultural transformation, especially in terms of views on how to establish social and community relations. It is worth considering how the conception of culture as static and insulated contributes to its treatment of migrants as simply importing certain worldviews to Australia.

While forced marriage prevention continues to rely on this bounded definition of culture, it is also concerned with how "culture travels"—namely how migrants' transnational connections to their home countries matter to how they conduct their lives in Australia. Ethnographically examining forced marriage prevention is a window into understanding how "transnational culture" becomes an object of pre-emptive biopolitical policies. What does it look like to situate the individual as at risk of a "cultural practice" that is seen to travel across borders? Forced marriage prevention, then, not only provides linguistic and social support to victims from different countries of origin; it reconfigures how migrants' countries of origin matter in prevention. Migrants' origin countries are seen as the source of behaviors that are antithetical to Australian values. Culture becomes both something to be accommodated but also something that can produce and import morally suspect behavior. To the state, this difference is static and intrinsic, while to some practitioners, like Lori and others in the prevention sector, this difference is fluid and conditioned by the disorientations, economic precarities, ongoing traumas, and displacements of forced migration.

Research has shown how state-sanctioned multiculturalism has made marginalized groups visible with the caveat that they must adhere to certain expectations around how they present their cultural identities publicly (Appiah 1994; Gutmann 1994) Other ethnographies have shown how juridical spaces that adjudicate claims by Indigenous groups require them to perform their cultural identity in ways that do not reflect the complexity of their relationship to land and group membership (Hale 2002; Povinelli 2002). This ceiling to multiculturalism's politics of recognition reflects how the state continues to mobilize existing settler colonial logics of recognition that fail to take people's modes of creating sociality seriously (Asad 2003; Brown 1995; De la Cadena 2010; Giordano 2014).

Producing Family Relations as "Deviant"

Intimacy is of utmost concern to the state, including how it happens, where it happens, and between whom it happens (Berlant and Warner 1998; Canaday 2009; Povinelli 2006). While intimacy has tended to be spatialized within the domestic sphere, it is always of public concern and is policed in both the public and private spheres. In colonial contexts, for colonial administrators in emerging European empires, for example, the emotional investment and commitments that colonized peoples demonstrated toward their blood kin versus the family to which they may have been assigned to do domestic work were sources of existential anxiety and subject to surveillance (Stoler 1995; 2010; Stoler and Strassler 2000). Knowing the social and political implications of people's intimate relations in terms of their allegiance to national values is not limited to monitoring the relationship between colonizer and colonized. In settler colonial contexts, how the governing regime could know the intimate family relations of Indigenous populations has been inextricably linked with the state's own existential concerns around how to maintain its power. This has taken new forms in contemporary settler colonial Australia in the wake of demographic shifts through increased migration from the Muslim world (Dastyari and O'Sullivan 2016; Elder 2016; Gouda 2008; Phillips 2009; Stanley 2016).

Intimacy is difficult to define, especially given its conflation with the private sphere. However, the definition provided by Nicole Constable (2009, 29) best captures the relational dynamic in question: "The term 'intimate relations' refers here to social relationships that are—or give the impression of being—physically and/ or emotionally close, personal, sexually intimate, private, caring, or loving. Such relationships are not necessarily associated with or limited to the domestic sphere, but discourses about intimacy are often intertwined with ideas about gender and domesticity, gifts as opposed to markets." In this definition, intimacy is not spatially confined but constitutes an intersubjective relation bound up in affects of care and love. At the same time, this definition of intimacy is also rife with power relations that reflect gendered constructions of space and sociality. Liberalism for example works with the premise that the intimate relations of private personhood cannot appear as "matter out of place" (Berlant and Warner 1998). Despite intimacy's relegation to the private sphere, it continues to be governed as a matter that has bearing on public issues of national importance. Intimate relationships, whether between immediate and extended family or marital partners, become seen as indicative of the state of social institutions in heteronormative societies: "A complex cluster of sexual practices gets confused, in heterosexual culture, with the love plot of intimacy and familialism that signifies belonging to society in a deep and normal way. Community is imagined through scenes of intimacy, coupling, and kinship; a historical relation to futurity is restricted to generational narrative and reproduction" (1998, 554). In the case of forced marriage prevention, it is not only that particular familial intimacies are being governed by the state; the governing of intimate kin relations can be traced back to policies designed to control the marital practices of Indigenous communities in the eighteenth century and "assimilate" them into White settler society, which entailed displacement from land and systematic family separation. What is also of significance is that the governing of transnational migrant intimacies is concerned with how those intimate relations travel outside the bounds of mainland Australia and what happens when people return. The exiting of migrants out of Australia and their re-entry following an overseas marriage might also mean the future arrival of new migrants on spousal visas. I refer to transnational intimacies to describe how kin expectations around marriage and relationships manifest across geographies—between Melbourne and Kabul; between Dandenong (a Melbourne suburb) and Islamabad; and between Narre Warren (another Melbourne suburb) and Tehran, among other examples.[19] The intimate kinship configurations that undergird forced marriage and are deemed illegible by the Australian state because they are marked by particular histories of war, displacement, and resettlement are overlooked at each step of the prevention process.

State technologies of governance have historically situated intimate kinship relations as a window and even a litmus test for the state's own claim to sovereignty and longevity. Furthermore, the state's preoccupation with how citizens are mobilizing kinship for access to citizenship and other rights have resulted in policies that monitor, surveil, and regulate different types of kinship relations (Borneman 2001; Carsten 2003; Faubion 2001; Franklin and McKinnon 2001; Mahdavi 2016; Weston 1997; Yanagisako and Collier 1987). To study the governance of kinship, then, is also to study what Seung-kyung Kim and Sara Friedman (2021, 454) call "family-adjacent legal domains that create normative frameworks for kinship, sexuality, and family rights," including the welfare sector. Kathryn Goldfarb (2021) has examined how child welfare caseworkers prioritize a child's future relationship with their absent parent as a desirable outcome, thereby dismissing everyday relationships children have with foster parents and other caregiving figures. These technologies of governance yield a common sense around what count as normative kinship relations and recognize particular configurations of kinship as more desirable or legally legible over others. I take Kim and Friedman's approach seriously. Namely, it is important to look at "how [family and intimate] relationships are incorporated into national projects of population management and national security: family . . . is not merely a 'privileged instrument for the government of the population,' as Foucault (2007: 105) argues, but also ideas and ideals about intimate relationality that are mobilized by citizens to redefine the very experience of governance and national belonging" (2021, 455).

Forced marriage prevention works to produce particular truths about which kinship configurations constitute deviant forms of citizenship. The use of marriage by migrant communities is layered with economic and affective commitments and represents responses to the challenges of forced migration, ongoing conflict in their home countries, and increasingly stringent immigration policies in Australia. Kath Weston (1997, 106) notes that it is important to look at alternative kinship ideologies as not simply derivatives of or alternatives to a blood-centered kinship configuration, but as a historically situated transformation in and of itself. Other studies have emphasized how the production of kinship relations is structured by anxieties about the precarities of the future, both material and in the realm of legal recognition of different kinship formations (Friedman and Chen 2021). Migrant families' use of marriage to help extended kin via spousal visas also constitutes an alternative kinship arrangement. However, these arrangements have not been immune from robust critique from migrant communities in Australia. In that sense, they should not be romanticized as sites of morally clear responses to the structural obstacles of displacement or as antithetical to the responses of practitioners and the state. However, they do represent a response that is conditioned by structural inequalities that tend to be dismissed in the sector. For example, the Australian Muslim Women's Centre for Human Rights has released reports on early and forced marriage which have provided more nuanced explanations about what decisions led to parents and young adults to look to marriage as an easy solution to a complicated problem. These decisions often revolved around economic security and a desire for young women to start their own lives outside the confines of their parents' homes. The epistemic dilemmas that practitioners in prevention face concern making sense of these kinship arrangements as well as the emotional and affective layers that constitute them.

How these concerns get refracted through racial and gendered lines is also critical to understanding whose kinship relations matter to the state and why. As several studies have shown, state-led interventions that are predicated on the wellbeing of the family have tended to concern minoritized communities' kinship configurations, resulting in their further insulation and marginalization from public and political life (Friedman 2010; 2015; Howard-Wagner 2013; Parreñas 2001; Thai 2008; Yeoh and Lam 2005). However, there is minimal ethnographic research on the logics, discursive technologies, and relationships through which contemporary settler colonial states actually generate official knowledge about the intimate dynamics of the kinship relations of marginalized communities. In that sense, this book contemplates how violence prevention work is also the work of producing institutional knowledge about the intimacies inherent in everyday migrant life. Institutional knowledge, in this sense, refers to the development of profiles and standardized assessments of how the power dynamics within families, domestically and transnationally, matter to the state's expanding ideas of good citizenship.

How conceptualizations of autonomy and personhood function to produce marriage as the ultimate intimate event in settler colonial societies is also a key concern of this book. In *The Empire of Love*, Elizabeth Povinelli (2006, 16–17) writes that expressions of love in late liberal settler colonial societies function to reinforce the self-evident good of social institutions like marriage: "If you want to locate the hegemonic home of liberal logics and aspirations, look to love in settler colonies." European empires have historically dictated how intimacy is organized to enact their governance powers. What count as autonomous personhood and choice are organized around prevailing economic and social systems. What count as recognizable and legitimate forms of intimacy in liberal settler states are refracted through the myth that subjects are making full and free choices when they engage in certain kinds of legitimized intimacy. Intimacy, and what counts as legitimate intimacy, is a political question, and as Povinelli (2006, 13) writes, it has been cited "as the motivating logic and aspiration of dispersed and competing social and cultural experiments" including social policies and laws. The question then becomes: when does the event of intimate love actually happen, and what are the criteria we use to decide whether this event has happened? (2006, 14). In liberal states, certain forms of intimate dependency come to count as freedom, whereas others count as undue social constraint. Some are morally judged as choices, whereas others are seen as coercive (2006, 3). Forced marriage prevention is an example of how the intimate event of marriage re-emerges as a question of legitimate and illegitimate forms of sociality that not only discipline those who are seen as deviant, but also reinstantiate and redeclare the myths that liberal settler colonial societies tell themselves about their investment in individual choice, autonomy, and personal sovereignty. While settler colonial origin stories tell us that such societies are founded upon the aspiration for autonomy (religious, economic, or otherwise), such autonomy has historically meant the destruction, devaluation, and displacement of others and their ways of life and being. In Australia, the freedom of penal convicts meant the establishment of settlements that led to the destruction of Indigenous peoples, ways of life, and futures. Indigenous marital practices were regulated by the settler colonial state, and Indigenous peoples were also coerced into marriages with White Anglo people in the name of biological absorption, among other settler colonial technologies of racial engineering and control. The settler colonial state's foundation is one in which consent, as Audra Simpson (2017) has argued in the North American context, is a "ruse" that naturalizes transactions between Indigenous and colonizer that were never based on consent. The state's participation in imperial wars in Afghanistan and Iraq has displaced people who now seek safety and refuge in Australia, which views them as always already needing to prove not only their worthiness of refuge, but also their innocence, namely that they are not threatening to national security. As displaced people traverse oceans and land to reach refuge only to be met with denial of entry or rerouting to offshore detention centers, one is hard pressed to find under what conditions migrants are exercising true consent when it comes to their futures. For Povinelli (2006, 15), the intimate event becomes important to the liberal settler state insofar as it does not occur in the way it declares it is meant to unfold. How does its nonoccurrence come to be seen as the breakdown of liberalism itself, and what is being done to produce the world in the image of the dominant discourses of liberalism? Forced marriage prevention is one of many examples of an attempt to do just that.

Marriage and Liberalism

In Australia, as in most liberal settler colonial states, marriage is a key social institution through which access to rights and resources are ensured. Regulating marriage has been a key way that settler colonial states ensure the circulation of property, inheritance rights, and wealth within settler society. Studies of marriage in anthropology have focused extensively on how marriage functions as a technology of governance to regulate who gets access to resources and the benefits of full citizenship as well as personhood in the polity and other types of cultural spaces. Both older studies in anthropology (Lévi-Strauss 1949; Yanagisako and Collier 1987) and contemporary studies (Basu 2015; Borneman 2001; Rubin 1981) have illustrated how the preservation of hegemonic marital institutions functions to determine who is placed where in the social order. They have examined how such institutions also reshape the conditions of economic, social, and cultural possibilities for people and, thus, their lived experience of their identities and subjectivities, especially in the wake of new border control policies and notions of national sovereignty.

This book takes the position that an anthropological perspective on marriage must respect different social understandings of not only the institution itself but also the paradigms of choice and power that organize them, with an understanding that these matrices and paradigms are fluid, historically specific, and politically located. Within the anthropology of marriage, several studies have, in recent years, sought to complicate the idea that early and forced marriage among global South societies and the migrant communities that emerge thereof are static cultural practices based on social structures in which individual choice is not valued in favor of traditional and patriarchal forms of social control. Some have done this by examining the social, political, and economic histories and contemporary conditions under which early marriage practices within global South societies take form. Caroline Archambault's 2011 ethnographic study of early marriage among the

Massai community in Kenya reframes the discussion on early marriage from "a traditional cultural practice" to a "livelihood insecurity." She shows that Massai girls in Kenya are pulled into early marriages but that this is not simply the byproduct of malicious patriarchal structures; it is a response to economic insecurities and the legacies of underdeveloped educational systems. In the global North, Gender Studies scholar Nicholas Syrett's (2016) book *American Child Bride* chronicles child marriage within White American communities today, demonstrating that it is not limited to racialized communities. But beyond this, Syrett also shows that in White American communities, the legal benefits that child brides experience also coexist with exploitative consequences, generating moral ambivalence around child marriage in the rural South. In the French context, Jennifer Selby (2009) has problematized how choice is understood by second and third generation male immigrants of a Maghrebian background who are looking for spouses. She shows that, for such immigrants, marriage is a way of preserving certain cultural formations within the Maghrebian European diaspora. At the same time, the transnational brides who migrate to France to enter into such marriages experience freedom and coercion in ways that go beyond and are often not linked to the entry into marriage itself. For example, one interlocutor, Nora, notes that the call by her parents to get married is not coercive, but rather experienced as a form of freedom. For other brides, being able to migrate abroad to get married is experienced as freedom in that they can move out of their parents' homes and begin a new life with a different kind of autonomy. For others, transnational marriages are a way for women who were forced into marriages in their home countries to escape. Naomi Quinn (1982) has also shown that linguistically in the United States, marriage is discussed through specific metaphors that blur the lines between choice and duress. For example, people use the words "commitment," "struggle," "dedication," and "attachment" to describe their position to their spousal relationships. These words point to a willingness to subject oneself to certain ethical obligations in the relationship and to act on carrying them out. Alongside this, John Borneman (2005) has written that entering into a marriage turns a personal relationship into a fact that matters to the state and society in new ways. The act of entering into a legal marriage is a move to seek external validation, which is coercive in its own way (you must be married through the state to be afforded access to certain rights, recognitions, and resources). By entering into a contract with the state, the parties have put their own assets in a more vulnerable situation in case of divorce, for example. As Borneman (2005, 33) writes, "Choice and free will do not promise permanence and security. The issues of sexuality and love marriage are often framed as ones of choice, sexual or marital preference, but, of course, no form of human affiliation can be explained through individual choice alone." Similarly, Ellen Lewin (2004, 11) writes that marital ceremonies contextualize a relationship within a broader community and get recognition that solidifies one's place within a community outside of one's immediate one. Framing these as "love" marriage is one of many ways that one could make such moves understandable to a particular kind of audience. She writes, "Love is a code that makes otherwise alien behavior understandable within a shared cultural matrix—for both actors and audience" (2004, 11). What brings these studies together is that they recognize that to understand the power dynamics of marriage, one has to understand the positionalities of the subject, and what structures and social environments they are already embedded within and navigating. This book is inspired by these ethnographies, focusing on how autonomy is made sense of from the outside in the space of social welfare and how it is experienced by women negotiating their relationships with their parents and a range of citizenship and economic insecurities.

Methods

This book is based on a total of fourteen months of fieldwork in the state of Victoria, which is in southeast Australia. Taking place from 2016 to 2017, with preliminary fieldwork in the summer of 2015, this project sought to produce a qualitative account of how the law and educational initiatives around forced marriage were being implemented on the ground. As such, it demanded a fieldwork approach that was multi-scalar (Delaney and Leitner 1997; Strathern 1991; Tsing 2005) and multi-sited (Marcus 1995) at the local level.

I spent most of my time in either Melbourne proper or its suburbs in the Northeast and Southeast, which are densely populated with migrant and refugee populations. These areas have a range of social service organizations committed to family violence prevention which also began to take up forced marriage prevention after 2013. These suburbs included: Dandenong, Narre Warren, Roxburgh Park, Morwell, Shepparton, Noble Park, and Templestowe. Other suburbs I spent time in, but from which I have not included ethnographic data in this book, are: Broadmeadows, Brunswick, Endeavour Hills, Frankston, and Sunshine West. Victoria was chosen as the state in which to conduct research because it is considered to have been at the forefront of the domestic violence and women's refuge movements as well as at the forefront of developing infrastructures for family violence prevention. Victoria also resettles the most refugees per year (3,500–4,000; Victoria State Government 2016), and it was one of the first states to create a forced marriage network which brought together practitioners and experts from advocacy, casework, policymaking, and law enforcement.

This research was broken down into conversations with and participant observation of the work of different institutional actors who are key stakeholders in the forced marriage prevention sector. Methods were focused on understanding the stated beliefs, techniques, practices, and social relations among the following actors: direct service providers, policy advocates, state and federal law enforcement, and human rights and family law lawyers. This kind of data enabled an understanding of how social service actors are thinking about their work. As such, these methods were attuned to how people think about their work in the everyday

(Stewart 2007) as well as how different actors reproduce normality and regularity within their professions and social lives (Das 2006). In speaking with such actors, I was also concerned with the different structural constraints that shape what they could and could not do and say in their respective professional and social environments. I also interviewed people from the following categories: those who self-identified as victims/survivors of forced marriage; those who expressed they were at risk of being forced into a marriage; and young adults from migrant backgrounds who are currently grappling with the role of family in their intimate partner relationships. The last group I interviewed consisted of activists and advocates who were dedicated to tackling Islamophobia in different spheres of social life, including the ways in which gender-based and family violence were portrayed in the Muslim community. While this book is not focused on their work (which appears in a different article; Zeweri 2020a), their insights revealed that an anti-Islamophobia politics can refuse to replace negative stereotypes of Muslim women with positive ones. Instead, this group of women shifted the conversation to understanding how Islamophobia forces Muslim communities to represent themselves as assimilable rather than questioning the legal and political structures that make one an assimilated subject.

In conducting participant observation with direct service providers and policy advocates, I attended twenty-two trainings and information sessions around family violence, as well as nineteen trainings, meetings, and information sessions around forced marriage specifically. I interviewed eighteen direct service workers and twelve policy advocates who work with social service organizations that focus on family violence and are currently integrating forced marriage within their organizational purview. These practitioners have been working to administer trainings about the law and the practice of forced marriage to migrant women, educators, and community leaders within Victoria. Throughout my research, I sat in on and, at times, participated in information sessions they provided to women in various suburbs, attending to how they framed the practice as a legal and social issue. I conducted interviews with staff members to decipher how they understood forced marriage as a legal construct and mandate and how it intersects with their personal objectives to aid and educate local clients through culturally competent approaches. I also interviewed eleven migrant community leaders who are implementing forced marriage prevention education in their communities. These community leaders came from: Afghanistan, Pakistan, Iraq, and Syria. I interviewed six lawyers who work on a range of issues from family law to human trafficking to asylum cases. In addition, I attended trainings around family violence led by state hospitals. These trainings were windows into how family violence is increasingly being treated as a public health issue. There was also insight into how forced marriage and particular familial configurations had consequences on people's physical and mental well-being.

I also engaged with members of different law enforcement communities. I interviewed and met with two Victoria State Police Officers and two Australian

Federal Police (AFP) officers to discuss the challenges of implementing the forced marriage law. I interviewed two of Victoria's MCLOs who serve as intermediaries between the police force and local immigrant communities. Most MCLOs have built strong bonds with youth, women, and families in their assigned communities, due to their language skills and shared religious and ethnic backgrounds. I also observed two forced marriage awareness-raising trainings administered to a local high school by the MCLO. In speaking with two AFP members who are part of the Human Trafficking Investigative Team that investigated reports of forced marriage, I focused on how they navigate the challenges of responding to forced marriage cases, especially with regard to locating evidence and what would count as a successful prosecution.

I interviewed four victims/survivors of forced marriage situations and twenty-three young adults of immigrant backgrounds currently grappling with marriage and what their families' roles should be. (Out of these twenty-three, four were self-identified men and nineteen were self-identified women.) While the study's initial goal was to interview ten victims/survivors of forced marriage, it was challenging to get access to potential interlocutors. There are strict protocols and mechanisms that govern with whom and in what spaces victims/survivors of forced marriage currently in various support programs can have interactions and conversations. These conversations provided insight into how relationships are being thought about as both a partnership and a collective form of sociality in which the role of family is being carefully curated by young people. This group represents a particularly interesting demographic because they are quite aware of both how their upbringing has reproduced notions of patriarchy that breed situations of familial coercion as well as how these forms of oppression are being used to frame their communities as backward and threatening to the social fabric. My analysis is also informed by news articles, opinion pieces, and peer-reviewed articles in the social sciences that relate to forced marriage, migration, Muslim communities, and family violence initiatives in Australia. The names of all individuals have been changed within my analysis. I have not identified the names of certain organizations to protect their identities, but certain organizations whose presentations were made available to a public audience have been kept as is.

While I have outlined the many groups I interviewed, this book reflects a small portion of these conversations and interactions. It reflects moments I saw as particularly illustrative of broader dynamics in the prevention sector, and thus the reader will notice that certain people reappear throughout the book. The reader will also notice that, within a given chapter, locations will shift. This reflects the multi-sited nature of my fieldwork and the reality that forced marriage prevention did not unfold in one agency or in one community. It also reflects the time in which I conducted fieldwork, one in which agencies were still figuring out the social problem they were tasked to prevent. To understand a nascent social policy is to observe conversations, workshops, and professional trainings in multiple spaces that cumulatively produced this prevention system's regime of knowledge.

Book Layout and Australia as a Field Site

Before I offer an outline of each chapter, I will explain 1) what brought me to this project, 2) why I chose Australia as my field site, and 3) how I see this project contributing to anthropology more broadly and policy debates more specifically. Australia was a place I had taken an interest in for a number of reasons. Having grown up in the Afghan American diaspora, I was initially interested in understanding the Afghan diasporic experience in a place where Afghans had found community but that tended to be left out in American public discourse on Afghan diasporic life. As I did more research on this community's experience, I began to see how much Australia has been marginalized from public discourse and scholarship on migration more broadly. Australia's geographic proximity to East and South Asia has, over time, significantly shaped its self-awareness that it is a desirable migration destination. At the same time, its distance from the geographic "western world" has allowed it to undertake particularly restrictive border control policies while attracting minimal public critique beyond the Australian mainland and surrounding archipelagoes that have their own histories of being economically and territorially exploited by Australian colonial projects. In a place that values multiculturalism but has excluded migrants and refugees through increasingly militarized and deterrence-based border control policies (Hirsch 2017; Pickering and Lambert 2002; Weber 2007), I wondered how this paradox found expression in everyday life. During my preliminary fieldwork, I learned about refugee and migrant-targeted social service organizations and came across forced marriage prevention as a program that services were offering migrant communities. While volunteering with an organization that works with migrants with disabilities, I came to learn through sitting in on refugee health and cultural orientation workshops that forced marriage was an issue that the Australian government was trying to address in recent years with a greater focus on Muslim migrant communities.

Initially, I felt confused about what forced marriage prevention meant, but wanted to learn more. I wondered how precisely a government could judge whether a marriage was coerced. Having witnessed coercion into marriages in my own community, it was hard for me to imagine how a government or policing agency could intervene in stopping such marriages from occurring. I thought about extended family friends and could not see them as having done something that merited imprisonment and even potential deportation. I also found it strange that immigrant support services were tasked with carrying out prevention. I wondered if forced marriage was seen by the government as a migrant-specific issue and what migrant groups themselves thought about it. The more I spoke with social welfare practitioners, the more I realized that people were still working out the definition of coercion and how to know it was imminent. While the law had passed, what it meant to prevent coercion was unfolding in real time. I decided to focus my dissertation fieldwork on the unfolding of this policy in real time. Australia represents a case study in how different institutional actors in liberal settler colonial states look to social welfare to simultaneously foster human rights while also addressing threats to national identity.

A question I kept confronting during fieldwork from practitioners was "How will your research directly help our work with clients?" While an anthropological analysis is not designed to be a policy report, I situate this book as an analysis of how the moving parts of a policy apparatus work together to produce a truth regime around family, migration, marriage, and violence. I attempt to offer some ways forward in the last chapter. However, the book is more generally designed to activate questions that practitioners across multiple institutions of prevention can begin to consider more seriously and consciously as they do their day-to-day work. As is the case with workers across social welfare sectors in developed countries, there is little time to think about where one's work lies within a broader regime of institutional violence and a broader history of state-sanctioned violence. It is my hope that this book can help stimulate more critical reflection when, and if, that time is found.

Reflections on Positionality

I was initially welcomed into the forced marriage prevention sector through an organization that focuses on providing culturally sensitive social welfare services to migrant youth through Bridget, who introduced me to important practitioners at the level of direct service, policy, and law enforcement. Bridget was excited about the opportunity to reflect on her work in a more conscious way after I had explained what an anthropological perspective on forced marriage prevention would be designed to do. In discussing anthropology, I felt an obligation to say how my work could be useful to the sector given how much trust they had put in me to be privy to these institutional conversations. I explained that I wanted to better understand victims/survivors' lived experiences because this was a gap in advocacy research in the sector. I also wanted to understand how the sector itself was developing a shared language and praxis around forced marriage prevention. In making my case to be a participant at Victorian Forced Marriage Network (VFMN) meetings, I emphasized that I was interested in understanding how forced marriage as a legally codified category of violence was being defined on the ground. After explaining the anthropological project, practitioners perceived me as both someone who could understand victims/survivors' stories and as someone with whom they could reflect on their own experiences in the sector. The sector was curious about why an American graduate student would be interested in Australia of all places—practitioners, then, had a sense that they operated within a place considered somewhat detached from American-born research projects.

While practitioners were aware of my anthropological investments in the question of gender-based violence and migration, some also saw me as sharing their goal of eliminating forced marriage. They saw my anthropological investments as coexisting comfortably with a presumed desire to prevent forced marriage. It was a challenge trying to explain that, while I was trained in feminist critique of categories like honor-based violence and the universalizing assumptions of the violence against women movement, I also knew that such critiques did not always reflect the assumptions that those involved in the day-to-day work of policy brought to their own work.

When it came to migrant community leaders, my ethnic and religious background, as well as the fact that my own parents were immigrants to the United States, helped me to make connections with community leaders. As someone who identifies as raised in an Afghan Muslim immigrant family, I shared many of my interlocutors' ethnic and religious backgrounds. Some community leaders were skeptical that I was focusing on Muslim migrant communities because it did not seem fair to assume that forced marriage only happened in those communities, a discourse that they believed the advocacy sector had already been perpetuating. I had to explain that my focus centered not on why forced marriage occurs in Muslim communities, but why this demographic has disproportionately become an object of state and policy questions through the window of these categories of gender-based violence. I also made sure to be transparent that, in fact, I was not serving as a mouthpiece for practitioners, but that I was trying to facilitate a space where they could critically reflect on their own practices and the systemic expectations under which they operated. Both social welfare practitioners and migrant community leaders saw my position as a "cultural voice" but for very different reasons, and thus assigned very different expectations around the outcome of my research. While some practitioners expected that I would produce a report that would give an intimate look at the cultural dynamics of forced marriage, community leaders thought I would offer a critique of the sector that recuperated culture as "not backwards," since it would be a professional risk for them to do the same. I ended up producing a draft report for the VFMN that focused on why forced marriage prevention was not capturing the nuanced realities of its intended beneficiaries. While this book focuses primarily on the knowledge practices of the forced marriage prevention apparatuses, there are several conversations and interviews with young adult Muslim Australians and community leaders I have not included. This is because they do not directly address the prevention apparatus itself but, rather, how social welfare thinks about recently arrived immigrant and refugee communities and their struggles with sustaining and renegotiating familial ties, fulfilling models of good citizenship, and attempting to navigate new types of intimate relationships.

Chapter Layout

This book is composed of seven chapters total, including this introductory chapter. Chapter 1 attempts to connect multiple histories to illustrate how social welfare, anti-immigrant policies, and policing become converged in the forced marriage prevention apparatus. Thus, it looks at the histories of violence against women and forced marriage globally and their expression in Australia. It examines how the settler colonial state has policed Indigenous marital and familial relations and communities more broadly and how this sets the groundwork for the policing of immigrant communities through maritime border control policies. Chapter 2 examines how the forced marriage sector, through scenario-based trainings, produces truths about who the typical victim of a forced marriage is and why this typical victim signals a threat to the integrity of Australian values around family and citizenship. Chapter 3 takes a closer look at how educators at secondary schools are pulled into the work of forced marriage prevention vis-à-vis their students. It looks at cases in which school staff are learning how to conduct forced marriage risk assessment. The dilemmas that educators experience regarding whether to disclose that a student is at risk to the AFP reveal that forced marriage prevention's linkage with the criminal justice system puts school staff in impossible positions where disclosure of their suspicions means automatically putting their students and their families in the hands of a criminal justice system that is already biased against Muslim Australians. I show why school staff choose nondisclosure to take their students' everyday realities more seriously. Chapter 4 examines how victim/survivor narratives are institutionally managed within the prevention system and how their own narratives of familial violence exceed biopolitical forms of storytelling. Chapter 5 analyzes the ways in which young adult Muslim Australian women, who were almost coerced into a marriage or who experienced familial coercion during the marriage process, narrate their relationships to their family and to the family violence prevention apparatus. Their narratives deprivilege state models around what successful family violence prevention looks like, models that assume power takes the form of domination and empowerment takes the form of separation from one's family. Chapter 6 concludes the book with an overview of what this analysis means for anthropological debates around assimilation of migrant communities, how kinship matters to contemporary biopolitical projects for migrants, and recommendations for the prevention sector.

Readers will notice that the book does not engage with the question of marriages relating to minors as it does with marriages relating to adults eighteen and over. In 2015, an amendment was passed to Australia's forced marriage law which noted that those who are sixteen and under (minors) could not consent to a marriage because "they cannot understand the nature and effect of a marriage ceremony" (Amendment to the 1995 Criminal Code) and will be assumed to be in a forced marriage. This was an important protection for people under the age of eighteen.[20] However, forced marriage was still seen to be a problem for women who were considered legal adults and the sector spent a great deal of resources conducting prevention education for this demographic. While much of prevention education did see minors as most susceptible to victimhood, I will not be discussing their experiences, because I chose to interview those who were eighteen and older. I do not spend as much time discussing the intersection between Child Protective

Services (CPS) and forced marriage prevention, though this relationship is a key node in the prevention sector. There is much to be said about the assumptions prevention makes about the experiences of children including those from racialized communities as sites of corrupted innocence (Castañeda 2002; Malkki 2010; Ticktin 2017).[21] This is outside the scope of this book, but it is worthy of further research because forced marriage prevention is heavily invested in conceptions of childhood, and human development.

The 2013 law is one of several moments when Australia has vigilantly tried to protect marriage as a symbol of national identity and as a signifier of citizenship. The creation of coercion into marriage as a crime, however, marks a distinct way in which migrant behavior, kinship relations, and sociality were made knowable and governable through the institution of marriage. In this book, I examine how the gray area between consent and coercion, between mobility and immobility, and between freedom and constraint emerge as more visible yet remain marginalized in social welfare. Forced marriage was seen as a problem for Australian values that originated within migrant home countries. Through this research, I chart how the debate on forced marriage is less about the rights people should have in marriage and more about what kinds of socialities make a legitimate marriage. In that sense, this analysis does not uphold a particular ideal of marriage as healthier or better. Rather, I aim to show how marriage becomes a filter through which belonging, political inclusion, social deviance, and, ultimately, the humanity of migrants gets contested and reconfigured into violence against the nation-state.

1

A Genealogy of Forced Marriage Prevention

In this section, I present a genealogy of "forced marriage" as a legal and political category of violence shaped by global, national, and local political circumstances, demands, and constraints. The chapter will begin with an overview of the global discourse on forced marriage and its emergence within the violence against women movement in the late 1990s. This is followed by an analysis of how Australia's approach to forced marriage prevention has been distinct from other Western European and North American contexts. Then, the chapter examines key court cases, news stories, and policy debates in the lead up to the 2013 law. Lastly, the chapter examines how the concern with coercion and consent lies at the nexus of settler colonialism, immigration, and family violence prevention, philosophically and institutionally. In that section, I introduce how the governance of migrant marital relations has a deeper history in the state's policing of Indigenous communities.

The goal of this chapter is not to present forced marriage as the effect of a linear set of consecutive events. Rather, it is to show how a category of violence forms and comes to signify different concerns in different historical moments. In that sense, I frame this chapter as a genealogy of the truth regime that I described in the introductory chapter. I take inspiration from Michel Foucault's (1977a, 143) idea of genealogy as an "effective history." Foucault writes that such a history would cease to be preoccupied with a search for origins. Rather, it would embrace contingency and "the dispersed effects that coalesce around a particular social phenomenon." Thus, by looking at the emergence of forced marriage as produced by intersecting conditions of possibility, this chapter situates the current policy around forced marriage in Australia as the convergence of multiple institutional and discursive histories.

Global Discourses of Forced Marriage

With the advent of the Universal Declaration of Human Rights (UDHR) in 1948, the right to marry has been solidified as an internationally recognized human right. Article 16 of the UDHR states, "(1) Men and women of full age, without any limitation due to race, nationality, or religion, have the right to marry and to found a family. They are entitled to equal rights as to marriage, during marriage, and at its dissolution. (2) Marriage shall be entered into only with the free and full consent of the intending spouses. (3) The family is the natural and fundamental group unit of society and is entitled to protection by society and the State." The UDHR inclusion of marriage, then, also declares that it is an institution at the core of family, which, in turn, is the premise of society itself (United Nations General Assembly 1948).[1]

The Convention on the Elimination of All Forms of Discrimination Against Women (CEDAW; United Nations General Assembly 1979) also notes that women and men share the same rights in entering into a marriage, noted in article 16(b). The International Covenant on Economic, Social, and Cultural Rights (ICESCR) declares that marriage must be entered into with the "full and free consent of the intending spouses." The International Covenant on Civil and Political Rights (ICCPR; 1966) harkens back to the UDHR, which notes that men and women of marriageable age have the right to create a family and enter into marriage with free and full consent of intending spouses.[2]

Advocates often cite such human rights documents as providing internationally recognized clauses that require signatories to ensure that their laws are protecting people of marriageable age's right to fully and freely enter into a marriage.[3] However, as with most human rights documents born out of United Nations frameworks, they do not account for all the social and political circumstances under which marriage becomes a viable option for people in different contexts, especially the material conditions under which full and free choice are not possible.[4]

While the Australian forced marriage prevention sector mobilizes international human rights language around child marriage, it also frames prevention through the language of violence against women (VAW). During the 1990s, the UN Economic and Social Council (ECOSOC) followed a recommendation by the Commission on the Status of Women (CSW) which declared that VAW is a direct result of women's unequal status in society and that states had to have consequences as well as prevention initiatives around VAW in the family (Merry 2016, 46–47). Committees like those who created the CEDAW also framed gender-based violence as a form of social discrimination (2016, 47). In 1992, CEDAW "placed violence against women squarely within the rubric of human rights and fundamental freedoms and made clear that states are obliged to eliminate violence perpetrated by public authorities and by private persons" (2016, 47). It served as a powerful way to hold governments accountable to the various platforms and conventions they had signed around the issue (2016, 49).

The provisions of CEDAW were buttressed by the 1994 creation of the role of the special rapporteur on violence against women as part of the UN Commission on Human Rights, which would be tasked with gathering information related to violence against women (2016, 47). The inaugural rapporteur Radhika Coomaraswamy helped to sediment evidence and knowledge around VAW as a global problem. Under her tenure, the definition of VAW also expanded to incorporate a wider set of harms:

> The original meaning of violence against women—male violence against partners and others in the form of rape, assault, and murder—was expanded to include intimidation and psychological harm; humiliation; female genital mutilation, cutting, and excision; gender-based violence by police and military forces in armed conflict as well as everyday life; violence against refugee women and asylum seekers; trafficking in sex workers; sexual harassment; forced pregnancy; abortion, and sterilization; female feticide and infanticide; early and forced marriages; honor killings; and widowhood violations, among others (2016, 48).

The expansion of the definition to include other forms of gender-based violence further situated it as a question of not only women's suffering but also their freedom over charting the course of their futures in the public and private spheres.[5] Another fundamental moment in the global discourse of VAW was the Fourth World Conference on Women in Beijing in 1995, during which VAW was named as a violation of human rights and fundamental freedoms. The Beijing Platform for Action defined VAW as "any act of gender-based violence that results in, or is likely to result in, physical, sexual, or psychological harm or suffering to women, including threats of such acts, coercion or arbitrary deprivation of liberty, whether occurring in public or private life" (Merry 2016, 48). A whole range of public and private acts were encompassed by the definition of gender-based violence here, including sexual abuse during war, forced abortion, and female infanticide.[6]

In Australia, violence against women and gender-based violence is considered a public health issue and a pervasive social problem (Australian Human Rights Commission 2018; Department of Social Services 2016; Vidal 2018, 6). According to the Australian Institute for Health and Welfare (2022) and the Australian Bureau of Statistics (2016), one in six women in Australia have experienced physical or sexual violence from a current or previous cohabiting partner and one woman is killed every nine days by a partner. Having attended several seminars and public events on family violence and domestic violence prevention, I noticed that gender-based violence was treated as a social epidemic and a public health issue, with over A$1.1 billion of the federal budget allotted to domestic violence prevention in 2021. The state of Victoria has committed more than A$3 billion to reform family violence prevention and response (Fitz-Gibbon and Meyer 2021). It is important to point this out, because domestic violence in particular is considered an issue that cuts across race and class in Australia and has been less susceptible to being tied to any one ethnic group. While the global definition of violence against women has expanded to include forced marriage and honor-based violence, these are often left out of the public conversation in Australia on domestic violence, and, with the exception of select organizational approaches, tend to get explained through the lens of culture and interpersonal relations rather than issues of structural violence. Forced marriage and honor-based violence tend to appear more frequently in family violence prevention, which focus both on intimate partner violence and violence committed by other immediate and extended kin. From my experience attending seminars and trainings on both domestic and family violence led by national and local community organizations, it was clear that domestic violence trainings more seriously considered structural factors such as poverty, homelessness, and unemployment in the committal of violence in a relationship. Family violence trainings targeted to migrant communities specifically tended to focus on individual characteristics and cultural factors that contributed to interpersonal violence. While I did not conduct a systematic or quantitative study detailing these differences, the latter approach seems to have more heavily shaped the forced marriage prevention sector's framework for explaining violence.

Forced Marriage as a "Migrant-Specific Problem" in the Global North and West

Australia's approach to forced marriage prevention draws from transnationally salient discourses of forced marriage as a form of gender-based violence (Gangoli and McCarry 2008; Gill and Mitra-Khan 2012; Quek 2012; Wilson 2007; Uddin 2006). Its approach to the issue also resonates with similar approaches taken by countries in North America and Western Europe, which tend to treat forced marriage as a problem of migrants' inability to assimilate. Forced marriage debates in Europe have been in existence since the late 1990s. In the post-9/11 landscape which was marked by rising xenophobia throughout migrant-receiving countries in the global North and West, migrants from the Middle East and South Asia were increasingly depicted in Parliamentary debates as importing "alien practices" and exceeding multiculturalism's politics of tolerance. Such debates have intensified in the early 2000s and increasingly organized around the binary of western versus Islamic values. With the advent of Samuel Huntington's theory of the "clash of civilizations," the dichotomy of the "West" versus the "Islamic world" was mobilized to portray Muslim majority countries as sites of religiously-sanctioned terrorism (Appiah 2016; Mamdani 2002). This notion reverberated to the immigration policies of global North and Western countries which came to see Muslim migrant men, especially those who were not eligible for "skilled migrant" visas and were not as valuable for their labor power, as security threats to the nation (Beydoun 2018; Fekete 2016; Gusciute, Mühlau, and Layte 2020; Rana 2007; Rytter and Pedersen 2013). Through policy, popular media, and academic discourse, Muslim migrants were treated not only as threats to an abstract notion of security but also as threats to western culture, civilization, and values. The panic around Muslim migration in the early years after September 11 focused not only on threats of terrorism but also on the "importation" of "illiberal ways of life" that exist at the level of the family. The reframing of Muslim migrants, especially refugees, as potential national security threats has coincided with the circulation of news stories documenting particularly brutal cases of gender-based violence committed by Muslim immigrant men against their daughters (Dauvergne and Millbank 2010; Grewal 2013; Volpp 2011). Such stories have framed this violence as a symptom of increased migration and the importation of depraved cultural values across borders.

Such conceptions of immigrants as vectors of threatening cultures have shaped how European states have approached their own forced marriage legislation. As of today, roughly half of EU member states have created specific legislation that renders forced marriage a crime, which, in part, follows recommendations by the Istanbul Convention of 2011. These member states include: France, Denmark, Norway, the Netherlands, Sweden, Switzerland, Germany, Belgium, Australia, Hungary, and Spain. Prior to creating such legislation, though, several states used immigration and age of consent laws to legislate around coercion into marriage. For example, Belgium, Denmark, and the Netherlands modified their age of consent laws through raising the minimum age of marriage. Germany, Norway, and the Netherlands are among countries that have historically used immigration laws to monitor migrants' beliefs about forced marriage before taking steps years later to make it a criminal offense (Bredal 2011). What these contexts share is that the attempt to address forced marriage began through regulating migrant travel abroad and family reunification policies, and it eventually culminated in specific laws making the offense a federal level crime.

Australia's approach has taken inspiration from EU forced marriage prevention infrastructures, but also borrows from the U.K. model. The U.K. model, however, was not always rooted in criminal legislation and has a longer history driven by community-based models. In the 1990s, forced marriage was treated as an issue of gender inequality in Britain. It was driven by the grassroots work of organizations such as the Southall Black Sisters (SBS), an immigrant women-led community initiative that sought legislative and community-based protections around a wide range of gender-based violences. It emphasized the role of social and economic inequality in underage and forced marriage. In 2007, Britain created a specific civil protection order around forced marriage which SBS members have identified as a "vital component of the protection that is available for persons at risk of a forced marriage" (Southall Black Sisters n.d.). In 2014, the Anti-social Behaviour, Crime and Policing Act made forced marriage a criminal offense in England, Wales, and Scotland. This law, coupled with the increased culturalization of the issue—much to the SBS' dismay—in media and policy discourse led to the pinpointing of South Asian Muslim communities as the site of forced marriages in the United Kingdom. Around the same period, the U.K.'s Forced Marriage Unit (FMU) was created to investigate and prosecute reported cases. Australia has looked to the FMU and the

United Kingdom for guidance in developing its own criminal justice approach to forced marriage, in some ways not realizing how the framework for coercion became culturalized and disconnected from structural inequalities when it became criminalized.

What is unique about the Australian case is that it immediately created a federal law to address forced marriage rather than amending existing child protection, marriage, and trafficking laws. One reason may be that the government sought to stop forced marriages occurring within the borders of Australia as well as those with an overseas component. Another reason why amending trafficking laws was not an option may have been because Australian federal authorities could not travel to another national jurisdiction to stop a marriage already happening in that context, because that could run the risk of violating international sovereignty laws. While the AFP could and did cite existing federal legislation around child trafficking to prosecute those attempting to take a minor overseas (which only applied to the attempt and not the completed action), this would not allow prosecution of cases in which the actual marriage already occurred or in which the victim was not a minor. In the current situation, the federal law has not yet successfully prosecuted any individual for attempting a forced marriage despite two attempts to do so, one of which is ongoing in the Melbourne County Court and involves a woman from Shepparton. In the first case, the husband of the bride and the imam who officiated her wedding were charged and convicted of conducting a marriage of someone who was not of marriageable age and solemnizing an invalid marriage (because it occurred with a minor).[7] While attempts were made to charge both people with carrying out, or being party to, a forced marriage, due to lack of evidence, the charges were changed to the aforementioned violations of the 1961 Marriage Act. Because gathering evidence to prove that a forced marriage has occurred is so difficult, the federal law, since 2013, has functioned less as a tool of justice and more as a tool to send a message to migrant communities.

Another distinction between the EU and Australia's addressing of the problem is that, while EU states certainly operate with racialized ideas of immigrants and minority communities, unlike Australia, EU supranational institutions have more say and influence over how such states (except for the United Kingdom) continue to legislate and create policy around the issue. The United States has also taken measures to tackle child marriage, specifically through advocating that individual states change their laws to increase the permissible age of marriage to eighteen without any exception. Organizations such as Unchained at Last and the Tahirih Justice Center are working to increase understanding of forced marriage as a form of family violence and abuse while building the capacity of existing programs to assist victims; dedicate funding for new forced marriage-specific resources and programs; ensure access to civil protection orders for forced marriage victims; strengthen state laws on the age of consent to marry; implement safeguards in federal immigration laws for marriage-based visas; and ensure that criminal justice options are available to forced marriage victims (Tahirih Justice Center n.d.;

Unchained at Last n.d.). The U.S. approaches are distinct from Australia in that legislation around family matters and marriage happens at the state level.

The 2013 Forced Marriage Law and Legal Precedents

In Australia, various rulings around coercion in marriage in family courts have helped to sharpen what counts as coercive familial behavior and who within a family could be held accountable. Such court cases also helped to solidify what conditions constituted the violation of consent while entering the marriage. The case of *Kreet v. Sampir* (2011) was significant in defining such conditions. In this case, an Australian-born woman, Ms. Kreet, asked the Family Court to void her marriage that occurred in India in 2009, because it was consented to under duress. When Ms. Kreet travelled to India, she was under the impression that she was going to marry Mr. U., her Australian boyfriend. However, when she arrived, her parents took away her passport and introduced her to Mr. Sampir. Ms. Kreet's father told her that her boyfriend's sisters and mother would be raped and kidnapped unless she married Mr. Sampir, after which Ms. Kreet agreed to marry him and sponsor his partner visa application. In this case, Judge Cronin concluded that, because the Marriage Act of 1961 did not define duress, it was taken to mean any form of oppression or coercion that erases consent (Burns and Simmons 2014, 977). This case was an important moment that contributed to expanding the definition of psychological coercion at the hands of familial pressures. The Judge also cited Judge S. J. Watson's ruling in the case of Re: Marriage of S: "The emphasis on terror or fear in some of the judgments seems unnecessarily limiting. A sense of mental oppression can be generated by causes other than fear or terror. If there are circumstances which taken together lead to the conclusion that because of oppression, a particular person has not exercised a voluntary consent to a marriage, that consent is vitiated by duress and is not a real consent." Judge Watson had granted the nullification of a marriage between an Egyptian man and a younger woman. The judge determined that the woman was threatened in the sense of being "caught in a psychological prison of family loyalty, parental coercion, sibling responsibility, religious commitment, and a culture that demanded filial obedience" (2014, 978).

In the case of *Madley v. Madley* (2011), a sixteen-year-old Australian female citizen applied for a court order in Family Court to prohibit her parents from removing her from Australia to marry a man living in Lebanon. What is interesting about the *Madley v. Madley* case is that not only was her fear of her physical safety considered as evidence that she was coerced into a marriage, but so was her fear of her mother's reaction to her saying "no." This case, then, was an important step in defining coercion (and the violation of consent) as based on a fear of parental reactions and responses. It was also a scenario in which the act of coercion was seen to be carried out by multiple people. The definition of duress has been reshaped to now include the web of familial pressures that result in psychological pressure on an individual. The judicial interrogation of "duress" has resulted in court rulings accounting for the more insidious ways that consent may have been violated in situations where family typically plays a role, including marriage. As legal scholars Jennifer Burn and Frances Simmons (2014) point out, it is only in the last few years that Australian family courts have commented on how social or familial pressures, including psychological coercion, could invalidate a person's ability to freely consent to marriage. Previously, courts refused to nullify a marriage unless there was the threat of immediate danger to one's physical body. However, the move to account for various conditions under which consent is rendered violated now recognizes what political theorists Anne Phillips and Moira Dustin (2004, 531, 537) call "the force of moral and emotional blackmail." These cases, along with other cases of the Family Court and the Federal Circuit Court of Australia, allowed these bodies to issue protective and preventive orders for children at risk of forced marriage (based on the Family Law Act of 1975), which includes being placed on the Family Law Watch List and asking the AFP to seize the child's Australian passport if they were being taken overseas (Askola 2018, 16).

Another important aspect of the cases of *Kreet v. Sampir* (2011) and *Madley v. Madley* (2011) is that they both drew upon Australia's Marriage Act of 1961, federal legislation stating that any marriage solemnized without the full and free consent of both parties is rendered null. However, policymakers argued that the Marriage Act was not enough to prevent the marriage itself from occurring, because it could only be referred to after a marriage took place. Concern with the event of marriage itself generated legislation designed to deter someone from entering a marriage (rather than rendering it null and punishing a party to the marriage after the fact). How was this shift produced by and reflective of broader existential questions that animated policy discussions about the future of Australia as a destination for refugees and asylum seekers from the Muslim world? Forced marriage became a site where these questions were grappled with on the national and global stages.

Legislative Debates on Forced Marriage

In this section, I explore how forced marriage is treated as a culturally distinct expression of family violence and a criminal issue as well as how it comes to represent a symptom of migrant mobility. For policymakers, forced marriage was seen not only as a social welfare issue but as an issue of national identity and security.

A more recent history of legislative debates around forced marriage reveals that legislators were less concerned with how coercion was experienced than with how it offended Australian moral sensibilities around family, domesticity, marriage, gender, and sexuality. In a Parliamentary debate in 2012, MP Michael Keenan of the Liberal Party and acting shadow minister of justice, customs, and border protection at the time framed the issue as a threat to Australia's status as a modern nation: "Clearly, in modern-day Australia, we have no place for this type of violence, intimidation and deprivation. As a community, we do not accept, under any circumstances, the crimes of slavery, trafficking and forced marriage. These forms of abuse have absolutely no place in Australia" (*Parliamentary Debates* 2012). MP Craig Kelly situated it as a problem produced through migration from the Middle East and South Asia that, in fact, pose a threat to Australian citizen girls born in Australia: "Sadly, we have recently seen forced marriage arrive on our shores. There have been cases, apparently, where Australian girls have been taken overseas to countries where they have no legal protections and are forced to marry against their will. In many cases they are even forced to marry members of their own family. We have seen a recent *ABC Four Corners* program, titled "Without Consent," which cites several cases of young girls living in Australia who were forced into unwanted marriages back in Pakistan" (ABC News 2012). MP Teresa Gambaro of the Liberal Party, and shadow secretary for citizenship and settlement at the time, framed forced marriage as a problem of religious cultures: "It becomes difficult because many religious cultures, unfortunately see it as acceptable; and many cultures see the marriage of a 12- or 13-year old as acceptable. However, there is one underlying principle: It is not acceptable in this country" (*Parliamentary Debates* 2012). Nicola Roxon, who introduced the forced marriage law to Parliament and who was attorney-general at the time, expressed why the introduction of this amendment was so critical and historic: "Marriage should be a happy event, entered into freely between consenting adults." Here, Roxon's words frame marriage as the ultimate "intimate event," the way the event of normative love is formed at what Elizabeth Povinelli has called the intersection of the autological subject and the genealogical society in explaining heteronormative love in settler colonial states under late liberalism (Povinelli 2006, 4). Roxon's words harken to Povinelli's point that, in liberal settler states, marriage is undergirded by the myth of the fully consenting subject whose consent is signaled by the fact that she enters marriage "after falling in love." This consenting subject is juxtaposed against the "genealogical society" defined as the set of inherited institutions, norms, and traditions that impose a constraint on her freedom. Thus, entering into marriage for love is seen as a way of instantiating her sovereignty as a subject and a gateway into creating a heteronormative settler future in which the subject can fully exist in her autonomy. Roxon went on to say, "Forced marriage places young people at risk, and can result in many harmful consequences including the loss of education, restriction of movement and autonomy, and emotional and physical abuse. Some critics have asked, 'Won't this just force this underground?' I say to them that it is already underground and it cannot afford to stay that way. As Attorney-General it is my role to make it completely clear that in Australia, marriage must be entered into freely, without duress or constraint" (*Parliamentary Debates* 2012). Further analysis of Parliamentary debates reveals, however that concerns over the autonomy of subject were also concerns over the integrity of Australian ways of life and its borders. Legislators and media reports framed forced marriage as a hidden "epidemic" that was overtaking Australia, drawing upon a particular geographic imaginary that saw Australian society as invaded by the practice, even though statistics on its occurrence were cursory and incomprehensive (Deery 2017). The subject of invasion was both society itself and state laws, making the response to forced marriage both legal and discursive. In an article titled, "It is the young flesh they want," published in June 2014 after the forced marriage law's passing, it is noted that "Girls as young as 12 or 13 are disappearing from schoolyards, packed off to the countries of their parents' birth to wed men they have never met, while others are taken from their homes in southern Asia or the Middle East and brought into Australia to marry" (Barrowclough 2014).[8]

Following MP Nicola Roxon's 2012 introduction of the forced marriage law, the Senate Legal and Constitutional Affairs Committee of Australia created an inquiry around the proposed amendments to the Criminal Code of 1995, including the proposed amendment around forced marriage. The response was rapid, and several local community and legal organizations sent submissions, including the Australian Immigrant and Refugee Women's Alliance, the Victorian Immigrant and Refugee Women's Coalition (VIRWC), and the Australian Muslim Women's Centre for Human Rights. VIRWC recommended that forced marriage be treated as a civil rather than a criminal offense. AMWCHR pointed to the many reasons that drive forced marriage, including the economic precarities associated with building a new life in Australia. These organizations argued that criminalizing the practice risked alienating Muslim migrant communities who were being disproportionately targeted by the legislation. Specifically, these organizations posited that the following would happen should the law be implemented: a) victims would not report because they did not want to subject their parents to criminal investigation; b) disclosures would result in more students being surveilled at school; and c) criminalization would undermine existing efforts within communities to address a range of coercive practices and patriarchal systems that put unfair burdens on women to maintain family stability (Almarhoun and Nasr 2013). Despite the consensus that making forced marriage a criminal offense would do more harm than good, Parliament passed the law in 2013. In doing so, the law defined what constitutes a "forced marriage" in the following way: "For the purposes of this Division, a marriage is a forced marriage if, because of the use of coercion, threat or deception, one party to the marriage (the victim) entered into the marriage without freely and fully consenting" (2013 Amendments to 1995 Criminal Code, sec. 270.7A).[9] Coercion is defined explicitly as: "(a) force; (b) duress; (c) detention; (d) psychological oppression; (e) abuse of power; (f) taking advantage of a person's vulnerability."

Another key part of the legislation was that it was nested under the "Slavery, Slavery-like Conditions and People Trafficking" section of the 1995 Criminal Code. Doing so made it easier for some legislators to make the case that forced marriage should be treated with the same evidence-gathering and risk assessment tools as child trafficking. Treating forced marriage as a type of trafficking would institutionally make it easier for the AFP to include it as part of an existing set of issues it manages rather than to develop an entirely new set of procedures and to address it. Eventually, forced marriage became a part of AFP's Counter-Terrorism, Trafficking, and Narcotics Unit given its overseas component. However, in practice, it is not just the AFP that plays a role in stopping coercive marriage abroad. Other government bodies are also involved, especially if a case entails trying to help an Australian citizen leave the country where they are being held against their will and had been married. These bodies include the Department of Trade and Foreign Affairs as well as the Department of Immigration and Border Protection.

The passage of the 2013 law marked the beginning of a whole set of programs and initiatives designed to prevent forced marriage. The federal government's allotment of funds to national and local direct service organizations were part of its larger *National Action Plan to Combat Human Trafficking and Slavery* released in 2015, which dedicated over A$150 million to anti-trafficking initiatives (Department of Home Affairs 2015). From 2008 to 2015, the government dedicated over A$4 million to civil society organizations and other direct service organizations under the umbrella initiative of preventing human trafficking and slavery. This includes A$3.9 million distributed equally between Australian Catholic Religious against the Trafficking of Humans (ACRATH), Anti-Slavery Australia (ASA), Project Respect, and Scarlet Alliance, as well as A$500,000 for ACRATH, ASA, and the Australian Muslim Women's Centre for Human Rights to prevent and address forced marriage from 2014 to 2017; in addition to $250,000 for the Australian Red Cross to develop research, a client kit, and a service provider training program (Department of Home Affairs 2015), which are all major organizations that work directly with clients to prevent them from being coerced into marriages and providing educational workshops to migrant communities throughout Victoria. In 2020, The updated *National Action Plan to Combat Modern Slavery, 2020–2025*, allotted A$1.67 million to seven organizations, three of which would specifically work on addressing forced marriage in Australia (Department of Foreign Affairs and Trade 2020).

The Support for Trafficked People Program (STPP) was an important actor in the emergent forced marriage sector, because it was the main refuge for victims of forced marriages and those who were at risk of being taken abroad. However, as the primary federally funded and created program, it was tied to the criminal justice system. Entry into the STPP required victims to cooperate with AFP to receive support for ninety days, after which their support would end unless they continued to cooperate with AFP to pursue the investigation. The first forty-five days of the STPP is a recovery and reflection period designed to enable the victim to stabilize their situation and make an informed decision about how they want to proceed with the investigation. However, making victim support conditional on their cooperation with the criminal justice system was changed in 2019, when ARC increased the number of days of support from ninety to two hundred. The program is funded by the Federal Department of Families, Housing, Community Services and Indigenous Affairs, and the Red Cross has been managing it since 2009.

Two years into the law's passage, reports of dwindling disclosures made to AFP and zero prosecutions prompted the Australian legislature to think more closely about introducing stipulations about age within the 2013 amendment. Justice Minister Michael Keenan went on to introduce legislation that would make it clear that those under sixteen could never be presumed capable of consenting to a marriage. This would make anyone organizing a marriage for a minor, no matter how consent was solicited, guilty of committing a federal crime. Those who committed this offense, according to Keenan's proposed legislation, would incur penalties equal to slavery offenses (Australian Human Rights Commission 2015).[10]

Cultural Competence in Family Violence Prevention

In order to understand how family violence in migrant communities was seen as a product of cultural beliefs, it is important to understand how the idea of cultural competence makes its way into social welfare discourse. In the 1970s, multiculturalism emerged as a guiding political and social ethos for Australian public institutions, especially in the wake of the 1973 renunciation of the White Australia Policy, a collection of laws excluding non-White and non-western European migrants from entering Australia. Multiculturalism also found its way into migrant-targeted social welfare. Initially, these services centered on providing interpreter and translator services for what were first known as people of Non-English Speaking Backgrounds (known as NESB groups). In 1996, Culturally and Linguistically Diverse (CALD) was introduced to replace NESB when the Ministerial Council of Immigration and Multicultural Affairs (MCIMA) determined that NESB was no longer suitable to capture the myriad ethnic groups living in Australia. Specifically, the Council noted that NESB is a term with many different definitions; it groups people who are relatively disadvantaged with those who are not; it is unable to separately identify the many cultural and linguistic groups in Australia; and it has developed negative connotations (Sawrikar and Katz 2009). Sawrikar and Katz (2009) point out that the category of CALD, however, was limited in how it addressed these shortcomings:

> CALD's acknowledgment of the uniqueness of different (minority) groups detracts from the fact that in its common use, the term still refers to the same groups as NESB—those who are different from the majority; it is simply less transparent about the fact that there is a majority from which others are seen to differ. The mismatch between its function of celebrating diversity and its common categorical use for the non-Anglo Australian majority population, can still lead to relational exclusion among minority ethnic Australians who may feel both linguistically and culturally different from what constitutes being 'Australian' (2009, 3).

CALD, then, reflected a bigger issue with multiculturalism—that is, does the recognition of difference translate to equality or does it further "other" newly and recently arrived migrant groups? Other questions and debates that the CALD category have raised include: when people are considered CALD, along what lines are people pinpointed as different and from whom? Does CALD view culture as some kind of intrinsic and immutable part of someone's identity? And if so, does the category turn people's lived experiences into static and essentialized identities? It is important to note that the emergence of CALD also coincides with serious changes in immigration policy and in migration flows to Australia. In the mid-2000s, as skilled migration and humanitarian refugees from the Middle East and South Asia increased to an average of 13,000 per year compared to between 9,000 and 10,000 in the 1990s, CALD appeared frequently within official policy agendas around family violence. However, CALD is not only a common part of the family violence lexicon. It is also a key conceptual apparatus practitioners use to explain the causes and circumstances that produce family violence.

In the mid-2000s, several family violence organizations emerged to help migrant communities, including the Victorian Immigrant and Refugee Women's Coalition, Safe Steps, the Southern Migrant Resource Centre which served southeast Melbourne's suburbs, the Multicultural Centre Against Family Violence (MCAF), and the Centre for Multicultural Youth. Other organizations, such as the Women's Information and Referral Exchange, Wellness Springs, and Relationships Australia were key players in developing culturally appropriate family violence services. The magistrates' courts responsible for reviewing and granting family violence intervention orders also hired more translators, interpreters, bicultural workers, and community specialists to help people from different migrant communities navigate the application for Family Violence Intervention Orders.

Within the social service sector, the definition of family violence underwent an important shift in Victoria with the 2008 amendment to the Family Violence Protection Act (FVPA). The amendment included several additions in terms of what counted as family violence and who counted as perpetrators. First, it provided a broad and detailed definition of family violence beyond just physical abuse, including economic, emotional, psychological, spiritual, and financial abuse. The act also expanded to people who could be considered victims, broadening the definition of "family member" to include family-like members, as well as who can be considered a perpetrator to family-like members. In addition, the preamble recognized non-violence as a fundamental social value and violence as a violation of human rights. In contrast to the definition of family violence in the 1989 law, the 2008 version was concerned with the multiple expressions family violence took. The Act, for example, made it a civil offense to do anything that caused a person to fear for their safety or well-being or that caused a child to hear, witness, or be exposed to the effects of family violence. Overall, the FVPA of 2008 expanded what types of power dynamics amongst kin members counted as violent in the eyes of the law, including coercion and duress.

Advocates have argued that emotionally or psychologically abusive acts that control or dominate a family member and that cause them to feel fear for their safety are two key foundations upon which forced marriage fits the definition of

FIGURE 2 A wall of passports highlighting Australia's commitment to multicultural policies at the Victoria Immigration Museum in Melbourne.

family violence. For example, in 2018, Victoria included forced marriage as a statutory example of family violence in Section 5(1b) of the FVPA of 2008, making it one of two states (along with South Australia) to define forced marriage within legislation on family violence within state law. This law has been seen as a key framework through which to cement the status of forced marriage as a unique example of family violence, along with other forms of violence like dowry-related abuse. The inclusion of forced marriage into the act was the result of much advocacy among nongovernment organizations (NGOs), the Victorian Multicultural Commission, and several multifaith advisory groups that saw statutory inclusion as a key step toward getting more funding and government support for social welfare initiatives solely dedicated to addressing this issue.[11]

The 2016 Victoria Royal Commission into Family Violence's report was a pivotal moment in solidifying the idea that CALD communities were more vulnerable to family violence, thus further culturalizing the issue. The report noted that "multicultural communities face the biggest challenges in getting help" (Banasiak 2016). The commission released 226 recommendations the Victorian government approved to undertake. The government subsequently allotted A$1.9 billion to implement them. A key finding of the commission was that migrant women were disproportionately at risk of forced marriage, female genital cutting, and honor-based violence, because they were more intensely subject to community and familial expectations. However, in the findings, the reasons migrant women face these challenges were attributed to restrictions on their mobility placed by their communities, taboos around seeking help for mental and emotional health, and their own failure to recognize what they are experiencing as violence in the first place (Neave, Faulkner, and Nicholson 2016, 100, 156, 187).

Media reports also mobilized the Royal Commission's findings to support their own claims of culturalized violence. A report in *The Age* has covered the release of the findings, citing the brutal murder of Sabah Al-Mdwali, a twenty-eight-year-old woman who migrated from Yemen to Canberra by her husband, Maged Al-Harazi, as an example of how CALD communities faced higher risk of violence at the hands of their intimate partners (Gorrey 2017). The article also discusses how Al-Mdwali's local Muslim community actually encouraged the couple to get back together and mediated a peace between them when they were experiencing marital troubles, implying that this mediation is one of the proximate reasons for her murder.

Although forced marriage has been included within FVPA less as a cultural practice and more as a form of familial coercion, it reappeared recently as a culturally specific form of violence within the Australian Government's *Fourth Action Plan of the National Plan to Reduce Violence against Women and their Children* (Department of Social Services 2019b; Vidal 2018, 9). In the plan, forced marriage was included within "complex forms of violence and harmful cultural practices, including female genital mutilation/cutting, dowry abuse and human trafficking" (Department of Social Services 2019b, 6). This rendering of forced marriage shows that, at the federal level, it continues to be more associated with migrant cultures than at the state or territory level.[12]

Other reports, however, did acknowledge the role of systemic barriers in shaping women's vulnerability. The *Sydney Morning Herald* reported that "Social isolation, cultural and family pressures, stigmas around divorce, language barriers, visa arrangements, reluctance to seek outside help, unemployment, lack of transport and difficulty securing housing have been identified as hurdles to victims seeking help." The article went on to say:

> ACT Victims of Crime Commissioner John Hinchey says culturally and linguistically diverse (CALD) women were less likely to report violence and less likely to leave a violent relationship than other Australian women. 'Achieving safety is a difficult process for any woman in a violent relationship—but it is even harder for CALD women,' Hinchey says. Domestic Violence Crisis Service ACT chief executive Mirjana Wilson can't say domestic abuse happens more often in culturally and linguistically diverse communities, but those women are over-represented among the service's clients (Gorrey 2017).

While different family violence prevention organizations such as Safe Space and the Multicultural Centre Against Family Violence have a wide array of research on the causes of family violence in CALD communities, there remains a prevailing and underlying common sense that non-White immigrant communities are more susceptible to family violence and its victims less apt to report. What is less considered are the structural factors that prevent some migrant women from reporting. These include past negative experiences with racialization through contact with policing authorities and fear that putting oneself in contact with police could put their temporary immigration status, or those of their partners, in jeopardy. One lawyer I interviewed at a gender and human rights clinic at an organization that provides immigration support for asylum seekers mentioned that it is very difficult for asylum seekers to report instances of domestic violence if they are still waiting for their asylum claims to be reviewed.

The lawyer mentioned that in recent years, her organization received several cases in which a wife and husband who had arrived in Australia via boat in the mid-2000s had applied for asylum through a joint application. In the meantime, they would be on bridging visas (a kind of temporary holding visa one has while waiting for one's asylum claim to be reviewed). If the woman's husband was abusing her, their applications would be immediately separated, his bridging visa would be cancelled, he would be deported, and his application for asylum would be permanently jeopardized. If he was the main source of financial support for the woman, she would be left with little to no resources, leaving her with no source of financial or housing support. Here, it is not that a migrant woman would not report simply because she comes from a migrant background and a submissive culture, but because there are material losses and risks associated with reporting, which are connected to a broader regime of asylum and deportation.

The Depiction of Forced Marriage as an Immigration Issue in Australia

After the forced marriage law passed, prevention efforts were concerned with questions of migrant assimilation, Australian sovereignty, and the limits of the state's jurisdiction over migrant mobility. Family violence prevention is another example of how social welfare is mobilized to create immigration policy (Park 2011). On one level, overseas marriage becomes a concern to the state because of how it might serve as a gateway for spousal visas. The extent to which Australia can intervene in marriages that take place in other countries is also a question that is raised with forced marriage prevention. Something the AFP was struggling with was how exactly to remove victims from their home countries beyond simply working with the Australian Embassy in that country. While they could not send Australian personnel to the country, they could communicate with the victim to organize their flights back to Australia, but ultimately escaping a coercive situation was up to the victim and whatever resources they had at their disposal. This inability to physically intervene overseas led some in the AFP and social welfare to call for more intense scrutiny of spousal visa applications—this was an area in which they felt they could intervene. At a VFMN meeting in May 2017, I was struck by several practitioners' calls to implement new provisions to the existing forced marriage law or to existing immigration laws that would threaten cancellation of a spousal visa. This assumes that the coerced party viewed the visa as the coercive element in the transaction when in some cases, participating in a relationship after applying for a spousal visa was seen by the coerced party as more coercive rather than facilitating the entry of the individual into Australia.

While such an amendment has not yet been passed, it is worth noting that 2017 saw several proposals from the federal government and the Ministry of Immigration around more stringent scrutiny of prospective migrants' value systems, specifically their views on forced marriage and family violence. The state's preoccupation with migrant assimilation as an issue of incompatible cultural values found expression in 2017 when Prime Minister Malcolm Turnbull and Immigration Minister Peter Dutton announced that they were proposing serious overhauls to the Australian citizenship test. The questions would be designed to assess migrants' beliefs around religious freedom and gender equality, which were framed as distinctly Australian values. In April 2017, Turnbull proposed that any new arrivals to Australia had to prize "Australian values" and show their commitment to the nation when they applied for citizenship. As of 2020, aspiring citizens would have to declare how committed they were to Australian values by declaring what their attitudes were toward gender equality. Example questions now include: "In Australia, are people free to choose who they marry or not marry?" In addition, those migrants who had a documented history of family violence could be wholly barred from citizenship. They would have to demonstrate an integration into Australian society by joining community organizations and showing evidence that they were employed and that their children were in school (Rachwani 2020).

Turnbull's stated motivations for reforming the test was to "put Australian values at the heart of citizenship processes and requirements." He continued, "Membership of the Australian family is a privilege and should be afforded to those who support our values, respect our laws, and want to work hard by integrating and contributing to an even better Australia." Dutton noted that applicants had to view citizenship as "a big prize." He continued, "Our country shouldn't be embarrassed to say we want great people to call Australia home. We want people who abide by our laws and our values and we should expect nothing less" (Dziedzic and Belot 2017). Thereafter, Dutton noted that, in order to assess migrants' commitment to Australian values, questions would be included on respect for women and children, with a specific focus on early and forced marriage, female genital cutting, and domestic violence. According to scholars Linda Briskman and Scott Poynting (2018), amid ongoing debate about "Australian values" and how migrants could assimilate into society, this proposed test was met with widespread approval among right wing nationalist groups like Reclaim Australia.

Histories of Marriage Regulation and the Settler Colonial State

"How, then, did Australia become so similar in its culture and ethnic makeup to a society at the other end of the world? . . . The whole thing was carefully and deliberately planned within the context of the global British empire. It is still being planned now that the empire has gone, using immigration as a method of controlling population change. This has been just as true for governments claiming to believe in the free market as for those subscribing to planning and social engineering" (Jupp 2007, 7).

This quote is from James Jupp, an Australian historian who has chronicled Australia's immigration policies as an expression of the existential anxieties of state-making. The making of the settler colonial state has its origins in the 1600s with surveys and missions by the Dutch East India Company which sought land and resources that would set the precedent for future expeditions. The settler project of dispossession begins in 1770 and 1788 with the violent incursion of James Cook on Kamay/Gamay (later renamed Botany Bay in what is today New South Wales) and the subsequent importation of 1,300 penal convicts led by Captain Arthur Phillip in 1788 in the same area. The creation of Australia as a settler colonial nation state is deeply entangled with the preservation of Whiteness and the forms of sociality associated with it (Carey and McLisky 2009). Settler colonial forms of governance and economic systems of private property were based on the destruction of Indigenous communities, systems of knowledge, and the separation of families. The policing of who Aboriginal and Torres Strait Islander people could marry has been a key technique the state has used to preserve Whiteness and settler colonialism as a political and economic system. Australia's origin story is one of a society engineered to both expand the British imperial state's influence in the South Pacific and create a space where British debtors could be punished, yet simultaneously redeemed, by participating in settlement and agricultural labor on stolen Indigenous land. Historian Angela Woollacott (2015) has written about the extent to which British settlement in Australia was part of this ethos of societal establishment that rendered Australia a unique colonial experiment compared to other British colonies. By the 1820s, Australian colonies were actively sought out by British settlers, many of whom were former administrators and bureaucrats of the British empire and had been stationed across the imperial world. Australia's history as a convict penal colony is telling in how the balance between freedom and coercion was a key anchor for Australian nationhood. Situated as a site where Britain could house its "extra" and "unwanted" debtor and convict population, New South Wales and Tasmania became places where prisoners were coerced into labor in exchange for the promise of freedom and resettlement.

What began as British penal colonies for convicts and rebels would become an attractive long-term destination for British settlers who saw the appeal of unpaid laborers and easy accessibility to a remarkable amount of land (Woollacott 2015, 1). In the 1850s, most of the Australian colonies had transitioned from penal settlements to a more structured government and a "free settler society" (2015, 2). "Free settlers" were globally oriented and aware of existing racial hierarchies in the world they sought to reproduce in Australia. Settlers were able to engineer the societies they wanted by moving within the mainland and saw the progress of Australia and their own prosperity as inextricably linked to the future of the British Empire in other colonies. Settlers' theft of Aboriginal land and the subsequent forms of violence and displacements of Aboriginal communities is at the heart of the contemporary Australian nation-state's founding. Settlers were not only Anglo-British but also German and from other parts of Western Europe. They eventually identified as Australian during the shift from penal colony to settlement and saw themselves at the forefront of shaping these new colonies as part of a larger British Empire (2015, 10). As Woollacott (2015, 11) notes, "Displacing and criminalizing Indigenous people . . . were justified by the settlers' belief in the superiority of Christian white Britishness, and buttressed by the knowledge that they were part of a global British ascendancy." According to Jupp (2007, 16), "The Australian population was planned and engineered to a greater extent than is true for almost anywhere else. Assisted passages continued to be used but were opened by international agreement to other nationalities after 1947." The planned nature of Australian society reverberated in its approach to immigration in the twentieth century. According to Jupp (2007, 7), Australian immigration policy has, over the past 150 years, relied on three pillars: the maintenance of British hegemony and "White" domination; the strengthening of Australia economically and militarily by selective mass migration; and state control of these processes. This is all to say that

Australian settler colonialism was initially formed through the settler's conception of Australia as part of a broader imperial project based on White supremacy and attendant notions of intrinsic superiority. These initial self-conceptions continue to reverberate in the domains of policy, law, and social welfare.

It is necessary to explain how Australia's nationhood as a predestined fact has informed its approach to immigration, specifically its logics of border control on the mainland and in the surrounding maritime region. I point to the logic of border control to show that the state's pre-emptive attitude toward migration has historically been haunted by an anxiety around the precarity of Australian sovereignty—the imminent threats to it by external "others" (migrants) and internal "others" (Indigenous communities). While this ethos marks the foundational violence of settler colonial states, the inevitability of "Australia" lends its claim to sovereignty a unique bent that helps to explain why non-White migrants are seen as threats. Suvendrini Perera (2009, 61) writes, "the seemingly self-evident nature of Australia—as a unitary, sovereign geo-body whose boundaries naturally coincide with its continental landness—is undone, or at least put into question in several ways, by its colonial history." As an island with clearly defined maritime borders, Australia has been represented in political and nationalist narratives as the realization of a predestined prophecy—a territory that was waiting to be discovered. It has been viewed as a configuration of land that, in its clear demarcations on the map, was meant to be settled. In various cartographic illustrations, it is not simply the contours of the Australian nation that are illustrated but also the idea of a predestined Australian identity (2009, 18). As Perera (2009, 18–19) writes, "The Australian nationalist imaginary is predicated on the construct of the island-continent, that is, of a singularity understood as whole and self-contained . . . [these] imaginaries depend upon an anachronistic and ahistorical assumption of a pre-existing territoriality, a country ready made, already there." Australian settler colonialism begins with the erasure of Indigenous life. Through codifying the notion of *terra nullius* (the land belonging to no one) in law, Australian statehood is based on the premise that the landmass itself was always already there for the taking, the notion that land and water perfectly meet to produce a ready-made sovereign entity where other terrestrial and maritime borders do not have to be negotiated. The idea of Australia as the pre- destined space of European discovery and civilization has influenced its immigration policies historically. If Australia is pre-made and pre-existing, then the threats to it are also pre-made and pre-existing, ready to be found like the land itself. The fantasy that Australia was destined to be a White nation was key in the government's rejection of migrants in the early 2000s and in rerouting them to offshore detention centers later in 2002, 2008, and 2012, which were only shut down in 2019. According to Australian anthropologist Angela Mitropoulos (2015), the border is a system of classification, and in that sense, its integrity relies upon seeing migrant movements near it, toward it, and even after they have reached it in terms of the extent to which they pose a risk to the nation-state itself, shaping a pre-emptive response (Weber 2006; Weber and McCulloch 2019; Wilson

FIGURE 3 Poster circulated by the Australian Government to prospective asylum seekers in Afghanistan, Sri Lanka, and Indonesia, among other countries in South and Southeast Asia, designed to deter them from seeking refuge in Australia via boat (Australian Government).

and Weber 2008). According to Sharon Pickering and Leanne Weber (2014, 18), Australian border control is now trying to anticipate the "risky traveler" before any actual journey to the border has commenced, thereby situating communities in the global South as threatening in their "potential" to travel.

In this section, I give an overview of how Australia's outlawing of forced marriage and its disproportionate policing of Muslim migrant communities retains many parallels to how the state has intervened in the marital practices of Indigenous communities. That is not to draw an identical line between the two cases as there are both obvious and subtle differences between them. Muslim migrants are, arguably, also entangled in the settler colonial project in complicated ways as they live on Indigenous land and participate in settler colonial systems of power to various degrees. While their claims for political recognition and fair treatment are not tied to ancestral connections to land in Australia, many asylum seekers, including Hazara Afghan refugees, have been displaced as a result of their own status as Indigenous minorities suffering from state-sanctioned persecution. However, both Muslim migrants and Indigenous communities share experiences of being policed and seen as threats and as part of backward and regressive cultural milieus. This policing has taken the form of different kinds of surveillance that focus on everyday public comportment, and on the health of their familial relationships and religious beliefs, through programs like the Countering Violent Extremism program which began in 2010.

In fact, as some anthropologists have argued, Australia's strengthening of multicultural policies and programs have often been accompanied by intensified laws that govern migrant entry into the nation-state. Analogously, the strengthening of multiculturalism in the 1970s and 1990s, while opening up new opportunities for land claims by Indigenous communities, also produced new forms of government oversight on the expiration of such claims and stringent evidentiary requirements to prove such claims (Lea 2020; Povinelli 2002). Overall, settler colonialism as a project of preserving Whiteness as a racial and social identity, but also as a political and economic system continues to shape structural inequality in the country (Dunn and Nelson 2011; Forrest, Lean, and Dunn 2016; Hage 2000; 2011; Howard-Wagner 2013; Kowal 2008; Povinelli 2002).

Historically, marriage has been a site where the very future of the settler colonial project is grappled with. Marriage practices become key to the settler project of consolidating land and constructing lines of inheritance of this land. The regulation of coercion into marriage among migrants today, while less rooted in a concern with land, is still rooted in a concern with how the social mores and behaviors of society will erode if certain conditions of entry into marriage occur. Forced marriage also poses a threat to Australian sovereignty, in that the violence of concern is transnational and cannot be tracked or monitored entirely by Australian law enforcement apparatuses.

Historically in Australia, the principle of rescue has been used to justify the settler colonial project, which is an ongoing one. Indigenous marriage practices were systematically subjected to policies framed as rescuing Indigenous communities via controlling interracial marriage or insidiously punishing the offspring of interracial marriage, known as "mixed bloods." Laws like Victoria's Aborigines Protection Act of 1886 introduced all-encompassing regulations on the lives of Indigenous communities, including where they lived, their employment, and whom they could or could not marry.[13] In the state of Queensland, the Aboriginals Protection and Restriction of the Sale of Opium Act 1897 forbade Indigenous women from marrying a non-Indigenous man without the permission of an Indigenous protector. In the Northern Territory, the Aboriginals Ordinance 1918 restricted marriages between Indigenous women and non-Indigenous men. The logic of such acts reflected the White Anglo state's anxieties around miscegenation and the threat that a "hybrid colored population" posed to the creation of a racially homogeneous White Australia (Ellinghaus 2003, 192; Howard-Wagner 2013, 220). Other laws took the approach of "biological absorption," which entailed coercing Indigenous people to marry into White Anglo families to facilitate offspring that would eventually be considered White.[14] This was often paired with separating children from their Indigenous mothers. While each state's policies were different, they ultimately reflected a desire on the part of White Australian policymakers to "civilize" Indigenous peoples whom they had uprooted through a tactic of biological absorption of the mixed-descent population.

The policing of Indigenous familial relations continues today under the guise of rescuing Indigenous children from their "unfit" parents and family members. In 2007, the Northern Territory Intervention was ordered by the Howard administration into alleged rampant child sexual abuse and family violence. A state of emergency was declared to employ military force to remove children from their families and communities (Howard-Wagner 2013). At the time, Howard called the alleged family violence as affecting the whole of Australia and as a universally recognizable stain on the country's history: "We believe that our responsibility to those children overrides any sensitivities of commonwealth/territory relations" (Everingham 2017). I raise this history in order to show that the regulation of marriage and familial relations through a logic of protection and rescue is not a new mode of governance and has its precedent in settler colonial relations of domination. This is a history that school staff and the social service sector is also highly aware of, and some have pointed out that the state's criminalization of forced marriage in 2013, while targeted toward Muslim migrants, was an extension of these logics in new form.[15]

I situate the state's criminalization of forced marriage and its attendant educational campaign as, on some level, an extension of the logics of these forms of policing, though not entirely the same. For example, the state is concerned with the long-term social consequences of marriages that were entered into under particular circumstances, rather than the act of coercion in and of itself. These long-term social consequences include the increase in domestic violence and other forms of gender-based violence within the marriage. This is similar to how the state was concerned not with the act of marriage itself, but the production of racially mixed offspring within the Australian population. Both concerns are also reflective of the state's anxieties around how well Indigenous and Muslim immigrant populations can assimilate. However, there are key differences in the state's concern with Indigenous versus Muslim migrants' marriage practices, to which I cannot do justice in this chapter. But one worth pointing out is that there is not the same concern with coercive marriage as a gateway into a racially impure population. However, during fieldwork I did overhear practitioners voice concerns over the effects of such marriages on the physical and cognitive development and potential disabilities of offspring of inter-cousin marriages which the state conflates with forced marriages (i.e., the idea that most forced marriages are probably inter-cousin marriages).[16] Additionally, the state's concern with forced marriage is entangled with a concern about protecting Australia's control over its borders; some documented cases of forced marriage (though it is unclear if these constitute most forced marriages) take place overseas, where Australian female citizens are coerced to marry men in their parents' home countries.

The history of family violence prevention in Australia can also be tied to the state's relationship with Indigenous communities. While it is difficult to pinpoint an originary moment to the emergence of the category "family violence," its definition was organized around and formed through conceptualizations of Indigenous communities. According to Australian scholar Suellen Murray (2007), definitions of domestic violence have changed over the last three decades, and in the 1970s, the Australian Government's Royal Commission on Human Relationships examined the idea of "family violence." The definition put forth was that family violence included "acts of violence by one spouse against the other spouse or against children" and focused squarely on physical violence, including marital rape. The inclusion of violence against children was a key difference between these early notions of family violence versus those of domestic violence, and it stemmed from government evaluations and assessments of Indigenous relations with children (Theobald 2011, 3). However, the definition became more expansive in the 1990s to include violence perpetrated by a broad spectrum of family members, not just male partners (Murray 2007, 66).

The use of the family violence concept represents a shift in the conceptualization of violence in the private sphere. Family violence, in its initial iteration and due to its concern with Indigenous ways of life, served to pathologize violence because it assumed that violent behavior could be traced back to the family itself as an isolated unit (Ramsay 2007, 262). According to Jacqueline Theobald (2011), in Victoria, the term "family violence" was generated by the state government to indicate that violence can occur by other family and community members. The term was adopted "with the intention of capturing the complex and interacting features of violence experienced by predominantly Aboriginal and Torres Strait Islander women and children . . . [and can be used to] acknowledge the continuing currency of 'domestic violence' as a descriptor for violence perpetrated by an intimate partner and 'family violence' as a preferred term for many indigenous people" (Wendt and Baker 2013, 512). Thus, family violence itself marked a distinct expression of violence unique to Indigenous communities—different from domestic violence's newly progressive iteration—one that was intrinsic to the family rather than shaped by social conditions and that occurred beyond the conjugal couple and other familial networks.

At the same time, family violence services came to increasingly focus on the multiple vectors of kinship relations and dynamics that shaped Indigenous experiences of family life. While services did try to expand their understanding of Indigenous kinship relations, they tended to focus on how they were part of broader coercive and abusive social and cultural forms in Indigenous communities. The go-to solution was often pinpointed as separating the abused victim from their family, with little regard for the consequences of separation. Aboriginal and Torres Strait Islander-specialized services took a different approach: "Aboriginal women's services' goals were different from those of their Anglo counterparts. For them, the breaking up of the family would be the last resort' in responding to family violence. The refuge movement came to acknowledge that the 'Aboriginal women's major struggle' was 'with the general Australian community as a whole' as much as men's violence" (Theobald 2011, 164–165).[17] In 2006, the Australian Government began an initiative under the Keating administration to work with states and territories to create initiatives to address Indigenous family violence. The Commonwealth Department of Family and Community Services began funding various state departments to set up transitional housing for Indigenous women and children facing homelessness due to family violence (Wendt and Baker 2013, 513). The Australian government's *National Plan to Reduce Violence against Women and Their Children 2010–2022* (Department of Social Services n.d.) explicitly states the need to support Indigenous communities to create local strategies around the prevention of family violence and sexual abuse.[18] Recently, there has been a move to create more Indigenous staff openings for social services in policy agendas, such as the Special Taskforce on Domestic and Family Violence in Queensland Report (2015), *Not Now, Not Ever: Putting an End to Domestic and Family Violence in Queensland*. These specialized services have distinct funding streams and policy agendas. These plans also made family violence a social issue that required what is known as a "whole of community response." Similar to how domestic violence was resituated as an obligation of the community and the state, family violence in Indigenous communities was deemed a social ill that affected all of society and, therefore, required all of society to help eliminate and prevent it.

In family violence prevention discourse, family violence is seen as having a distinct expression among Indigenous communities that requires specific warning signs. A paper by Jane Lloyd (2014, 99) aims to track the characteristics of domestic violence-related homicides of Indigenous women in Central Australia to develop a profile of such deaths in these communities, including the events that led up to them. She aims to identify the "distinctive socio-cultural features that influenced and enabled the violence." A key premise of this paper and other reports

FIGURE 4 Family violence prevention protest. This sign emphasizes the violence of family separation in predominant family violence prevention approaches, Melbourne, 2016.

around domestic violence-related deaths in Indigenous communities is that these communities are already at risk of higher mortality rates compared to non-Indigenous populations (Kowal 2015; Lloyd 2014, 100; Rowse 1990; 1998; Saggers and Gray 1991; Sutton 2009; Tatz 1972; Tonkinson 2007; Watson 2010).[19] According to Lloyd (2014, 103), Indigenous women are nine times more likely to be victims of homicide than non-Indigenous women. She describes violence as "embedded in intimate partner relationships" in Indigenous communities and the unspoken rules around sexual relationships beginning at a young age (2014, 100). In her article, there is also an underlying narrative that government-led interventions into Indigenous communities in the form of "humanitarian interventions" have been key to alleviating domestic violence and child sexual abuse. The 2007 Northern Territory state military intervention resulted, according to Lloyd, in more welfare payments to women, thereby increasing their financial autonomy and the safety of Indigenous children. She also writes that the co-mingling of men and women in family "camps" beginning in the 1980s resulted in increased familial violence. The cohabitation of multiple generations and different sexes posed a serious problem for community safety (2014, 101).[20] The paper's implication is that Indigenous communities needed state intervention against social ills that began in their homes.

In situating Indigenous family violence as a social ill, prevention policies depicted Indigenous communities as needing to be further researched in terms of rates of violence. The approach to preventing domestic and family violence in Indigenous communities is based on the premise that it occurs at disproportionately higher rates in Indigenous communities than among White Australians, due to a number of exacerbating factors, including: alcoholism, drug use, and mental health issues. The disparities between Indigenous and non-Indigenous health have been the subject of much social welfare intervention. According to Emma Kowal's (2015, 10) ethnographic study of health interventions into Indigenous communities, the statistical gap between Indigenous and non-Indigenous health is also tied to imaginaries of citizenship for Indigenous peoples. This gap "holds the promise of a future where full citizenship rights can be enjoyed (at such time when the gap is finally closed)." The "gap" is not only a reminder of ongoing colonial oppression, but it has also been used to signal the inability of Indigenous communities to take responsibility for their communities' health and well-being (Kowal 2008, 342). Kowal writes that, when Indigenous statistics are "extracted and compared to 'non-Indigenous' ones, "biopolitical strategies encounter discourses of community control and cultural appropriateness." As a result, health and social welfare practitioners are constantly confronted with the question of: "is an elimination of this gap also the erasure of cultural distinctiveness?" (2008, 343). Thus, emphasizing a health problem within Indigenous communities has several consequences that can easily be reinscribed within discourses attributing such gaps to Indigenous culture. In a similar way, multiculturalism discourses have functioned to depict family violence as a distinct area of concern in migrant communities that is even more difficult to overcome as a result of their cultural beliefs and values.

Increasingly, migrant communities find themselves in a social welfare landscape that provides funding and support to migrant-led organizations that can demonstrate that they are invested in transforming culture and tradition. Less focus is placed on funding for anti-racism and immigration reform as a pathway to addressing family violence and coercion into marriage.

In fact, among the concerns about family violence were also concerns about Indigenous communities practicing early and forced marriage. In numerous news stories and TV interviews, these communities were portrayed as creating the problem of child sexual abuse by promising young girls at birth to different male relatives in the name of "traditional custom" (Howard-Wagner 2013, 227).[21] Indigenous communities historically have been seen as sites where trajectories of childhood have been corrupted through poverty and sexual violence. According to Prentice, Blair, and O'Mullan (2016, 241), sexual and family violence is amplified by several factors in Indigenous communities, including living in remote and rural areas. Rates of this violence in Indigenous communities are reported to be two to five times higher than in the non-Indigenous population (Bryant and Willis 2008; Wundersitz 2010). Indigenous women are also said to experience higher rates of domestic and family violence overall (Al-Yaman, Van Doeland, and Wallis 2006; Mouzos and Makkai 2004; Wild and Anderson 2007), with women living in rural areas at even higher risk than those in urban Australia (Wendt 2009). Such reports have contributed to and been mobilized to govern Indigenous communities via military force in the name of humanitarian ideals of care, which, over the past decade, have transformed into an emphasis on ideals of self-responsibilization and self-empowerment in Australian social welfare.

In her analysis of the 2007 Australian government's military intervention into the Northern Territories following reports of rampant child sexual and family violence, Deirdre Howard-Wagner frames this moment as signifying a particularly nefarious form of governance of Indigenous lives. In the 2007 intervention, the state framed its duty of care as equipping Indigenous communities with the means for self-responsibilization in order to eliminate family violence and child sexual abuse through military force. Howard-Wagner (2013, 217) quotes Prime Minister John Howard's speech right before the intervention that children in the Northern Territory were "'living out a Hobbesian nightmare of violence, abuse, and neglect.'" The government went on to frame family violence in these communities as a result of welfare dependency and alcoholism and the failure of Indigenous communities to fulfill their social and economic potential. As Howard-Wagner (2013, 218) notes, through declaring a state of emergency in the Northern Territories, "a zone of exception was established." "The discursive construction of Indigenous communities of the Northern Territory as failed social enclaves in which violence and child sexual abuse was rife allowed for new disciplining, prohibitive, and corrective practices" (2013, 218). Here, the work of policing was tied to the work of social welfare and humanitarianism. The federal government went on to increase police presence in the area; implement harsh penalties around alcohol consumption and purchase as well as pornography; surveil people's movements through photographic identification laws; and make welfare payments contingent on proof of other factors, such as sending one's children to school or employment. This was done in the name of facilitating Indigenous autonomy and participation in "mainstream Australian society" (2013, 218). The idea that increased policing is a technology of social integration continues to find expression in the discourse surrounding forced marriage prevention. While forced marriage prevention focuses less on increasing a physical police presence in immigrant communities, there is an increased emphasis on equipping different social actors with the tools to identify what now have been legally codified as deviant behaviors on the part of parents. Many campaigns emphasize forced marriage as a problem because it is "illegal in Australia." The ability of migrant women to identify what now lies in an existential state of illegality and report it to an authority figure like a teacher signals not only their autonomy but their ability to socially integrate their families into the Australian nation.[22] Here, the ability to embrace the logic of illegality is the pathway toward self-realization and autonomy.

Colonial legacies of different kinds of policing often shape how security policies are implemented (Jaffe-Walter 2019, 450). Social welfare organizations that specialize in Indigenous well-being are often perceived by these communities to be reproducing past colonizing practices and are not easily trusted (Funston 2013).[23] Many Aboriginal-Torres Strait Islander organizations, such as the Aboriginal Family Violence Prevention Legal Service, treat family violence as a social injustice that is a legacy of the state of ongoing violence of settler colonialism itself (Cheers et al. 2006). However, there remain services that continue to pathologize family violence in Indigenous communities, situating this violence as born out of misguided social traditions, social isolation, and deviant social practices. Many of these cases are family-violence related. Family violence was also, then, inextricably linked to the settler colonial project for Indigenous people. The pathologization of violence in Indigenous communities diverts attention from structural inequality in their causes. This pathologizing of violence is resonant with how migrants today are seen as vectors of family violence caused by backward cultural and social traditions.

There are fundamental historical and structural differences between Indigenous experiences of the violence of state governance and those of recently resettled migrant communities, as well as the possibilities available to both for resistance or systemic reform. However, my focus on Indigenous experiences seeks to shed light on the ongoing practices of settler colonial forms of governance that continue to impact Indigenous people and migrants today. It is not to say that one should look to migrants to identify how settler colonial forms of governance are still operative, because they continue to operate on the lives and bodies of Indigenous communities. The pathologization of culture—that there are specific cultures of moral depravity requiring intervention and that social problems appear in communities who do not know how depraved they are—all coalesce within the settler colonial project and continue in how family violence is addressed today in migrant communities.

2

The Threat of Suffering

Configuring Victimhood in Forced Marriage Scenario Planning

Forced marriage policy is unique in that it was only after the law passed that practitioners began to develop standardized ways to identify at-risk individuals. Beginning in 2014, the prevention sector was steadfastly working to generate a profile of victimhood in and across multiple sites of learning, teaching, and intervention. Through examining scenario prevention trainings for direct service workers and advocates, this chapter questions how such profiles are constructed and what they mean to those who participate in their construction. In this chapter I show how scenario trainings, far from taking an evidence-based approach, employ essentializing cultural markers to construct narratives of Muslim migrant women as at-risk subjects, which reflect the state's language of moral anxiety around migration from the Muslim world. By examining scenario trainings (both the scenarios themselves and the conversations around them), I argue that: a) despite their attention to cultural detail, they use such cultural specificity to place migrant lives into limiting scripts, and b) they emerge as affectively charged technologies of power that reinforce and discipline how practitioners think about migrant women's suffering as threats to institutions like the family and citizenship.

Scenarios are used in all kinds of practice-based professional spaces as teaching tools. They communicate to professionals-in-training several things, including how the configuration of certain variables leads to certain outcomes and how to address them using intervention tools unique to that profession. In contrast to the idea that they represent impartial predictions of the future, scenarios can be deeply political forms of knowledge that reflect society's anxieties in a given historical moment. In spaces of government-funded social welfare professionalization, scenarios can also reflect what the state views as threats to national identity. Scenarios, then, serve to aid policies in imagining what undesirable futures for society look like and what outcomes should be avoided. As Winifred Tate (2020, 87) has written:

Policy production is a central site in which multiple futures are deployed in the present, haunted not only by the past but also by fears of possible things to come. These imagined futures constrain and shape the possibilities for action in the present. Some of the possible futures that weigh most heavily on the present are threats, imagined future dystopias, and the making real of worst-case scenarios. Through scenarios, modeling, and other forms of threat assessment and prediction, dystopian visions are constructed as possible futures that present policy must militate against.

Scenario trainings, then, are spaces within which real people can relate the imagined future of the scenario to their own lives and their moral and political ideologies. They are also spaces within which practitioners can, on a more visceral level, temporarily bring to life what an actual crisis and its fallout would feel like. They call upon social welfare practitioners to not only be compassionate to victims, but to see victimhood itself as a threat to national imaginaries of family, individual autonomy, and the nation's borders. Through mobilizing select cultural essentialisms, scenario trainings develop narratives about who is at risk and why, which practitioners are expected to treat as standardized narratives. In that sense, scenario trainings not only produce knowledge about potential victims; they also produce knowledge about the broader social world in which they exist.

In this chapter, I turn to how scenarios function as epistemological devices that configure how violence happens and how the conversations spurred by them are concerned with assessing potential threats to the victim herself and to Australian social norms more broadly. Scenario trainings not only teach people how to recognize specific situations as coercive; they also communicate how these situations matter to society. Through models drawing upon long-held gendered and culturally essentialist tropes about Muslim migrant communities, scenarios introduce what arrangements of familial relations should be cause for concern. I argue that embedded within forced marriage prevention scenario trainings are future-oriented nationalistic political and moral anxieties, declarations, and assessments of the state of Australian social norms around the family, the individual, and the nation-state's borders. In highlighting scenario trainings as part of the real-time implementation of what, at the time, was still a new policy, I show that practitioners participate in identifying the victim as both a vector of suffering and a vector of threat to social values. As such, scenario trainings interpellate practitioners as prognosticators who take up the responsibility of identifying potential sources of moral crisis. I use "interpellate" because it accounts for how people are subject to state apparatuses (ideological and repressive in the Althusserian sense; Althusser 1970). This allows for a decentering of practitioners' intentionality and a focus on what power relations they are pulled into—the politics of preserving Australian social norms around family and proving oneself worthy of belonging within the Australian nation-state.

Knowing Victimhood and Making It Matter

Ethnographies of care-based interventions and social welfare spaces have examined how to identify a victim. Social welfare settings that are tied to juridical and therapeutic institutions deploy criteria for what constitute legitimate forms of suffering. In doing so, they focus on how people are excluded from care because they do not meet the criteria for proper victimhood (Fassin and Rechtman 2009; García 2010; Razack 1995; Stevenson 2014; Ticktin 2011). In this chapter, I ask what happens when identifying victimhood is based on the hyperinclusive premise that everyone is always at risk of being a victim. I posit that forced marriage prevention scenario trainings are spaces that make young adult women's familial arrangements matter in particular ways for social welfare and the future of Australian conceptions of freedom and consent. In this chapter, I ask how scenario trainings develop standardized procedures to identify at-risk victim subjects and how victim subjects are conceived as vectors of threat to Australia's future.

Security Logics in Social Welfare

Much anthropological literature on scenarios has examined contexts of biosecurity, military exercises, and public health and development crisis management (Lakoff 2008; Rose 1998; Samimian-Darash 2022). Biosecurity is the study of threats to life, including public health threats to the human and nonhuman world. However, its philosophies of risk mitigation and identifying threat are not foreign to philosophies used in social welfare and spaces of care. Studies of scenario planning have examined how scenarios function to account for and mitigate risk in situations of war, geopolitical conflict (Masco 2014), domestic military operations (Samimian-Darash 2016), and collective intelligence around climate change, digital security, and economic stability (Faubion 2018). Other notions of scenario planning have focused less on spectacular scenes of crisis and more on long-term issues that are seen as chronic but still portend imminent vulnerability (Chen and Sharp 2014). In this chapter, I offer another example of the social life of scenarios that unfolds in the social welfare setting, an as of yet under-explored space in the literature on scenarios. The scenarios and scenaristic conversations I introduce are not mechanistic dialogues that ask how different variables affect different outcomes. Rather, they create scenes of what the social problem of forced marriage prevention looks like and define why it matters to the future of Australian society. Scenario trainings in forced marriage prevention *produce* marital coercion as a social crisis rather than *test* different interventive mechanisms. I offer that scenario planning in social welfare shares concerns about who counts as vectors of risk and threat, the past familial relations leading to risk, and what it means for the future of the nation. As Carlo Caduff (2014, 112) has written, scenarios can also be part of a "discursive machinery of mythical production" that calls upon the past and future. Forced marriage scenarios are certainly not the same as apocalyptic scenarios in biosecurity planning in that they do not address biological threats to the population. However, they are similar in that they diagnose and produce society (and in forced marriage prevention's case, liberal values) as existing in a moment of imminent failure. As Caduff (2014, 114) writes, "the staging of apocalyptic scenarios is another proof of power's . . . mimetic faculty. Power's task, in the mimetic theater of collapse, is to learn how to use the terror of terror as effectively as possible and reach an optimal level of public anxiety." In this way, scenarios can help to convert feelings of insecurity into *assessments* of insecurity (Barker 2012, 701).

It is important to mention that in contrast to biosecurity, forced marriage scenario contexts do not test how certain variables, configured in different permutations in a victim's life, will or will not yield certain outcomes. The variables explored (i.e., one's relationship with one's parents and extended family and how much control the victim is under in other aspects of her life) are not presented so that practitioners predict whether someone will be forced into a marriage. Rather, the scenarios are meant to illustrate the "worlds" within which coercion into marriage will occur. In its concern with risk, the hypothetical quality of these trainings suggests a form of scenaristic planning that exemplifies what James Faubion (2018) calls a "parabiopolitical sophiology," a helpful analytic in its concern with scenario formation. In his discussion of the FORESIGHT program—a long-term project that centers around the future of the European Union—Faubion offers a theory of "scenaristic governmentality" that exceeds the logic of a best/worst case dichotomy (2018, 6). This is apt, because many scenario planning exercises cannot develop metrics around predicting what sorts of outcomes correlate with what sorts of inputs. As Limor Samimian-Darash (2016, 361) writes within the context of Israeli government scenario planning exercises, there are multiple *dispositifs* of governance, some more invested in calculating precise risk factors and probabilities and others with accounting for the uncertain and the unknown—finding ways to make the unknowable slightly more graspable. Yet whether we call the creation of scenarios in forced marriage prevention *risk assessment* or *planning for uncertainty*, it is true that the sector's attempts to conceptualize the future require constructing the social realities in which it seeks to intervene. In the scenarios I analyze, there is an attempt to develop a mechanistic understanding of what kinds of family relations yield coercion into marriage and to create stories about what happens within families to account for the prevailing sense in the sector that there existed a lack of knowledge about migrant communities.

This chapter, then, focuses more on the world-building efforts of scenarios (Masco 2014, 206) and how they are undergirded by frameworks that bring the language of risk and nationalism together. Scenarios, in this context, produce the intimate contours of the social problems they claim exist *a priori* to their modes of apprehension. In constructing the victim of forced marriage as produced through the importation of foreign practices specific to migrants, scenario trainings treat the victim as a site of suffering but also, in her victimhood, a vector of threat with the potential to injure Australian social norms. The mobilization of these scenarios reflects forced marriage prevention as an affectively charged practice of knowing and constructing migrant realities.

Contextualizing Scenarios within Forced Marriage Prevention

When they first emerged in 2016 and 2017, scenarios on forced marriage were not entirely based on actual interactions practitioners had with victims. A major reason behind this was that, up to that point, zero prosecutions had been carried out under the law (a reality at the time of publication as well). This meant that there were no examples of cases being reported to direct service agencies that then made their way to the AFP, resulting in the prosecution and conviction of the organizers of a marriage. Due to confidentiality protocols, there was also little research at the time on cases of the AFP successfully preventing coercion into marriage or the specific tools practitioners used to respond to reported or suspected cases. Rather, the stories featured in training manuals were, themselves, amalgams—they pulled pieces from individual stories featured in news articles of young Muslim girls taken overseas to be married and from select aspects of practitioners' own experiences with clients. Many scenarios were aspirational in their depictions of what the response to reports of coercion would look like. In that sense, they had a distinctly future-oriented disposition. This outlook took concern with how to stop a marriage from coming to fruition but also with protecting the future of Australian social norms. But to take up that future-oriented attitude, scenarios had to first diagnose the nature of the problem itself by painting a picture of who the victim of a forced marriage was. Such select stories offered what came to be known as quintessential examples of forced marriage.

Before delving into the scenarios, it is important to point out that the 2013 law situates the violence of forced marriage as encapsulated by a set of bounded, consecutively ordered events culminating in the subject giving her (coerced) consent. However, in prevention trainings, scenarios depict coercion as a product of not only a set of consecutive events but also of migrant families' ongoing struggles to assimilate to Australian life while preserving familial culture and traditions. This is because a key part of forced marriage prevention trainings was to help practitioners understand the general environment in which coercive familial practices took place and how that set the stage for the criminal act itself. Knowing when an individual was at risk of being coerced into a marriage meant that practitioners were taught to be on the lookout for these "cultural struggles." As a result, "cultural struggles" were the social problems that practitioners discussed, while the individuals in the scenarios were rendered part of the background.

Identifying Risk

Who was being protected through these trainings? This was a key question I considered on the train ride from Melbourne to Morwell in November 2016 to attend a training led by an anti-trafficking organization. Morwell is part of the Gippsland region in the LaTrobe Valley in Southeastern Victoria, which is one of thirty-six areas designated "Refugee Welcome Zones" in the state as of March 2016. With a population of about 73,000 people, 79 percent were born in Australia (Alcorn and Bowers 2018) and 62.7 percent have both parents born in Australia (Australian Bureau of Statistics 2016). Morwell is one of several regional areas in which refugees were being resettled through government programs. A local chapter of a national organization that provided shelter and refuge for unhoused groups and other vulnerable groups had increasingly been hearing of secondary school teachers who suspected that students were at risk of being taken overseas to be married. Some students had even used the shelter's services to have a few weeks of separation from their families. As a result, the Morwell branch of the organization asked for a training session on forced marriage for local social service providers and teachers. I was eager to know what this first training would reveal about how forced marriage was being treated as a social and community issue.[1]

The training was administered by Alice for schoolteachers, caseworkers, youth workers, community leaders, and health practitioners. It consisted of a presentation on the forced marriage law but also explained and solidified the definition of forced marriage as a readily identifiable event that occurs throughout Australia. The latter part of the training was a set of exercises in which practitioners would be given scenarios and they would have to identify what parts of the scenarios raised red flags. These red flags would help trainees identify how that person was at risk of being coerced. However, the trainees were not asked to raise red flags (at least not at first) based on a set of metrics of what constituted coercion into marriage. Rather they were asked to rely on their intuition to identify aspects of the story that stood out to them. They were also asked to think about what constituted the proper form of intervention to prevent the marriage from happening and thus ensure, at the very least, the short-term safety of the victim.

I arrived at the training and saw that Alice was beginning the presentation. Alice had been working with a Melbourne-based social service organization which was at the forefront of providing direct service and education work around human trafficking for almost two decades. She had seen forced marriage prevention as an extension of her work in this space. This experience had shaped her views on why forced marriage was a problem connected to migration and Australia. For Alice, forced marriage was a symptom of a broader problem that migrants brought with them and suffered through at the same time. Victims, according to Alice, were members of families struggling to assimilate to western cultural ideas. The idea that coercion into marriage was a migration issue would emerge later in the scenario training. For now, Alice began speaking about the warning signs of an "at-risk" person to an audience of about twenty people, all of whom were women across five rows of tables. Alice was at the front with training literature stacked in front of her. She began the PowerPoint, each slide giving a more detailed glance at what it meant to be forced into marriage. Alice enunciated every word she spoke, and it was clear that she had given this presentation several times before. There was something very simple and direct about her delivery. I found myself nodding throughout, almost convinced that the definitions of coercion and consent were clear cut, universal, and made sense as objective truths. She stated: "A forced marriage is a marriage that is entered into without the individual's full and free consent. It occurs in all cultures, not just one. It is against the law in Australia. It destroys the futures of young girls as it can lead to early pregnancy, domestic violence, and domestic servitude." The succinctness of the statements drew the audience in—to their surprise, forced marriage seemed to be much more straightforward than some had suspected, especially those who had never heard of the term or had only heard of the practice as occurring in the global South. The questions that first propelled me into this project crept up again as I focused in, my attention caught by the clear-cut world being painted on the white board. After the overview Alice provided, the participants were asked to read the following story from a Forced Marriage Educational Curriculum in development at the time—a set of training materials Alice spearheaded for secondary schools throughout Australia to use:

> Ayla is a 17 year-old high school student in Australia. Ayla's teacher notices that Ayla seems depressed and has taken a lot of time off school for overseas travel. Her teacher also observes that Ayla's family seem to be very strict and controlling. Ayla always has someone with her outside school hours and the teacher has heard from Ayla's classmates that she isn't allowed to go out with friends without a family member going with her. When the teacher asks Ayla if she is okay, Ayla says that her parents took her to visit relatives overseas. When they arrived, her parents told Ayla that she would only be able to go back to Australia if she agreed to marry her cousin, whom she had never met. With no passport or money, Ayla was forced to marry her cousin overseas so that she could return to Australia. Ayla's parents have also told her that, when she turns 18, she will have to sign migration papers for her cousin so that he can come to Australia to live with her. Ayla tells her teacher that she feels like a slave and never wanted to marry her cousin. Ayla says that she feels trapped and is scared about what might happen if she tries to leave. Ayla asks her teacher for help. Ayla's teacher contacts the AFP for help. Although Ayla does not want her parents or 'husband' to be prosecuted, the AFP is able to help her access support, including safe accommodation, financial support, legal advice and counselling. As a result of this assistance, Ayla is able to work towards establishing the future she wants for herself. (Australian Catholic Religious against Human Trafficking 2020)

The scenario above, while it seems like it could represent anyone, contains several markers that signal a particular kind of community as the protagonists. Prior to the passage of the 2013 law, a select few news stories in the Australian press had either involved young girls marrying a cousin or a man they had never met, usually within Pakistan or Afghanistan. The reference to inter-cousin marriage was clearly drawing from such depictions, despite the fact that no statistical evidence pointed to a higher rate of such marriages within Muslim migrant communities living in Australia. Another important component of this scenario is that it is only Ayla's teacher who assesses her situation—it is her teacher who makes the judgment that her family is strict and controlling. We do not learn much about Ayla's understanding of her family relations except for her declaration that she feels like a slave and does not wish to marry her cousin. We do not know if this has been a long-held feeling of subjugation or something that has emerged with this marriage proposal situation. However, the scenario includes assessments that her family is generally controlling, because they do not allow her to go out. This conveys that coercion into marriage for the purposes of migration happens in a family that manages their child's friendships and social relations, and inter-cousin marriage is the form this configuration of coercion takes. In other words, this scenario mobilizes facts that are clear indications of coercion but often do not map on to the complexities of how such coercive relations unfold on the ground.[2]

Practitioners I interviewed certainly heard about young women who had been involved in inter-cousin marriages and women who had applied for spousal visas for extended family members including cousins shortly after their marriages. They had also come across young females who felt coerced into making choices around living with their parents and having to abide by curfews and rules about whom to socialize with. Thus, the individual components of the scenario are not outside the realm of practitioners' interactions with clients prior to the passage of the law. However, the scenario presents a configuration of violence that gives the impression that forced marriage comes in a neat amalgamation of family relations, coercive patterns, and sequential facts knowable through the prism of existing government warning signs and tropes associated with Muslim migrant communities, including the prevalence of inter-cousin marriage. For example, educators shared in a different training that some of their students wanted to participate in marriage toward the end of secondary school because it would create a legitimate pathway for them to leave their parents' homes, where they felt controlled in terms of their friendships, social lives and everyday financial choices. For those women, their home lives checked off many of the warning signs, including parents who controlled their finances and social lives and an upcoming overseas marriage. However, some did want to participate in marital relations to begin families and lives of their own. In this way, marriage, even one that was proposed and organized by one's family members, could be used as a vehicle through which to leave the everyday forms of control one's family had on one's everyday mobility and social life.

Rather than accounting for these complexities, the scenario was a one-to-one reflection of the official warning signs that someone is at risk of a forced marriage, according to the government-produced forced marriage pack for social service agencies. Part of the reason for this, I contend, was that scenarios are supposed to create worlds that require intervention. Scenario training is designed to teach practitioners how to effectively intervene. In this case, intervention included calling the AFP, developing a safety plan with the client if they were already a client of that organization's social support services, and potentially referring the matter to Child Protective Services (CPS). However, the latter would often refer the case back to AFP, because they had final jurisdiction on criminal prosecution and referring the victim to the ARC's STPP services for aid and support. When these nuances are introduced, the need for intervention would be put into question. During the training, the attendees concluded that the scenario with Ayla mapped on to the following official government warning signs:

- Ayla's teacher notices that *Ayla seems depressed and has taken a lot of time off school for overseas travel.*
- Her teacher also observes that *Ayla's family seems to be very strict and controlling.*
- Ayla always *has someone with her outside school hours.*
- The teacher has heard from Ayla's classmates *that she isn't allowed to go out with friends without a family member going with her.*
- When the teacher asks Ayla if she is okay, Ayla says that *her parents took her to visit relatives overseas.*

These warning signs, the attendees concluded, mapped on to the following official signs that someone was at risk:

- The person's family has a lot of control over the person's life, which doesn't seem normal or necessary (for example, the person is never allowed out or must always have somebody else from the family with them).
- The person seems scared or nervous about an upcoming family holiday overseas.
- The person is unable to make significant decisions about their future without consultation or agreement from their parents or others (Attorney-General's Department n.d.).

The scenario then, employs a set of characters and protagonists to transport the warning signs onto a potential real-life person. The character of Ayla is constructed as an amalgamated embodiment of these warning signs to help practitioners better know how they would appear in an actual human being. The scenario of Ayla creates a world of distinct components that mirror government documents, discourses, and anxieties around migration and the importation of deviant social practices more than it accurately reflects the nuances of a specific case.

Here, I want to step back from the training at Morwell and pivot to another training in which the reasons for marriage and familial interdependence do not fit within emerging institutional frameworks about the victim's familial relations. At a workshop on forced marriage prevention in downtown Melbourne organized by the Australian attorney-general's office, a direct service practitioner named Farah, who works at a center focused on helping migrant women from the Middle East and South Asia, explained to me the vast array of reasons that she witnessed female clients being married. She mentioned that a forty-five-year-old woman of

FORCED MARKAGE

Forced Marriage: INFORMATION SHEET

> **For information about forced marriage**, visit <www.mybluesky.org.au>. You can seek free, confidential legal advice, or report possible cases of forced marriage, by contacting the national forced marriage helpline, *My Blue Sky*: call 02 9514 8115, SMS 0481 070 844, or email help@mybluesky.org.au. If you want to report someone in, or at immediate risk of, a forced marriage, call the Australian Federal Police on 131 AFP (131 237). In an emergency, dial Triple Zero (000).

What is forced marriage?

Everyone in Australia is free to choose whether to get married. Forcing anybody to get married is never acceptable and is a crime in Australia. A forced marriage happens when a person gets married without **freely and fully consenting**, because they have been **coerced, threatened or deceived**, or because they are **incapable of understanding the nature and effect of a marriage ceremony**, for reasons including age or mental capacity. Some types of coercion are obvious and easy to identify and can include the use of physical or sexual violence or refusing to let somebody leave a particular place or location until they accept the marriage. Other types of coercion are less obvious because they involve psychological and emotional pressure. These types of coercion can include making a person feel responsible for, or ashamed of, the consequences of not marrying, such as bringing shame on their family.

Forced marriage is a slavery-like practice, a form of gender-based violence and an abuse of human rights. Anybody can be a victim of a forced marriage, regardless of their age, gender, sexual orientation or religious or cultural background. The crime of forced marriage applies to cultural, religious or legal marriages that occur in Australia (including where a person was brought to Australia to get married), as well as where a person is taken from Australia to get married overseas.

It is important to know the difference between a forced marriage and an arranged or sham marriage. While an arranged marriage involves the introduction of potential spouses through the involvement of a third party or family member, it requires the consent of both parties, who can agree or refuse to marry. A sham marriage is a fake marriage willingly entered into by both parties for fraudulent purposes.

How can I tell if someone is in, or at risk of, a forced marriage?

If someone you know is in, or at risk of, a forced marriage, they may have difficulty telling you about their situation. However, a combination of the following signs may indicate that a person is in a forced marriage, or at risk of being made to enter into a forced marriage:

- a sudden announcement that the person is engaged
- the person's older brothers or sisters stopped going to school or were married early
- the person's family have a lot of control over the person's life which doesn't seem normal or necessary (e.g. the person is never allowed out or always has to have somebody else from the family with them)

FIGURES 5A AND B Official warning signs that someone is at risk of being forced into a marriage as part of the forced marriage information pack circulated to direct service providers (Australia Attorney-General's Department).

- the person displays signs of depression, self-harming, social isolation and substance abuse
- the person seems scared or nervous about an upcoming family holiday overseas
- the person spends a long time away from school, university or work
- the person often doesn't come to, or suddenly withdraws from, school, university or work
- the person doesn't have control over their income
- the person is unable to make significant decisions about their future, including without consultation or agreement from their parents, and/or
- there is evidence of family disputes or conflict, domestic violence, abuse or running away from home.

It can be difficult to identify the signs of forced marriage and these descriptors are not intended to be exhaustive. You should always seek help and advice as soon as possible.

Lebanese descent who recently was resettled as a refugee in Australia was being coerced to marry a widower living in Lebanon. Her children and extended family felt adamant that she needed someone to take care of her daily needs given the difficulties of starting a new life without support in a new country. Farah also mentioned that people living in Australia were being pressured to sponsor spousal visas for their cousins stuck in refugee camps in Pakistan and Iran, displaced as a result of being persecuted and targeted by the Taliban as a result of working with US/NATO forces during the ongoing war in Afghanistan (2001–2021). Other clients were confronting drug addictions, depression, and anxiety. In these cases, marriage was thought to be a step toward entering into a set of relations with someone who would be able to provide them with the care they needed. Farah noted these were not clear cut examples of "familial control" in the way the warning signs suggested.

The workshop pivoted to discussing a scenario from the Attorney-General Forced Marriage Information Pack for Community Organizations and Service Providers. The scenario of Ayla from the Morwell training reappeared in the AG conversation. After the groups discussed the scenario among themselves, the moderator asked for each group's responses. Farah mentioned that she would try to understand the interdependencies that existed within Ayla's family that she did not see as mutually exclusive from also prioritizing her well-being. In an attorney-general's workshop on forced marriage, a Victoria State police officer (VicPol), who also identified as Lebanese Muslim, mentioned that she would try to reconfigure the physical contact that Ayla could have with her family members to provide Ayla with a safe environment. She mentioned that she would file a family violence intervention order (FVIO) to take the father out of the house and put the girl back in the home. Farah interjected by asking, "What if the mother doesn't want the father to leave the home since he is the only source of income and the guy who drives people around everywhere? This will create a lot of instability in the family and really disrupts the family home." The VicPol officer said that she would simply give the mother a referral to a domestic violence shelter. Farah looked on with disbelief and disappointment. She mentioned to the other participants at the table that in trying to prevent a forced marriage, family members who were financially interdependent would be separated and individuals who may not have had anything to do with coercing the marriage would be funneled into the criminal justice system. Farah's conclusions suggest that the sector should not deny the presence of coercion but might do well to understand the interdependencies that animate the victim's relationship with her family before developing a definitive and potentially life-altering solution. Farah's refusal to treat the victims in the scenario as one-dimensional figures whose relationships could be easily rearranged conflicted with the criminality framework the police officer employed that saw individuals as variables to be removed and rearranged in an equation. Farah seemed to feel misunderstood and replied, "What do successful outcomes look like? Everyone is an individual so everyone has a different idea of a successful outcome. The key here is to ensure that people have options; having been believed and heard might be a successful outcome for someone. Or perhaps being able to have an independent life and resetting contact with their family." For Farah, success could be open ended, an ongoing experiment within families that did not have to take the form of permanent separation from one's community. While scenarios produced certain essentialisms about victimhood, they also in this case provided fertile ground for debating how to identify and intervene in coercion.

In September 2017, I attended a migrant-led community workshop hosted by the ARC in Dandenong. Community leaders came from a range of countries, including Afghanistan, Iraq, Sri Lanka, Pakistan, and South Sudan. Community leaders communicated a range of reasons marriage was seen as a viable option for parents who had recently arrived in Australia. One Afghan community leader, Sheila, who was recruited to be part of the group because she conducts workshops about resettlement and support services for Afghan Hazara refugees in Southeast Melbourne, noted the following: "Asylum seekers and migrants go through so much. They have so many problems with their visas, and their kids. . . . There is a huge amount of problems they have. Most of them spend their money back home on their family here. It's really hard and sad." While Sheila acknowledged that pressures around marriage was a real issue among people she interacted with, she did not frame such pressures as tied to culture and tradition. She framed them as shaped by attempts to help extended family members flee Afghanistan by having one of the older children apply for a spousal visa. This would, in turn, relieve the family already resettled in Australia of the economic pressures of sending money back home. Sheila's remarks prompted a conversation among the rest of the community leaders about the pitfalls of treating forced marriage as an immigration issue. Another participant mentioned that people were afraid of being deported, which made them less likely to report that they were in a coercive situation. Sheila went on to mention: "I'm from an educated family. If my parents force me to get married, the first thing I would do is go to an imam and ask him what I need to do because I don't want to hurt my parents, I don't want to go to the police. I need help." Two other community leaders mentioned the hesitation they noticed among their friends to report to the police or to their teachers. One leader mentioned, "Some of my friends at university will come talk to me. . . . They don't want to go to counselors. . . . Some of them think when they report to school authorities, they will be seen as looking for favors. If a counselor reports to faculty or department about this student that disclosed, that will make students feel bad. Students would rather talk to friends. . . . Sometimes at night they call me and start crying to me and tell me what they don't want the authorities to know." In response, someone said, "Our students won't go to counselors because it's like, you don't know me or my community and counselors don't know how students give meaning to the word 'consent.'" Such assessments complicated the idea that a lack of reports were simply tied to a misunderstanding or lack of understanding of Australian laws or because victims themselves were unaware of what was happening to them.

Figured Subjects

In her analysis of Danish schools who are using integration programs for Muslim immigrants, Reva Jaffe-Walter (2015) provides a useful analysis of how Muslim youth come to be treated as "figures" rather than multidimensional subjects. She writes that, "Figured identities are abstracted and distilled notions of identity—cultural stereotypes—that carry with them a set of specific narratives, expectations of behavior, and charters for action. A 'figured world' is defined as 'a socially and culturally constructed realm of interpretation in which particular characters and actors are recognized, significance is assigned to certain acts and particular outcomes are valued above others'" (Jaffe-Walter 2015, 4, quoting Holland et al. 1998, 52). Jaffe-Walter (2015, 5) argues that students were not recognized in terms of their identities and experiences. While this is no doubt true, this contention also assumes that knowing more about students' identities and experiences would prevent social welfare from treating them like figures. Forced marriage prevention itself is unique in the extent to which it is concerned with producing knowledge about the less publicly visible details of migrant relationships with family; it is an example of how social welfare becomes concerned with the deeper details of community lives and yet misunderstands those it seeks to help. Social welfare's deeper investment in the microdynamics of communities can still produce knowledge that renders the subject as a figure and as shaped by cultural tropes. In that sense, I offer a slightly different iteration of Jaffe-Walter's idea of "figured identities." I find the term "figured subjects" more fitting, because it reflects and recognizes the fact that, in technologies of social welfare, like scenarios, individuals are not only being assigned one-dimensional identities, but they are being depicted as subjects. They are represented as people who live in culturally specific circumstances under a set of power relations. While the specific nature of these power dynamics is flattened in scenarios, the fact that these power relations are at the foreground of these scenario narratives gives some practitioners a false sense that they are truly understanding their clients. Figured subjects can be produced through discursive procedures that make their lives knowable using existing racialized and gendered tropes, existing state-sanctioned language around victimhood in family violence, and the idea that an actionable future based on such tropes has to be constructed.

In scenarios, the human turns into a character, and certain interactions she has with her family come to matter more than others. For example, while it is jarring to read that Ayla's parent accompanies her to school, are there ways that Ayla also exerts power in the family? What happens when Ayla goes home to her family? What precarities do Ayla and her family confront in their everyday lives that have made marriage an entertainable option for her parents? And if Ayla is experiencing a coercive and violent familial environment, what other structures reflect this coercion in addition to the prospect of inter-cousin marriage? These questions are important, but they are not legible within the parameters of the scenarios that are confined to discrete events and moments rather than long-standing relationships, genealogies, and histories of displacement.

Scenaristic Threats

Back at the training in Morwell, one attendee noted, "People like Ayla" are "all around us." What does it mean to say that "people like Ayla are all around us" in a context when the extent of a problem is not known and its contours are in the process of being figured out? Here, the Ayla scenario is presented as a tool to know one's clients better, while being applied as a universal identifier of other potentially problematic cases. Key to producing Ayla as a knowable figure is the environment in which she resides. Ayla's story, then, was treated in terms of a set of relevant signals to caseworkers. In fact, it also triggered caseworkers to think back to their previous cases to determine what red flags they may have missed. The scenarios, then, despite being designed to better interject into the future, rely on the excavation of components of past client stories to determine other aspects of Ayla's family situation. For example, one training participant, now a community advocate, noted that she had a client who mentioned that her parents wanted her to get engaged because they had suspected she was dating someone outside of her ethnicity. While the case with Ayla did not mention a relationship with someone else as a reason for her parents' decisions, the participant drew from her own life experience to explain why cases like Ayla might occur. An actual case, if even temporarily, fills in the gaps for the hypothetical case.

The scenario, then, despite its focus on a specific case, takes on a universalizing function in the training space. The story gets mobilized as portable and as representing the realities of numerous potential individuals and families from migrant backgrounds. In that sense, the scenario typologizes through specificity—showing forced marriage as a cumulative event rooted in certain kinds of familial arrangements and in culturally specific yet static worldviews.

The idea of the simulacrum is helpful to understanding the epistemology of the hypothetical victim subject laid out in these scenarios. According to Jean Baudrillard (1994, 166), a simulation is "the generation by models of a real without origin or reality: a hyperreal." The "real is produced from miniaturized units, from matrices, memory banks, and command models—and with these it can be produced an indefinite number of times. . . . It is nothing more than operational. . . . It is hyperreal: The product of an irradiating synthesis of combinatory models in a hyperspace without atmosphere" (1994, 167). This entails a "liquidation of all referentials" or their artificial resurrection within signs and various combinations of them (1994, 168). Simulacra are copies that portray things that had no original form. Baudrillard's description is apt to describe the reality-generating function of these scenarios, which, in this case, operates at multiple scales. There is the reality of the individual that is generated, the reality of her family life, and the reality of the origins of this practice. For Baudrillard, these simulacra do not have their origins in an empirically verifiable reality and instead rely on caricatures of who people and their social worlds are. To know victimhood in this context is to take the simulacrum as a substitute for reality—to develop a profile of what could happen. There are successive phases of a simulation:

1. It is the reflection of a basic reality.
2. It masks and perverts a basic reality.
3. It masks the absence of a basic reality.
4. It bears no relation to any reality whatever: it is its own pure simulacrum (1994, 170).

Eventually, the simulacrum leads up to the simulation bearing no relation to any reality whatsoever. I posit that forced marriage scenarios lie somewhere in between the second and third phases. On the one hand, scenarios mask and distort situations of actual coercion into marriage, but they do not unfold in the neat and tidy culturalized ways that the scenarios make it seem. On the other hand, scenario trainings give the impression that forced marriage is a national moral crisis. Alice noted this at the beginning of the training, with little to no data on which referrals of forced marriage reflect coercive situations. In this sense, scenarios mask the absence of the reality of moral crisis.

Treating scenarios as simulacra allows us to see how an epistemology of victimhood can end up substituting potentially complex facts with a predetermined repertoire of diagnostic possibilities, thus making representations rather than social truths the basis for prevention efforts. In Australia's forced marriage sector, it is the representation of violence that victims and their families are seen to be living in—the simulations that come to count as reality. In the context of a policy around which minimal empirical data exists, prevention workers, advocates, and policymakers, encounter the victim subject and the world which she inhabits through the scenario.

Defining Forced Marriage as a Migration Issue

In this section, I discuss how, in practice, the scenario training is a space that frames victimhood itself as part of a broader set of concerns about Australian social values. This makes marriage and coercion matter to practitioners through the language of family values and good citizenship. It is important to note that practitioners were not only being asked to think about Ayla's specific case but to use it as an entry point to think about forced marriage as a national moral crisis. More specifically, the training framed forced marriage as a problem unique to migrants through discussing the struggle that most victim's families have with cultural assimilation.[3] I argue that by engaging with scenarios in trainings, practitioners come to see themselves not only as direct providers of care but also as people committed to preserving Australian values.

Back at the training in Morwell, Alice explained that there were certain "types" of familial conditions that correlated to coercion into marriage, marked by an inability to adapt to the host society's cultural worldviews, or a failure of assimilation: "That's the problem—the real fear a lot of families have around this issue—the westernization of their children. First generation children who are taken offshore for a forced marriage have, I guess, become more articulate than their parents and former generations. So, in a way it makes parents more vulnerable to the fact this child won't consent." Here, it is westernization and the dissonance between first generation children and their parents that are seen to lead to parents' decisions to govern and discipline their children in particular ways. Alice's explanation goes on to highlight that there are certain components of forced marriage stories that are formulaic: "Another figure that has a lot of control that does not get a lot of air play [in discussions on forced marriage] is 'the cousin' who is going to take the girl away. In some situations, it's the older brother, but the older male in the family is the one who is going to be taking her offshore to be married. And there is an incredible bond between the father and the cousin. And the reality of the situation is that the girls are married to another first cousin because they want to strengthen that immediate family and extended family." Here, Alice points to kinship vectors and power dynamics that she sees as universal to forced marriage cases. She discussed this following Ayla's scenario analysis, thereby including this explanation as part of the "world-building" effort of forced marriage prevention. Here, Alice interpellates the victim subject as part of a particular set of kinship relations. Various extended family members, such as the cousin and his relation to the victim subject's father, are key kinship vectors that are supposed to tell practitioners about the young girl's risk of coercion. After presenting the scenario, Alice continued that "Ayla was an Australian citizen and her case shows that it's happening in Australia." A nurse raised her hand and asked, "Is it really happening in Australia? How often? I never thought this would be happening in Australia." Alice replied that they did not have any statistics but that practitioners knew it was happening based on the calls they were receiving.[4]

These were both responses common in many trainings I attended. Despite the uncertainty around statistical evidence for the frequency of forced marriage, there was a marked shift that took place in the conversation—the shift from a discussion of the specific circumstances of Ayla to that of its frequency within the state of Australia itself. What did the story evoke for practitioners in the room? Ayla's story evoked a set of concerns in excess of itself. *Who* the potential victim was seemed to matter less than *what* they represented.[5]

Attendees identified the attorney-general's warning signs out loud after reading the scenario. They discussed remedies for Ayla that centered on removing her from her family situation, finding her temporary housing, and assigning her to a caseworker who could help her develop a short and long-term safety plan. However, the conversation again quickly drifted into a discussion of disbelief about the extent to which this practice was happening in Australia. Caseworkers brought up how they saw the practice happening in particular among Afghan communities. A schoolteacher brought up that she had suspicions about it among recently arrived refugees at her school. One participant noted that families do not know that this "is the law in Australia," and that this behavior could be explained "as a coping mechanism that parents use when they see their children becoming westernized." They continued that marriage was a way to preserve cultural values. In addition to the details of the scenario itself, forced marriage was becoming defined in this training as part of a desire to preserve a homogeneous understanding of culture but also an act of willfully ignoring Australian law. The inability to find place and identity in a new setting is born out of an intrinsic connection to one's cultural worldview which, in turn, gets spatialized. Cultural worldviews are intrinsic, yet when they travel, they become converted into threatening socialities.

Scenario trainings not only involve imagining a response in relation to the details of the hypothetical case. The case itself is rendered meaningful and intervenable only through the conversations that happen around it. These conversations view migrant social relations as sites of illiberal moral values. I contend that, in this training, forced marriage was not seen and produced as an act of gender-based violence but one of violence upon Australian society. On one level, the scenario does what all scenarios do, which is to typologize through specificity—to offer an example of what could be plausible if certain conditions are in place. The reality-generating force of scenarios, combined with how the practitioners in the training engaged with them, moves this fact pattern from a way of knowing to a way of generating forced marriage as an existential threat to Australian social norms. Practitioners learn not only how to read in between the lines but also why the fact pattern is important. The training, then, conveys the broader social issues at stake that go beyond human rights and gender-based violence.

I now turn to the scenario of Ani and the discussion around it, which I argue reflects a discursive conversion of victimhood into a spatialized threat that resides in the mobility of migrants. Alice presented the scenario of Ani, told from the perspective of her friend, and had the practitioners read the story to themselves:

> Ani and I have been close friends since primary school. We tell each other everything. That is, until recently.
>
> I had noticed that Ani seemed to be going through a bad time. She was taking time off school and I knew she wasn't sick. She had always been a good student but she wasn't doing her homework and was actually failing assessments. This wasn't like her at all. She was losing weight; I could see that her clothes were getting baggy.

I tried to talk to Ani about my observations and concerns but she just shut down. I suggested that she should talk to her mum if she was worried about something, but she just hung her head.

Ani and her family were so close. Close in a different way to my family. I guess in her culture having strict parents is part of the deal, and I got that. Ani's family thought that being strict and having really high expectations showed the way they loved Ani and her brothers and sisters.

My concern for Ani's wellbeing began to grow when I noticed that Ani was taking less interest in her personal hygiene and grooming. She had always been so fussy. When I mentioned that something seemed wrong, Ani just exploded. She told me to mind my own business and she left me standing there with my mouth wide open.

Later that night Ani contacted me by text. She had a sneaky pre-paid phone that she hid from her family, as they didn't approve of having mobiles. In her text she told me that she thought her parents were planning something for her: something bad. I texted back that we really needed to talk about this and we should meet a bit earlier in the Library before school.

I couldn't believe it when Ani arrived. She had obviously been crying; she told her parents she didn't feel well. She was physically shaking and she had dark circles under her eyes. We sat down, and as I held Ani's trembling hand, she told me she suspected her parents were planning to make her get married.

I was gob-smacked as Ani and I were only 15! I tried not to show how upset I was; I just sat there and listened. Ani was to go with her older cousin on an overseas trip; we knew that. Now, however, Ani had put the pieces together and she feared that her overseas trip was actually an excuse to marry her to an older man over there.

Ani was so upset that her parents, whom she loved so much and who loved her so much, could possibly do this. She knew that they still had friends with whom they had regular contact in their home town. She didn't know what to think.

She told me that she had shared her fears and suspicions with her grandma, with whom she had always had a special bond. Her grandma had started sobbing herself, telling Ani not to say anything to anyone . . . that her parents loved her, that she must do as she was told, that she could never disobey her parents.

She then went on to tell Ani that if any of the plans went wrong that she would die of the shame of it all. Ani was afraid for her beloved grandmother's health; she had a weak heart and was on so much medication.

Ani thought about her mum and dad who had sacrificed everything to come to Australia to give their family a chance at a good life. She felt totally trapped by the circumstances, but she did not want to be forced to get married so young. Ani begged me to keep her confidence and I nodded my agreement, but felt a sick feeling growing.

I couldn't stop thinking about Ani's predicament. I knew that our friendship had always rested on the trust that we shared. But I also knew that I could not sit by and just let this happen to her. I realised that I had to tell someone who could help with the situation; I had to find a trusted adult who would have the knowledge to help Ani deal with this situation. The person would have to understand the impossible family situation that Ani was facing if this wasn't handled right. I knew that I had to act quickly but sensibly because who knew when Ani's grandma might let her parents know that she was aware of what was going to happen.

It is important to mention that this scenario is much more aware of the complexities of family relationships than the previous scenario in that it allows for the possibility for close familial relations to precede the act of martial coercion. For example, Ani and her grandmother are close. There is also a recognition of parental love and Ani is seen as having mixed feelings about her parents' decisions. Alice asked the participants to think about what vulnerabilities Ani faces during the time period before she would actually be taken overseas to be married. She gathered participants' responses and noted: "She is a young female, has an unfinished education. She's got decreased social networks whatever decision she makes so she can't stand up and argue against it. . . . Her health is at risk. She is losing weight and has no interest in food." After an attendee asked what would happen if Ani was taken overseas, Alice responded: "There is the risk of interrupted studies, suffering, losing weight, her physical and mental health are at risk. The new husband and cousin both represent unknown risks to her physical safety and we don't know whether they are good, loving, kind men. They might be but they also might not be, so that's a big risk."

Alice undertook a particular reading of how Ani's cousin and new husband could potentially increase Ani's risk of suffering. They are both the known and the unknown—we know they are members of the potential victim's family, yet we do not know how and if they will coerce her into a marriage. Yet in Alice's interpretation, they still pose a threat because of their existence as authority figures in her life. It is in the space of the unknown that training participants inserted their own readings of what could happen next to Ani.

One participant noted that if she were Ani's friend, she would try to turn to the grandma for help in convincing the parents to not go through with the marriage. Another interjected that this could backfire, because Ani's grandmother seemed to be aligned with the parents' point of view and might alert the parents that Ani was collaborating with her friend to escape the overseas trip. Another participant mentioned that no matter how understanding the family seemed, it was always a mistake to involve the extended family members in a plan to do away with the marriage—family mediation was out of the question, especially when it came to their role as caseworkers. Up until now, the participants had been discussing Ani's case on its own terms, with little reference to Australian society.

The discussion then moved from what intervention would look like to why coercion into marriage is a problem for Australian society. The participant continued that if a student discloses that they feel at risk to a teacher, they may be victimized and shamed by their family: "That's a real thing—honor-based violence is real and is a real problem in Australia too." Here, Ani's situation is reinscribed within the discourse of honor-based violence. In summing up the participants' analyses, Alice continued that the interruption of Ani's life and the possibility of a forced marriage is "unacceptable in Australia." In these types of cases, "the cousin and the brother are important figures because they are concerned about the girl's honor which is how a lot of these cases begin."

As scholars have noted, honor-based violence tends to be used as a catch-all label to connote a range of violences, with the common factor being migrants' cultural and religious backgrounds (migrants who identify as Muslim and come from the Middle East and South Asia) (Abu-Lughod 2011; Gill and Brah 2013; Grewal 2013; Yurdakul and Korteweg 2020). In recent years, honor-based violence has been tied to discourses of national security, Muslim migration, and geographic imaginaries of the Middle East/North Africa (MENA) and South Asia regions as sites of hyperpatriarchal violence. Lila Abu-Lughod (2011, 44) traces a genealogy of the category of "honor crime" and "honor-based violence." She argues that this category is produced as one of "spectacular cultural violence," animated by popular fantasy. It does more to obscure the actual experiences of violence experienced by women from the MENA and South Asia regions than revealing their conditions of possibility. The idea of the honor crime does political work to forge particular feminist solidarities and adherence to a set of value systems that set western women apart from those in the "third world." More importantly, it relies on an explanation of culture and values to describe violence against women that justify the uncritical acceptance of forced marriage prevention as a criminal justice response under the pretext of humanitarian reason.[6] The previous example reveals an instance in which honor-based violence gets spatialized as a form of violence that travels across borders. Alice's synthesis of participant remarks categorizes the case as a form of honor-based violence, thus removing it from a discussion of specific interventions that relate to coercion into marriage and connecting it to a broader set of categories associated with racialized Muslim migrants. The spatializing of honor-based violence in Alice's synthesis of participant remarks points to how Ani represents not only a suffering subject but, in her suffering, a threat to the Australian moral order itself. After hearing Alice's explanation, I realized that learning the signs of an imminent forced marriage also meant being confronted with the notion that Australia as a society was being threatened by suspect practices through these cases. Practitioners, through these trainings, were also being trained to understand the gravity of the problem as widespread in Australia—a result of migrant cultural practices that is also identifiable and preventable. In forced marriage prevention, violence amongst family is situated as a threat to the well-being of families themselves and as a threat to the values and morals of Australian society.

Prognosticators of Threat

In this section, I suggest that, in these scenario trainings, practitioners were hailed as prognosticator-like figures who could foresee the existential precarity of Australian values through identifying women's victimhood. Here, I introduce Frédéric Keck and Andrew Lakoff's (2013) concept of the "sentinel device," which inspires the idea of the prognosticator figure. A sentinel device is a signal of an impending crisis and form of vulnerability that can affect multiple people and contexts. Keck and Lakoff propose the idea of sentinel devices in the context of environmental threats, such as climate change, environmental radiation, emerging disease, and toxic chemicals. While their project is to invite a more thoughtful consideration of the potential for nonhuman animals to be considered sentinel figures who can aid in identifying potential environmental threats, their definition of the sentinel figure resonates with the kind of prognostication that scenario trainings value. They define the sentinel figure as presenting a "vigilant watchfulness that can aid in preparation for an uncertain, but potentially catastrophic future. The word derives from the Latin *sentire*, to feel or sense. Thus, the figure of the sentinel is bound up with both the problem of perception and the question of whether the detection of danger can successfully ward off a coming crisis" (Keck and Lakoff 2013). The sentinel figure is a virtuous one that has the potential to help humanity in its detection skills and watchful disposition. Forced marriage prevention scenario trainings are spaces in which, I posit, practitioners are called upon to detect the individual's risk of suffering as part of a potential threat to Australian social norms more broadly, and they are seen as good humanitarian actors for doing so. Thus, doing the work of care becomes entangled with the assessment of risk—both the risk to the individual and the risk to society. The work of preventive care becomes intertwined with ongoing spatialized imaginaries of Australia as vulnerable to foreign migrant practices. Practitioners, similarly, are being valued for their capacity to help prevent such impending doom, through identifying red flags in the victim's relationship with her family that signal something to the polity about the future of the nation-state. By thinking about the scenario through a risk assessment framework and discussing their reflections through a securitized migration framework, practitioners construct victim figures. The familial relations that such victims are a part of get converted into threats to the social order.

Hidden in Plain Sight: The Threatening Suffering Subject

Scenarios are dense, semiotic objects that reveal racialized and gendered assumptions about family, marriage, and what it means to be a good citizen. The trainings in which these scenarios are presented are spaces where forced marriage comes to matter to practitioners in new ways. In these trainings, forced marriage goes from being a form of gender-based violence to an importation of practices that injure Australian society itself. Scenario trainings, then, are not exercises in simply identifying violence; they are sites where conceptions of normal family relations and good citizenship are enunciated and where practitioners are interpellated as carers for victims and national values.

One could argue that scenarios are always going to be slightly exaggerated. I posit that the stakes of using exaggerated scenarios are high when they stand in for the realities of communities and the empirical evidence supporting the claim that forced marriage is a social crisis in Australia. I make this suggestion because, when the law was passed and during my fieldwork, the statistics on how many forced marriages occurred since 2013 have been contested.[7] However, in legislative debates, a common line of reasoning was that the lack of disclosures was an indication that forced marriage was prevalent because it was going underreported. Further, when sitting in on forced marriage network meetings, a key debate between community leaders and social welfare workers was whether communities knew that the practice was wrong. This often transformed into a conversation about the extent to which it was reported by victims.

Many of the scenarios put forth in forced marriage prevention manuals are supposed to represent potentially real situations. However, the scenarios themselves only lay out what will happen to the victim herself. Australian society is never explicitly mentioned as the higher order victim in these hypothetical cases. In fact, it would never be mentioned because these trainings represent what family violence prevention in Australia, and in other liberal contexts, call a "victim-centered approach" to social services. What Australia will look like if Ayla gets married is not a deliberate object of knowledge. However, the larger collection of stories from which Ayla's and other scenarios appear is part of a set of training material for schoolteachers, students, and other practitioners, which link forced marriage prevention to Australian values around healthy family relationships and personhood.

Scenarios in general can be considered carefully curated plausibilities of what has happened in the past, what is currently happening, and what could happen. Thus, they make three temporalities into objects of concern—the past, present, and future. The scenarios I described above, while curated, are designed to not only give the facts of the case but to paint a conditional world that produces victimhood as an accumulation of an already troublesome past marked by coercive familial relations, a violent present, and a threatening future for the individual and for the society in which she lives.

Using scenarios in family violence prevention training is certainly not new nor an uncommon practice in social welfare settings throughout the world. Scenarios are useful ways to put theory into practice—to test existing guidelines around response and intervention and to see where they fall short. However, analyzing scenarios reveals that they also function as world-building tools that not only allow practitioners to think about their response and intervention strategies but give them a window into their clients' lives. When coupled with existing tropes around Muslim women as suffering subjects, it is easy to see how scenarios could be used as tools to convert stories of suffering into indicators of threat. Shakira Hussein (2016; Hussein and Imtoual 2009) has analyzed how in Australia, Muslim women are seen as both threatened by forms of family violence that are intrinsically cultural or religious and as potential suspects and co-conspirators in the reproduction of this violence in how they socialize young men and undertake religious practices seen to promote violent ideologies. By turning to the scenario training space, I take this one step further by showing how, in a landscape that combines colonial social welfare with securitized migration, the very possibility of suffering Muslim women is treated as a national threat that erodes Australia as a site of freedom. It is worth asking: What worlds do scenarios build? What are the effects of creating such worlds in an environment that already essentializes who migrants are? Scenarios are powerful pedagogical tools that can fill in informational gaps that some practitioners have about the structural and intimate realities of communities. In doing so, such scenarios teach practitioners frameworks through which to understand and make sense of the decisions people make and how power relations work within a particular community. However, in doing so, scenarios can also produce misunderstandings of communities. In this landscape of care-based prevention and intervention, it is important to recognize how professional spaces diagnose problems as much as how they develop interventions for them. Through analyzing scenarios in migrant-targeted social welfare, we can better understand how they make communities matter to institutions and practitioners in particular ways. Scenarios compel us to ask when an apolitical ethic of care becomes a nationalistic politics of risk and threat assessment.

3

Reluctant Disclosure

Epistemic Doubt and Ethical Dilemmas in Prevention Work

Since the passage of the 2013 law, policy makers hailed schools as the new frontier for forced marriage prevention. Direct service workers with experience in family violence prevention were now tasked with heading forced marriage prevention and the responsibility of educating school staff about the law. In recent years, the federal government has also developed several contracts with social welfare (including family violence) organizations to deliver trainings on forced marriage prevention to public secondary schools, with mixed and contentious results. In this chapter, I examine the ways in which secondary school administrators, nurses, and teachers in Melbourne's suburbs were being taught to identify forced marriage as an emerging configuration of familial violence that has been codified in federal law. Specifically, I look at how such actors in two secondary schools (grades seven–twelve) grapple with the prevention sector's call that they disclose suspicions that their students are at risk of forced marriage to the AFP, the main body tasked with investigating reported cases. Through examining how school staff responded to forced marriage prevention trainings, I make two arguments: a) school staff's discomfort with the policy's demand that they conduct risk assessments on their students, which they view as a tool of migrant-centered criminalization, produces nondisclosure as a more ethical strategy of care for student well-being; and b) while nondisclosure refuses the mode of recognition demanded by this biopolitical project's risk assessment protocols, it does recognize the broader political conditions that structure some migrant families' perspectives on marriage. This includes intensified border control policies and economic precarity in the wake of displacement.

An ethnographic perspective on school staff's dilemmas can reveal dynamics that may be present in other, similarly situated biopolitical liberal governance regimes that have used social welfare as a frontier for assimilationist policies. First, this chapter focuses on how the epistemic assumptions about migrants' countries of origin that are baked into state-sanctioned social policies are contested by public servants. Such contestations illustrate how friction is generated in the interaction between school staff and direct service practitioners (Tsing 2005). They both address what, on the surface, is presented in policy language as a universally recognizable category of violence. In attending to this friction, the analysis complicates the idea that social policies constructed on the basis of "saving Muslim women" (Abu-Lughod 2002; 2013) are blindly adhered to and left uncontested by those who are tasked with implementing them. Rather, through examining the pedagogical space of the training, we see that social policies are actively negotiated based on a range of variables, including professional ethics, awareness of migrant lifeworlds, and the state's mobilization of cultural essentialisms. Aihwa Ong (1995) has examined how, in biomedical and biopolitical projects of immigrant and refugee medicine, patients resist the biomedical gaze that aims to govern diseased populations. Ong also shows how clinicians encounter limited resources, which makes it difficult to provide tailored care. This chapter, while not focused on a biomedical or clinical setting, foregrounds the care worker perspective and considers how practitioners turn the case on themselves. More specifically, I show that school staff are aware that predominant cultural tropes do not reflect the realities of their students' familial relationships and that forced marriage prevention is invested in a criminal justice and carceral response that focuses on identifying the criminal event and apprehending offenders. In doing so, the chapter adds another layer to what Sherene Razack (2004) has called the "imperiled Muslim woman" discourse in colonial social welfare. It illustrates how practitioners engage with this discourse, not as seamless messengers of the state but as professionals who see themselves as subject to a particular professional and ethical code. This code has, historically, been shaped by Australia's politics of cultural recognition but has the potential to support migrant communities in ways that go beyond the essentializing assumptions of such a politics.[1]

In illustrating practitioner attempts to move beyond these culturalizing assumptions, I show that school staff's critiques of the policy seek to neither ignore culture nor essentialize it.[2] They see how this policy frames itself as culturally unspecific but that in practice, it could end up disproportionately subjecting Muslim migrants and refugees to the gaze of administrators, students, and teachers at their schools. In that sense, practitioners contest the policy's demand that Muslim students' (especially young female students') behaviors and familial connections be read as simply the result of depraved cultural traditions and instead as responses to structural conditions around seeking asylum, crossing borders, and the human consequences of war.[3]

Here, I want to take a moment to distinguish staff decisions to avoid disclosure from attempts to avoid being labeled as racist toward students. I did not find that nondisclosure functions as a mode of "saving face" or ensuring that one is not held liable for potentially engaging in racializing behavior. While some staff did insinuate the policy is undergirded by xenophobia , nondisclosure is a mode of stepping back and attempting to comprehend what is actually happening to students rather than an attempt to avoid being labeled racist or what Ghassan Hage has called "a good multiculturalist" (2000). In other words, by disengaging, nondisclosure sets up an opportunity to re-engage in a more nuanced way that recognizes that student relationships with their families cannot be captured by state risk assessment tools but are deeply shaped by the struggle to cross borders, and the afterlife of displacement.

School staff's contestations of the policy are thus an entry point to imagining alternative ways to understand migrant lives and social relations that account for Australia's role in immigration policy and the global precarities migrants confront in the wake of war and displacement. Staff develop nondisclosure as an alternative to these frameworks and as a form of ethical care. Nondisclosure is an (imperfect) attempt to take people's differences seriously in a context where alterity has historically been pathologized as an importation of uncivilized and socially deviant outsiders. By extension, however, the debate about nondisclosure is also contained within multiculturalism's politics of recognition (Povinelli 2002).

Contesting Regimes of Care: Why Focus on Practitioner and Educator Perspectives?

Ethnography's deep dive into the culture of welfare (Edgar and Russell 1998) allows for a deeper understanding of the social effects produced by new approaches to human well-being without necessarily evaluating them as morally superior or inferior. According to Lisa Stevenson (2014, 3), care in biopolitical regimes can be defined as "how someone matters and the ethics of attending to the Other who matters." This definition of care allows more room to critically assess why certain groups become sites of concern and care for the biopolitical state and what kinds of interventions are sanctioned in the name of care. Specifically, school staff were asking themselves why forced marriage prevention cares so much about Muslim migrants and why people from certain countries of origin matter to the state. In this vein, this chapter examines school staff engagements with such approaches, which they view as exposing the subject to new forms of vulnerability through racialized assumptions about who they and their family members are.

Anthropological studies of care-based regimes, interventions, and policies have offered important insights into the power relations inherent in relationships of care. They have shown how state policies situate disclosure as a necessary requirement of care—and even a demonstration of compassion—but also as potentially harmful for people in different situations of vulnerability. Several anthropological analyses of care regimes have shown that disclosure of a person's vulnerability, physical or psychological, is not always a pathway toward relief. Rather, it can lead to revictimization (Campbell et al. 2001; Madigan and Gamble 1991; Taslitz 1999). These disclosures can sometimes render people visible as ineligible for the benefits of various political and legal protections, including citizenship and asylum. Scholarship has shown how this system can expose their "illegality" to border control institutions, such as Immigration and Customs Enforcement (ICE) in the United States (Dhingra, Kilborn, and Woldemikael 2021; Park et al. 2000; Park 2011; Pedraza, Nichols, and LeBrón 2017). Disclosure can also feed victims of violence into carceral systems that criminalize and deport them rather than offer tangible forms of support (Bernstein 2010; Mai et al. 2021) or that retraumatize them. Sameena Mulla's (2014) deft analysis of forensic examinations of rape victims in Baltimore has shown that the medico-juridical apparatus often requires victims to submit to invasive and retraumatizing bodily examinations and narrative accounts as a precondition for sustained medical and social support. While these analyses have shown the harmful consequences of care, less examined is how practitioners attempt to navigate the expectations around these interventions and how they are shaped by their own ethical standards and the broader discourses around cultural recognition and logics of race, gender, and culture that constitute their social climate. Practitioners cannot be reduced to agents of social policies who do not question the state policies they are tasked with implementing (Sharma and Gupta 2009). This chapter shows how practitioners, whose work is at the nexus of public service and social welfare, question and critically engage with the built-in epistemic frameworks (the cultural essentialization of migrants) and their attendant forms of action (in this case, disclosure) on which social policy is based. In doing so, this chapter also extends scholarship on what Michael Herzfeld (1992) has called the myth of the "indifferent bureaucrat." Herzfeld argues that indifference in bureaucracy is socially produced and can lead to practitioners becoming complicit in state-sanctioned violence. In this piece, I spotlight that what may seem like a form of indifference on the surface might, in some cases, be a mode of more seriously engaging with the subject. This turning away from viewing the subject as a biopolitical risk profile functions to shield them from the interventive and investigative procedures of criminal justice regimes which can render their lives vulnerable in new ways. Sometimes, practitioners critique the way these subjects matter to the state and want to stop them from mattering in these ways. Nondisclosure, then, is a way of removing the subject from the grips of certain institutional dimensions of care. What might come across as indifference, then, is not necessarily a mode of neglect, dismissal, or detachment. Rather, it signals an alternative kind of engagement—a move to reconsider and take the realities of the "other's" lifeworld seriously.

Migrant Mobility, Marriage, and the Limits of Risk Assessment Frameworks

Bridget, Alice, and I were escorted to our meeting with the school principal, a nurse, and a teacher at a secondary school in a northeast suburb of Melbourne which had recently seen a significant influx of resettled refugees from Afghanistan and Iraq. Alice thanked them for their time, and as we settled into our chairs, she began talking about the government-issued warning signs that someone was at risk of being coerced into a marriage. Many of these signs were adapted from the common risk assessment framework (CRAF), a national risk assessment tool that was used throughout Australia for victims of family and domestic violence. There were four CRAF warning signs that overlapped with forced marriage warning signs, but overall, the two risk assessment tools were quite distinct.[4] Warning signs that were distinct to this forced marriage risk framework included:

- The person's older brother or sister stopped going to school or were married early.
- The person's family has a lot of control over the person's life. The family must accompany them to social functions.
- The person expresses that they are scared about an upcoming holiday overseas.
- The person cannot make decisions about their own life.
- The person does not have control over their income.
- There is evidence of family disputes or conflicts, domestic violence, abuse or children running away from home (Australian Department of Home Affairs 2017).

What is notable about these warning signs is that, compared to the CRAF, forced marriage warning signs were less focused on the person's physical and emotional disposition in the present, which makes identifying that they are at risk more complicated. Forced marriage warning signs, by contrast, were more intricately connected to their family relationships—including, for example, the fact that the person's sibling stopped going to school or was married early or that there have been previous family conflicts. This requires "risk assessors" to connect the person's present demeanor with a presumed knowledge of her historical relationship with her family. For school staff, being able to responsibly judge if a person's family members controlled her mobility and finances, for example, demanded an understanding of behaviors and dispositions that were supposed to be readily visible to the "bystander." On the other hand, it demanded an understanding of the intimate family dynamics that were unrecognizable in an everyday school environment.

After Alice and Bridget reviewed the warning signs, one of the teachers asked in a confused and frustrated tone: "But how? How do we know that they are being *forced* into it? How do we know they are being forced to marry? How can you tell?" One nurse interjected and said that it seemed unfair to judge someone as being at risk because they were shy, timid, or quiet. She continued explaining why some of her students entered into marriages: "Some of the girls see it as a way to increase family size and thus support from the government; there really is no stereotype to reflect each girl's situation." Another teacher added that many students were still grappling with navigating decisions about marriage and felt a sense of disorientation around their identities. They were still figuring out what boundaries they could or could not push when it came to their parents. The nurse continued, "There is not one reason for why the girls want to get married. These girls are often on their own. These girls don't realize that when they get married, they will need to take care of their husbands' families, but in their mind, that's the easier option than staying at home." One by one, the staff began to push back against the notion that docility should constitute the sole metric with which to determine coercion into marriage, even as they reproduced other essentialisms about their students' lifeworlds.

Bridget, intently listening, then responded to the school staff with a sense of frustration, "You all are aware of child safety standards, correct? And the consequences for a failure to report?" The teachers responded that while they do report suspicions of other forms of family violence, they would have to be mindful in the case of coercion into marriage because they "know how it works." By this, the teacher was referring to the fact that a disclosure would mean the immediate involvement of Victoria police and AFP, especially in the case of a reported imminent forced marriage, because that was under federal jurisdiction. In fact, the referral system that had been set up since 2013 required any institution, whether it was a direct service provider or VicPol, to immediately call the AFP if they were notified of a suspicion that a coercive marriage was imminent. In other words, regardless of the specific situation of the individual, if "forced marriage" was part of that suspicion, the AFP would be immediately notified. For the school staff at the training, disclosure meant facilitating an encounter between the student, their family members, and the investigative arm of the criminal justice system.

Beyond this, school staff also feared that beginning an investigation could even lead to family members, especially those on temporary visas, being deported. This was especially the case, because in recent years, the government had implemented new rules that more heavily scrutinized the public behavior of migrants on temporary visas. In 2017, the Turnbull-led government introduced the Australian Citizenship Legislation Amendment which proposed that applicants for citizenship would have to declare their respect for "Australian values." Specifically, it would assess migrant attitudes toward religious freedom and "respect for women and children . . . questions about child marriage, female genital mutation and domestic violence." Thus, for school staff, disclosing that students were essentially vectors of risk was not simply a way to show concern and care. It could also potentially signal to state apparatuses, which were already concerned with their public and private comportment, whether or not their family members adhered to normative social values. The state's preoccupation with migrant character is reflected in a recent immigration directive carried out by Immigration Minister Alex Hawke. In March 2021, Hawke signed a directive ordering officials to use their discretion to cancel or reject visas if they failed a character test, which now includes whether they have been accused of trying to organize a forced marriage or have been involved in family violence under the Migration Act of 1958 (Direction 90). More specifically, the directive now includes the following as part of a "range of conduct that may be considered very serious" in the Australian government's consideration of one's character: "causing a person to enter into or being party to a forced marriage (other than being a victim), regardless of whether there is a conviction for an offence or a sentence imposed" (Direction 90, sec. b). What makes this directive unique is that it allows for the threat of visa cancellation or rejection regardless of whether someone has been convicted. Given that there have been no successful prosecutions under the forced marriage law, anyone accused of organizing a forced marriage would have their visa thrown into jeopardy. This makes it particularly precarious for those who are wrongly accused.

As the training continued, the principal noted that she had taken issue with the very use of the term "forced marriage." She said it did little to capture the complicated dynamics that her students were entangled in. Several students told her that they had agreed to marriages their parents were organizing for them with people overseas because they wanted to help family members trying to flee the threat of immediate persecution in their home country through a spousal visa. Other students had confided that their cousins were trying to find any way out of the economic and political precarities resulting from two decades of war and occupation in Afghanistan and Iraq. The students had explained that their family members had already escaped threats from the Taliban as well as ISIS-fueled violence in Afghanistan and found themselves in refugee camps in Pakistan and Iran, where living conditions were poor and the wait times for resettlement by the UNHCR were interminably long. For some, marriage was the best way out of prolonged political and economic precarity, and into the grips of a more hopeful future.

Here, it is important to mention that several students who attended this secondary school had the distinct experience of witnessing their fathers' failed attempts to reach Australia via boat in the 2010s and their subsequent incarceration in offshore detention centers on the islands of Manus and Nauru. Since 2013, Australia had tightened its borders in response to asylum seekers arriving through maritime routes from the Middle East and South Asia. As a result, the Australian state rerouted "unauthorized maritime arrivals" to offshore detention centers on these islands for several years. Some of the male asylum seekers who were eventually resettled in Australia ended up bringing their spouses and children over, but not their extended family members. Thus, for many of the children of these formerly detained asylum seekers, a spousal visa was one tool they could use to get their uncles and cousins into the Australian mainland, sparing them the violence of offshore detention.

While this was certainly not true in all cases, for some students, as teachers noted, marriage was not seen as an absolute form of repression. Rather, it was a way of facilitating the escape of others from repression in a global system of migrant governance that offered limited possibilities around mobility. In fact, in the case of Australian offshore detention, it actively sought to deter and punish it (Zeweri 2017; 2020b). What the principal was pointing to, then, was that the framework of forced marriage prevention assumed that all students who were engaging in martial practices were doing so under conditions of pure familial coercion. Such a framework did not allow for different conceptualizations of repression and freedom that were anchored in ethical obligations to others. Instead, it normalized liberal autonomous subjects who experience themselves as detached from social commitments and relations. In doing so, such a policy also silenced a discussion of the global regime of border control, including Australia's increasingly punitive policies toward migrants fleeing war and conflict zones and how they immobilized people. The teacher continued that given the extent to which students had expressed a desire to help their families, calling what they had experienced a forced marriage did not capture the conscious thought they put into supporting their immediate and extended kin. By the end of the training, school staff seemed skeptical about the disclosure process. They said that they would not be willing to disclose their suspicions without hard evidence that a student was facing a marriage they had expressed they did not want to be in.

Here, the principal saw their rapport-building with students as part of what it meant to be an effective and ethical educator, and what it meant to treat the school as a safe and inclusive space for refugee students that would not compound the challenges of establishing a livelihood in the aftermath of resettlement. This building of trust and safety sat in tension with school staff's roles as mandatory reporters. Mandatory reporters are required under Victoria state law to report if they have belief on "reasonable grounds that a child has suffered or is likely to suffer significant harm as a result of physical injury or sexual abuse, and the child's parents have not protected or are unlikely to protect, the child from harm of that type" (Victoria State Government 2017). However, what it means to "have a belief" was now being more explicitly delineated through the risk assessment guidelines in the hopes that school staff could use it as an anchor for their disclosures. However, the conversion from "having a belief" to pinpointing a student as at imminent risk of a forced marriage felt more like a conversion from one form of arbitrarily determined suspicions to another. By the end of the training, school staff seemed skeptical about the disclosure process. They said that they would be unwilling to disclose their suspicions without concrete evidence that a student was facing a marriage they had expressed they did not want to be in.

Here, I want to focus on how disclosure is thought about and contested among practitioners—a mode of intervention (or in this case, nonintervention) that does not often get closely examined in analyses of care. Practitioners entertain nondisclosure as an alternative act of care that attempts to inoculate itself from the potential violences (intimate and juridical) that might result from disclosure. Here, nondisclosure is an attempt to enact an alternative way of engaging with students' complex realities that cannot simply be read as detachment or turning away. Here, practitioners' decisions not to disclose is a turning away—but not from students' lives. Rather, it is a turning away from the expectation that they read students as embodiments of risk rather than as full subjects with complicated relationships to their family members. In that way, nondisclosure reflects a deeper (if at times, still essentializing) engagement with student realities and a decision not to reinscribe those realities within a framework of risk which could subject the student's parents to a criminal investigation and the threat of deportation. I posit that nondisclosure is a way of ethically engaging with the demand to create and assess a risk profile in the attempt to intervene in imminent violence; further, this decision is produced as viable through engaging more deeply with the complexity of students' realities. Thus, nondisclosure can function as a form of care—but one that does not subscribe to its bureaucratized form and is wary of making hard and fast decisions based on conventional risk assessment frameworks in the face of not knowing how to determine where a student lies on the risk spectrum.

Disclosure as the Erosion of Trust

In December 2016, I met Trevor, who worked in student services at a different secondary school in Northeast Melbourne serving grades seven through twelve. Established in 2003, the college is in a newer area in the suburb and has 1400 students. In the few years leading up to 2017, students from asylum-seeking families from Afghanistan, Syria, and Iraq began to constitute more of the student population. As the student services coordinator, Trevor believed that students should feel comfortable approaching educators or administrators without fearing that they would inquire further about intimate family details. Trevor had a good rapport with his students and valued his role as someone who could assist students with a broad spectrum of questions they had about classes, scheduling, and after-school programs. Throughout our meeting, students popped into his office several times. Trevor greeted them in Arabic, after which they asked him quick questions about their classes, an after-school meeting, or how to get a form signed. Trevor was able to answer each question consecutively with ease, a quickness that conveyed that he knew what each student expected from him without having to say much. He asked students how they and their families were doing, prompting them to take a seat in his office and have a quick catch-up about their plans for the week, classes, and upcoming extracurricular activities. In recent months, the school had organized several initiatives designed to integrate forced marriage prevention within the curriculum, including an applied theater workshop led by the office of Australian MP Maria Vamvakinou, an outspoken supporter of the 2013 law.

I asked Trevor if forced marriage was a problem that administrators were trying to more consistently look for. Trevor acknowledged that school staff had been more conscious of the practice over the past two years. He pointed out that December, the month we met, was a concerning time for school administrators, because families were starting to go on holiday and it was believed that young girls were more likely to be coerced to marry in their parents' birth countries upon traveling overseas. While he and other administrators were on high alert, he also pointed out that he preferred to wait until a student explicitly told him that they were engaged and going overseas before considering taking action, which, thus far, had not happened. Even then, he noted that he would follow the student's guidance and preferences on how the school did or did not get involved. There were instances in which a female student had asked Trevor to talk to her mother and father and explain that organizing a marriage to a man ten years older was detrimental to her future and that it would deprive her of future professional and educational opportunities.

Trevor knew that AFP's involvement ran the risk of beginning an investigation that would result in episodic investigator visits to the student's home and further anxiety for the student and their family rather than any sort of measurable benefit. To spark an AFP investigation would fundamentally go against Trevor's ethics because he viewed himself as creating a space of trust and safety for students. Despite the fact that some students' behaviors and familial relationships did coincide with the attorney-general's warning signs of an impending forced marriage and the grounds for disclosure to AFP, to Trevor, such signs were not enough to constitute the grounds for disclosure. In the case of some of his students, the decision to disclose to AFP was still based on an imaginary of what was really happening in a student's relationship with their family members. The implications of a disclosure were magnified for Trevor given that, at the time, zero people had been prosecuted by the state, despite the hundreds of investigations carried out. As a result, if the AFP did happen upon a case that carried enough evidence to be prosecuted by the federal government, it would inevitably get national media coverage. While it was statistically unlikely that Trevor's disclosure would be the one case that fulfilled this criterion, the imagined possibility of this was another deterrent to disclosing. For Trevor, disclosure based solely on the official warning signs could result in drawn out investigations and the erosion of current relationships with students.

While Trevor was reluctant to report to AFP based on a hunch and in the absence of enough information, he was also not in favor of teachers trying to interrogate students about a forced marriage on their own in order to make a determination about whether disclosure was plausible. He noted, "Really what we try to do is ask questions of the students about why they are going, what they are planning to do, rather than ask 'Are you going to get married when you go there?' And then we really try to get the administration aware and have them ask the right questions. The one thing you don't want to do is alienate families, and you do not want to have teachers act as investigators." He added that, oftentimes, teachers could already be quite nosy and that teaching them how to better investigate the nature of their students' familial relations could result in the erosion of student-teacher relationships. For Trevor, the question became: if teachers are now being called upon to both know and intervene in intimate family matters in ways they were not before, is there a line between caring for students and surveilling them? He noted in our conversation that "teachers should just do what they can to ensure the best interests of the child." At the same time, he added that they should recognize that students had already been dealing with Islamophobia in their everyday lives and didn't need it from teachers. Trevor wanted to ensure that his office remained a space where students could feel trust in their educators rather than continued scrutiny.

Trevor's reluctance around disclosure was based on a concern around reproducing patterns of racialized discrimination toward students. This reluctance can be read as an imperfect ethics of care that reflects the broader ethos of contemporary Australian multiculturalism. Emma Kowal (2015) has examined how nonintervention becomes an organizing principle of White Australian antiracism, specifically in relation to Aboriginal communities. According to Kowal, White antiracism, in an effort to avoid reproducing historical forms of discrimination and cultural insensitivity, takes on "a highly ambivalent attitude . . . toward their own agency," when it comes to intervening in social problems (2015, 71). In other words, there is a reluctance to intervene because of guilt, which ultimately becomes a barrier for antiracist liberalism to construct an ethical subjectivity in relation to racialized communities (133). For Trevor, nondisclosure becomes an imperfect tool he uses to at the very least avoid being complicit in policies that disproportionately target particular racialized communities.

In our conversation, Trevor mentioned that his job as an educator was separate from getting involved in parenting dynamics: "It's not really something we want to get involved with, and many teachers want to go and talk to parents directly and we sometimes have to tell them, that's not the best thing and that could make a situation worse. . . . Our job is not to be critical of parenting. Everyone has different mechanisms of parenting." Trevor added that, given that many of his students came from newly arrived families, an investigation would make what was already an uncertain immigration status even more precarious and would effectively ask teachers to function as arbiters of students' immigration status. Heide Castañeda (2008, 4; 2012) has shown that in Germany, doctors and hospital workers are required to report undocumented migrants to authorities. This is spelled out in legislation called the "Denunciation Act" that makes the provision of medical aid and other public services for undocumented people a crime. Tarek Younis and Sushrut Jadhav (2019) have discussed similar sentiments among British medical professionals tasked with identifying and reporting patients they felt may be susceptible to radicalization. In a similar way, Trevor found himself towing the line between ensuring he fulfilled his duties as an educator, which included creating an environment of trust and safety, and fulfilling the fairly new expectation that he report his suspicions. He would reflect on what a disclosure meant in a landscape where public servants were asked to adhere to contradictory demands by multiple institutions—to provide a safe and inclusive space for students yet also keep watch over their familial relationships; to listen to students discuss their anxieties yet fit those anxieties into a profile of risk and potential apprehension.

For Trevor, not reporting cases was a way to avoid an unsustainable precedent of having teachers intervene and surveil the intimate lives of their students. At the same time, he did feel the need to create some kind of meaningful architecture of knowledge within which to house the intuitions and suspicions that perhaps some other familial turmoil was taking place. Trevor's moral anxieties around risk assessment result in both a strong reluctance to report suspicions to authorities and an increased attunement to students' familial relations. His seeming disengagement was a form of re-engaging in different ways. He was hesitant to take on the role of the state-sanctioned assessor—the person who can make a solid conclusion about where his students fit within a spectrum of risk and coercion that he could then disclose to authorities. This ethics of nondisclosure is a way for Trevor to reconcile situations of concern with circumstances of invisibility. He admitted that he repeatedly encountered situations where students told him they would be taken overseas with a sense of concern. He decided to take the stance of listening to avoid putting himself in a position where he would have to judge whether and how all the details of the situation matter to the criminal justice and social welfare systems and the narratives that were legible to them. I read in Trevor's cautionary words and disposition a call to avoid entering a situation where one's intuition around coercion becomes the starting point for making further assessments.

Nondisclosure as a Mode of Engagement

Etymologically, "to disclose" comes from the Old French *desclos* which means "to open, to expose, to break, to unlock, to reveal." If disclosure is thought about in this way, then one can take more seriously the possibility that disclosure, in a social service setting, might also be seen as an act of exposure to new institutions and interventions, some of which may introduce new kinds of uncertainty and even potential harm even as they address other harms. Thinking about disclosure as exposure can illuminate the productive effects of power, and the different ways that individuals become vulnerable to other forms of unwanted intervention that compound already precarious situations.

While it might be easy to read school staff's decisions as simply a disengaged mode of looking away, this reading does not capture how their responses are conditioned by emerging knowledge infrastructures that undergirded forced marriage prevention. The epistemic anxieties of what was or was not coercion into marriage created new ethical dilemmas for school staff that revolved around how to make the distinction between a situation of violence and a different worldview, a situation of harm and one of the complicated power dynamics of interfamilial cooperation. We could say that educators were trying to navigate what Reva Jaffe-Walter (2015) has called technologies of concern in liberal educational discourses that try to foster the social incorporation of immigrant students but end up excluding and marginalizing them. School staff, while open to learning about risk assessment, hesitated to utilize it to make a final determination about a student's risk of coercion. Some questioned the very definitional pillars of forced marriage itself as a category of violence, including the nature of coercion, consent, and how the institution of marriage functioned in their students' lives, as ways to transgress and subvert the restrictive power of global border regimes. The broad spectrum of school staff reactions reveals that disclosure is a complicated decision that is not inherently good, bad, an altruistic form of rescue, nor a willful form of negligence. While it tries to resist certain epistemic assumptions, it runs the risk of resuscitating cultural relativism as a way of guiding care. Rather, nondisclosure is an avoidance of the possibility that the institutions use such disclosures as unequivocal grounds for interventions that can bring harm to people's lives and well-being. School staff's disclosures are increasingly entangled within multiple systems—the criminal justice system, which includes federal and state law enforcement, family violence prevention, and child protective services. Thus, to say that a student was a victim of forced marriage is also, then, a move to inscribe the student within a range of historically racialized institutions of policing. It would also put them in contact with an increasingly Islamophobic criminal justice system that sees Muslim Australians as socially deviant subjects.

By looking at school staff through this ethnographic lens, we can move beyond understandings of social welfare practitioners as simply agents of the state who seamlessly execute state policies without critical thought. Akhil Gupta and Aradhana Sharma (2009, 6) have shown that the state is multilayered, contradictory, translocal, and an "ensemble of institutions, practices and people in globalized contexts." In the same edited volume, Timothy Mitchell (2009, 169) has pointed out, "The network of institutional arrangements and political practices that forms the material substance of the state is diffuse and ambiguously defined at its edges." Forced marriage prevention in Australian schools is one domain in which state-sanctioned discourses on culturally specific forms of violence meet their ethical limits and produce refusals around particular kinds of action. School staff are also entangled within a flawed prevention system steeped in the policy and public discourse on Muslim migrants as always potentially criminal and Muslim women as always already potential victims. School staff dilemmas show the impossible choices that confront the public sector when calcified ideas of migrant criminality and Muslim women's victimhood meet increasingly intertwined criminal justice and social welfare systems. Practitioners make imperfect decisions; in doing so, they negotiate the politics of multiculturalism by relying on key ethical pillars of their professional status. Ethical dilemmas are central to social service work across the world. By focusing on the Australian context in which rescue has served as a pretext for social discipline, this chapter shows that rescue and risk assessment are questioned as systems of care. Nondisclosure is a way to step back and deeply reflect on the structural conditions that produce some choices around intimacy and kinship as more viable than others for displaced migrants. In focusing on the reasons behind nondisclosure, I highlight a form of care that attends to the possibility that the boundaries of personhood and sociality privileged in neoliberal colonial social welfare is deeply shaped by broader structures that regulate human mobility. These include the increasingly nationalist paradigms that govern Australia's securitization of its borders and the disciplining of its migrant communities well within the borders of the nation-state.

4

Phantom Figures

The Erasures of Biopolitical Narratives

"You know, you have to meet them—these two sisters. It is quite a story. They are so resilient. I think you could ask them a lot of questions." As Bridget and I conversed at a bustling Melbourne café about my research, amidst all the noise, I felt a sense of anticipation that I would finally be able to speak with people who had experienced the social welfare and juridical aspects of the forced marriage prevention system. My goal would be to examine what their experiences of the system were in order to present a more complicated understanding of its strengths and blind spots to practitioners. To date, there had been little research on victim/survivor experiences of the full breadth of forced marriage prevention institutions, including the role of refuges, the AFP, and the Australian Red Cross.[1]

Despite this new opening in the research horizon, I soon realized that getting in contact with the "two sisters," as they would be referred to by practitioners in the sector, would be one of the most complicated parts of my fieldwork. The two sisters were Australian citizens who had been taken to Pakistan to be married by their parents. Their parents had migrated to Australia from Afghanistan in the late nineties and had spent a few years in Pakistan, where many of their extended family ended up permanently staying. After being taken to Pakistan, the sisters were able to escape and return to Australia, with some help from the AFP and support from a local refuge in Melbourne. They were now working on finishing their secondary school studies in an undisclosed location in Melbourne and were no longer in contact with their parents. Many practitioners brought up the story of the sisters numerous times in public forums on forced marriage as an exemplary case. However, to preserve confidentiality, they were reluctant to share details of the case with individual non-caseworker advocates tasked with developing forced marriage awareness programs for migrant communities. As different iterations of the story were evoked in the forced marriage prevention sector, the "two sisters" became a "present absence" (Ho 2006). Their stories were everywhere, yet advocates had little knowledge about their lived experience. Despite the fact that multiple agencies had, at some point, been in contact with them and provided support, including housing, referrals to alternative schooling, and the overseas operation to return them to Australia, practitioners were hesitant to share details with other non-caseworker advocates looking to better understand victim narratives.[2] This paradox became more enunciated given that, in multiple VFMN meetings, a common refrain was that practitioners needed more research on the circumstances of actual cases handled by the AFP and STPP and on developing more effective support services.

As I came to see the frequency with which practitioners were preoccupied with both circulating and shielding the sisters' stories, I began to ask different kinds of questions. Why was the story of these sisters circulated as an exemplary tale despite the reluctance among practitioners to better understand the lived experience of victims/survivors? In this chapter, I examine: a) what the selective circulation of stories did for the prevention system's own sense of identity; b) the role of confidentiality as a professional ethic in sequestering victim narratives from advocates; and c) how ethnographic knowledge is valued within biopolitical narratives of violence.

In the first part of this chapter, I argue that the selective circulation of the sisters' stories equipped practitioners with a sense that they worked in a cohesive prevention system that, while constituted by distinct institutional logics, was united in purpose. This was particularly important given the multitude of agencies that were part of the VFMN and the distinct ways they approached prevention. For example, direct service agencies focused on identifying the kinds of power dynamics that existed within the families of Muslim migrant communities. The AFP focused less on dissecting community relationships and more on preventing the parties involved in the marriage from traveling abroad once they received a report from a direct service provider or an individual (though they also focused on domestic marriages). Thus, while social welfare providers had to focus on understanding relationships, federal police attended to "disrupting" particular events from transpiring. Because of these distinct goals, agencies often felt that they were talking past each other. For example, an AFP officer mentioned that they did not feel entirely comfortable or educated in how to deal with and address people's intimate family relationships and wanted to focus more on investigating reports and stopping overseas travel. In this situation of divergent goals, social service providers and AFP felt that they operated in their own practice-based bubbles. In such a landscape, the narrative of the sisters generated a common connective tissue between agencies—a sense that they were working toward the same goals. However, the circulation of such stories, coupled with the reluctance to allow victims/survivors to communicate with social service providers outside their immediate caseworkers, rendered victims as phantom-like figures about whom many partial stories were told but whose presence and firsthand accounts in institutional spaces remained invisible. While the sisters' stories functioned as vehicles to validate institutional cohesion, they were rarely featured in spaces where such accounts could meaningfully shape how coercion, marriage, and violence are explained in social welfare. At times, practitioners cited confidentiality as a key reason for why they did not want to disclose information to advocates about the sisters. Yet the ready public circulation of stories about the sisters represents not only the forced marriage system's imperfect adherence to confidentiality but also how it curates what types of stories matter to the maintenance of this biopolitical apparatus. In pointing to how confidentiality is vigilantly guarded yet imperfectly followed, I am concerned less with the performativity of bureaucratic ethics. As studies have shown, bureaucratic practices often exceed and transgress what is expressed in official language, documents, and public settings (Gupta 2012; Hull 2012; Raheja 2022) and work with particular implicit ideologies (Ballestero 2012; Das and Poole 2004; Taussig 1999). In this chapter, I attend to how the belief in confidentiality as a form of bureaucratic reason shapes the identity-making and cohesion-building practices of the prevention sector and how it creates a shared sense of purpose.

In taking concern with why information is kept closely guarded, I take a cue from Brian Rappert's (2010, 260) argument that ethnography should not interpret the absence of information simply as a barrier to knowledge. Rappert notes instead, it should attend to the productive effects of such omissions. Ethnography is poised to look at how "secrets" in a domain restrict information but produce other kinds of knowledge. "Although secrecy is often portrayed as the antithesis of transparency, it can have implications far beyond restricting who gets access to what. The manner in which secrets are kept can shape identities and organizational relations" (260). I also take heed of Michael Taussig (2003) and Ferdinand De Jong's (2007) insights that secrecy should be examined as a social practice, where it becomes socially relevant due to what it is doing through acts of telling (261). This "requires delving into complex relations of concealing and revealing" (264). As Joseph Masco (2014, 451) has argued in a study of U.S. national defense labs, secrecy is: "wildly productive: it creates not only hierarchies of power and repression, but also unpredictable social effects, including new kinds of desire, fantasy, paranoia, and—above all—gossip" (267). Analyzing secrecy, then, is not simply knowing what masks exist, but what these masks tell us about the kinds of stories systems of power are invested in producing.

In the second part of the chapter, I argue that when ethnographic information about the sisters' lived experiences was available, it was valued insofar as it could fit within a biopolitical narrative of coercion, intervention, and rehabilitation. The forms of knowledge deemed less significant to this biopolitical regime are those that unsettle neat profiles of victimhood and criminality. Biopolitical regimes of knowledge production convert people into cases who are knowable in particular ways. As Sameena Mulla (2014, 139) shows in her analysis of forensic exams of sexual assault victims, the case is a curated collection of knowledge—constructed in particular ways that bring together different institutional logics.[3] Ultimately, information from victims/survivors is not used to change how services are given but to corroborate existing criteria around what count as institutionally recognizable forms of violence. In this chapter, I shift attention from how victim narratives function in clinical and juridical settings of immediate care and service provision. Instead, I turn to how practitioners narrate victim stories to each other outside care-based settings and within professional settings. Focusing on such interactions reveals how certain narrative structures emerge as valuable. Turning to the circulation of stories in professional settings shows how victims/survivors are evoked when they are not physically present. It shows how their stories are important not only as objects of compassion and care but as forces that validate the existence of the sector as an effective institutional actor.

Constructing the Prevention System's Identity

In this section, I will lay out the various narratives that were presented about the two sisters, whom I am calling Homaira and Simin, that were circulated by prevention practitioners including direct service workers, advocates, and federal police. In doing so, I show the malleability of confidentiality as a form of bureaucratic reason. I do so not to say that practitioners were transgressing confidentiality's ethical norms but to focus on how these different iterations built a cohesive practice-based identity. Sharing the sisters' story in a variety of settings as an exemplary case allowed different practitioners to create a shared sense of purpose and identity unique to forced marriage prevention. Annelise Riles's (2006, 58) analysis of the dissonance between anthropologists and legal practitioners is instructive here. Similar to how lawyers have conceptions about anthropologists as knowers of culture, I observed that direct service agencies also have imaginaries about how other adjacent agencies work. For example, direct service organizations were having a difficult time convincing educators and other service providers whom they saw as frontline workers, to identify at-risk individuals. Part of the difficulty was due to frontline workers' uncertainty around whether or not forced marriage was a ubiquitous social problem due to a lack of statistics. At a VFMN meeting in 2017, a direct service worker asked an AFP officer about updates in the latest trends in reports to the AFP and investigated incidents. The officer responded that they could not disclose. The worker asked if the officer could provide a broad sense of the trends in referrals to the AFP rather than specific statistics, to which the officer responded they still could not disclose. For the AFP, prevention work was not about convincing people the problem was real. The officer dismissed the question but noted, "By the time we get involved, it's already at a crisis point." The worker responded, "We [the agencies at the meeting] are on a continuum though." The conversation was reflective of the dissonance between social service providers and the AFP. Direct service providers had imagined that the AFP was just as invested as they were in producing knowledge about forced marriage as a social problem and that agencies could collaborate on educating frontline workers that forced marriage was a true social crisis. However, in reality, the AFP was concerned with stopping a marriage from unfolding rather than producing definitive knowledge about the extent of the problem to convince others to intervene. At the end of VFMN meetings, agency leaders would often walk away frustrated, feeling a bigger chasm between their institutions' objectives.

However, when agencies would tell the story about the two sisters, the sense that agencies were collaborating toward the same goal re-emerged. To share their stories was to validate that practitioners had heard of this case and were building a unique institutional identity and memory of an emergent prevention system in real time.[4] The mention of the "two sisters" usually prompted nods and whispers among practitioners at VFMN meetings—people had heard this story before and some were directly involved in some part of the referral process. The exchange of these stories signaled that people were operating within one sector, even though different agencies had different responsibilities. However, it was not only the exchange of these stories that created a sense of united purposes, but also reflecting on the institutional mistakes and blind spots the stories revealed. Through engaging in this way, practitioners felt they were part of a unique system that was building a shared, if imperfect, practice.

In February 2017, I heard the first iteration of many instances of the story being circulated to different parts of the forced marriage sector. Bridget and I had spoken over the phone after she returned from a meeting with a domestic violence shelter that had housed the sisters. Bridget said that they were sixteen and seventeen.[5] The sixteen-year-old, Homaira, was excited about the prospect of going overseas to get married, while her older sister, Simin, was adamantly against it. They were going to be married to their uncle's sons, because their uncle had finiancially helped his brother (their father) to flee Afghanistan to a refugee camp in Pakistan. The marriage was seen as a way to pay off the debt. The sisters contacted Bridget's organization, asking for help in leaving their parents' home. Bridget told the story to a group of about thirty-five practitioners from CPS, direct service organizations, state and federal police, and ARC workers, expressing her frustrations about the case. After contacting her organization to help them find a way to avoid going to Pakistan, resulting in CPS involvement. However, CPS noted that they could assist Homaira, who was sixteen, but not Simin, who was seventeen, because her age made her ineligible for services.[6] This was especially frustrating because Simin was the one who explicitly vocalized that she did not want to go through with the marriage, according to Bridget. When Bridget contacted a refuge to take the sisters in, the refuge would not service Homaira because she was too young. Bridget continued that when they were taken overseas, they found the Australian embassy in Islamabad which could bring them back to Australia if they could pay for their flights. Bridget mentioned that the sisters must have had some sort of safety plan in place because they probably knew they would end up overseas. As Bridget put it, they both did an effective job of engaging Immigration and Border Protection and the AFP. Even though the girls were safe now and living in an undisclosed location, their father's side of the family in Melbourne were threatening them with violence. Bridget went on to describe how ineffective CPS and the domestic refuge were for refusing to help Simin and Homaira, respectively. Bridget expressed frustration with several aspects of the case. She felt disappointed that the sisters had to pay for their own flights out of Pakistan and that no follow-up was completed by the AFP to make sure that they were not being threatened by family in Melbourne for not going through with the marriage. At the same time, she was disappointed in the fact that Australian Border Protection did not get involved in stopping their travel earlier. For Bridget, the story of the two sisters exemplified institutional failure with the forced marriage service response system. After Bridget told the story, it marked one of the first times that practitioners in the VFMN talked about how each of their agencies would have handled the case. Having witnessed four VFMN meetings during my fieldwork, this was the first instance in which practitioners seemed to ask each other how their specific agencies would have responded, thus creating a sense of collective purpose while learning more about each institution's distinct approach and objective.

A few weeks later, I met with Greg, who was part of the AFP's Trafficking and Narcotics Unit (Melbourne headquarters), which investigated forced marriage referrals. He began to narrate a story of "two Pakistani girls, sisters," who were deceived about why they were getting married.[7] I was surprised to hear this story again given how reluctant practitioners were to disclose victim narratives in general to community advocates. He noted that the girls were led to believe that they were going to their brother's wedding in Islamabad. According to Greg, after arriving in Pakistan and staying there for a while, the sisters communicated and coordinated with the AFP and the Department of Immigration and Border Protection on a return to Australia. He added that their parents "were really lovely people, peaceful, and had no idea that what they were doing was wrong." Greg emphasized the parents' character and the institutions through which the sisters escaped. I was surprised that he painted a more complex picture of the sisters' parents—one which left room to recognize that the parents' actions did not reflect the love they had for their children. Greg's narration of the story was part of a broader point he was making to me about the AFP, ever since it was tasked with preventing and intervening in forced marriage cases. For Greg, the AFP was caught in an uncertain position. Forced marriage, in being categorized as a human trafficking-related crime and put under the jurisdiction of the Human Trafficking and Narcotics Unit, marked new terrain for his team. Forced marriage was considered a "victim-centered crime," which referred to crimes where individual experiences of harm were at the center of the investigation and in which evidence relied first on the victim's statement. It was only in the last ten years that Greg and the AFP focused on victim-centered crimes through trafficking cases. In conducting the investigation, Greg's goal was to demonstrate whether a victim had been coerced into a marriage. This required gathering the victim's statement and evidence about intentionality, such as wedding decorations, a dress in the victim's suitcase, or a religious marriage certificate, among other items.

In navigating this new terrain, Greg expressed doubt that he felt had no place in the "black and white world of law enforcement," as he put it. He said that, at times, he "felt like a social worker," attempting to navigate through the victim and her family's complex emotions. Trying to follow the letter of the law about family-perpetrated coercion into marriage while having to face the real people involved was fraught, especially if law enforcement was tasked with prevention or intervention. Greg pointed to how, on paper, the case of the sisters fit what a typical overseas forced marriage case would look like. However, after speaking with the girls and their parents, the evidence that there was an intention of coercion was not as clear cut. Greg mentioned that the parents themselves were being pressured by the girls' uncle (the father's brother) to marry because the uncle had helped secure the visas of their mother and father to Australia several years prior. The uncle, then, had expected the girls to marry his sons as a form of repayment. Thus, the AFP could not determine if the father and mother were actually the ones who coerced the girls into marriage or where the pressure around marriage even began. Greg's sharing of the stories in this context conveyed the dissonance he felt between his profession's expectations and the emotionally charged complexities of intervening in family relations.

While the aforementioned was part of an interview I had with Greg and was not part of a public circulation of the stories, he did bring up the sisters at a public workshop on forced marriage about three months after our initial meeting. Speaking to an audience of about one hundred people, Greg told the story of "two sisters who had managed to escape from Pakistan to Australia." He mentioned that the girls did not want their parents to be prosecuted under the forced marriage law. This was significant because the AFP was to take a victim-centered approach that required a victim statement to proceed with the investigation. The AFP decided that they could not move forward with an investigation or potential prosecution. Greg did emphasize that the AFP could, however, move forward with charging the parents with child trafficking, in which the intent to "move a child overseas" was all they needed for charges. Greg emphasized that after speaking with the sisters, who were worried about their parents' well-being and what would happen to them in Pakistan after their escape, charging their parents with this would only hurt the sisters' sense of security and recovery from this traumatic event. I noticed that, in this version of the story, Greg's narrative did not focus as much on the sisters' parents and their attitudes toward their children. He also did not point to the multiple expectations he was negotiating. Here, the narrative seemed designed to communicate to other practitioners that the AFP was a functional body that had to work within certain evidentiary and juridical constraints. In emphasizing AFP as a critical node in gathering the evidence to build a prosecutable case (in addition to removing the victim from an undesirable situation), Greg's presentation also functioned to illustrate the AFP's institutional authority to other agencies who were not used to engaging with them or were more comfortable communicating with state police thus far.

Following his explanation, Greg provided an overview of the AFP's capacities domestically and internationally to prevent forced marriage cases. This included their capacity to speak with victims; liaise with foreign law enforcement and Australian immigration authorities to assist with repatriation; to secure evidence held in or by foreign jurisdictions that could help to prove a marriage was carried out; to create a Passenger Analysis Clearance and Evacuation System (PACE) alert on someone's passport at an airport to prevent travel; and to provide referrals to domestic violence shelters for victims who do not want to provide statements in support of an investigation. Greg was trying to show that most of the AFP's resources and capacities were geared toward disrupting the events that immediately preceded an attempt to force a marriage and gathering evidence that could help Commonwealth Prosecution Services develop a case against the organizers of and parties to the marriage. Because of this, the AFP had to locate evidence that a) an attempt to coerce someone into a marriage had been made and b) the marriage took place. This narrowed the scope of facts that could count as evidence and explained the lack of prosecutions under the law, because it was difficult to procure such evidence. Greg then used the story of the sisters as a segue to illustrate the AFP's commitment to a victim-centered approach. The story of the sisters was a vehicle to make transparent to other practitioners the criteria the AFP had to fulfill to prevent and prosecute potential cases, which was new terrain. It made clear to practitioners in the room that, while individual officers like Greg may want to be attuned to the complexities of reported cases, the AFP had its own institutional logics to follow, ones that focused less on the moral character of parents and more on the details of the event itself. I could see how in this presentation, Greg did not grapple as much with his professional expectations and personal capacities. Yet rather than create a divide between agencies, Greg's presentation was effective in making institutional logics transparent for other practitioners in direct service organizations. It helped VFMN members feel like they were all operating under distinct sets of institutional constraints. The story of the two sisters, at the very least, reminded practitioners that they were all part of an interagency system that was working out, in real time, what each institution's role would be in preventing and disrupting a forced marriage. To evoke the sisters was, in a way, to evoke the broader purpose at stake.

A few weeks later, I met the director of the refuge where Homaira and Simin first went. In the director's recounting, Homaira and Simin decided to leave the refuge at Simin's urging. Simin had wanted to reconcile with their parents and was initially excited for the wedding, so she convinced Homaira to reluctantly return to their parents' house. When meeting with the director, I was struck by her recognition of the sisters' agency when retelling the story. She mentioned that the ARC, the AFP, and the refuge had told the sisters not to listen to their families and not to travel to Pakistan. She continued, "The girls here decide this and they are the only ones who can decide. But they decided to go with their parents. And then they found a way to get back home because they didn't want to go through with this." The director's recounting that followed focused on how the sisters mobilized their resources to escape the coercive situation. She mentioned that they had found access to their parents' safe to get money to purchase their return airfare and managed to get in touch with the Australian embassy to facilitate their return. The director said they were nurtured and loved by their parents, but "their parents had the wrong thing in mind for them." In the director's version of the story, the sisters were capacious people who made decisions for themselves, including the decision to leave through their own wherewithal and resources. However, the director saw this narrative as a symptom of a bigger immigration problem. She saw forced marriage as its own unique problem that not only required the law currently in place but also more explicit immigration interventions: "The law should say that anyone who is found out to be doing this, is going to get deported or have their visa/immigration status revoked. People should be deported if they do these things. Especially those who take these girls overseas. . . . You have people who are not willing to understand that in Australia you don't do these things. And there needs to be consequences." While the initial narrative recognized the complexity of their familial relationships, the director ultimately framed this story as a symptom of a broader immigration problem that could be solved through stricter legislation that made the threat of deportation a deterrent. For the director, the sisters' story was another example of migrants who exist in a state of illegality (De Genova 2002). At the same time, the director's framing re-emphasized the need for a unique and distinct forced marriage prevention sector. The sisters' story was the ideal example to justify the need for an interagency apparatus rooted first and foremost in a criminal justice approach.

The story of the two sisters was, in many ways, a "quintessential" forced marriage case. From the first reading, it checked the boxes for what events, types of travel, and family members constituted the type of case that was well publicized in the news media prior to the passage of the 2013 law. For one, it involved two Australian citizens whose parents had sought refuge in Australia from Afghanistan. Both sisters were underage, though one was young enough to be considered eligible for CPS' help, while the other was not. They had attempted to escape going on the plane to their parents' home country but were coerced into traveling after being promised lavish weddings. While abroad, they were deprived of their cell phones, locked in their family's house, and confronted with physical threats by their family members as they coordinated the weddings. The sisters were resilient enough to find embassy authorities, coordinate an escape plan, and flee back to Australia, where they are currently safe but still living under the radar. These were the makings of a harrowing story of the violence of cultural tradition, a tale of "honor-based violence," and the resilient victim-turned-heroine. These were exemplary of the kinds of stories that appeared in many professional training manuals and workshops to demonstrate what a forced marriage case looked like. On the surface, then, the story of the two sisters was dense with spectacle that mirrored the narratives of scenario trainings.

In that sense, the stories at a surface level provided an ideal vehicle through which practitioners could communicate their distinct institutional identities, blind spots, and shared sense of purpose in an emergent policy landscape. Whether it was law enforcement or social services, practitioners found themselves grappling with institutional failures, professional expectations in the juridical system, and validating the existence of a unique forced marriage prevention system that was addressing a migrant-specific problem.

A Logic of Sequestration

What is the experience of being asked to produce local and community-based solutions without being able to engage with the community one is asked to support? I would like to reflect on how advocates tasked with community-led forced marriage prevention navigate not being able to speak with victims of forced marriage who are using their organization's services. I turn to Lori whom I introduced in the beginning of the book. Lori was asked to create a community empowerment program around forced marriage for an organization that also provided refuge, financial support, and counseling. In her role, Lori had tried but failed several times to get in direct contact with victims the organization was helping. Lori's requests were oftentimes met with the response that victims' situations were sensitive and that caseworkers were the only people qualified to liaise between advocacy staff and victims themselves, to protect their identities. I argue that in Lori's case, such a logic sequestered victims from view, thus rendering them phantom-like figures. "Sequester" comes from the Old French "sequestrer," which means to set aside, remove, or confiscate. This version of the word also comes from the Late Latin "sequestrare," which means to place in safekeeping or to entrust (*Oxford English Dictionary* n.d.). Thus, it has embedded within its etymology both separation and care, distance and intimacy, an ethics of individual responsibility and trust in a bigger system that believes it must revert to keeping the victim from view to enact care.

As a new capacity coordinator, Lori was tasked with working with local community leaders to develop educational awareness workshops they could deliver to their communities. This meant understanding how communities themselves framed forced marriage and using that as a springboard to develop culturally sensitive educational programs. Lori said that she had never spoken with or been able to meet with a victim who was being serviced at her organization. She said she found it strange that caseworkers were so guarded when it came to discussing their clients with her, but they would openly talk to their clients on the phone from their cubicles right next to hers. Lori would catch bits and pieces of their conversations with victims. She had tried for months to convince caseworkers to coordinate a meeting between her and a caseworker's client. Lori wondered if caseworkers developed a sense of territoriality over client information or a paternalistic relationship with their clients, feeling as though they knew their true desires and were responsible for their protection. During one meeting at Lori's organization, a caseworker mentioned that even though a client may consent to telling their stories, they were so used to being submissive to authorities' requests that they would say yes because they felt they had to. Lori noted afterward, the idea that clients were blindly following authority or simply continuing to engage in submissive behavior patterns could easily lead to the idea that clients did not have the capacity to make thoughtful, clear, and nuanced decisions. While I did not spend time with caseworkers and cannot say for sure what was behind the reluctance, it is important to recognize that they are also working within constraints around what kinds of interactions they can facilitate between other practitioners.

A few months later, Lori and I met for coffee before the attorney-general's workshop for prevention and service providers in Melbourne. She told me that she was struggling with how to create a sustainable framework for understanding and working with community members without being able to ask victims how they experienced prevention services. Working in the prevention rather than the direct-response side of forced marriage put Lori in a very different position than someone like Bridget, Greg, or the caseworkers at her organization. She was tasked with expanding the sector's outreach to communities affected by forced marriage and with delivering educational workshops to community leaders in social services. However, while her job was not to directly engage with victims, Lori expressed that she could not develop an educational program for community leaders without understanding what specific challenges around family expectations, the resettlement process, financial insecurity, and isolation victims and their families felt. For Lori, communities were multilayered, and those who were being helped by the direct-response arm of the sector had to be seen as subjects who were tethered to multiple people. She felt that there was a general organizational hesitation to speak with and put forward victims' voices. This prompted Lori to think about creating a steering committee of different community leaders who could liaise with the people they serve and discuss forced marriage in a way that could be useful. It was clear to Lori that policy advocates and program developers were not being shielded from victims purely because confidentiality protocols demanded it. This was most acutely illustrated when Lori described how she would often hear caseworkers speak to victims on the phone just a few feet away from her. It was hard to avoid the circulation of information through the cubicles. Victims remained absent presences, legible through the nuggets of information passing through the administrative ether.

Lori continued that she was now trying to find alternative methods to get insights from victims about their experiences with the sector and their families. It felt as though she was trying to get in contact with someone who had been "quarantined," as she put it. For example, Lori came up with the idea to develop a set of questions that caseworkers could ask their clients who were being provided refuge by the organization. She also developed a document where she took general notes on what victims had been experiencing according to general and nonindividual-specific secondhand information caseworkers would occasionally share with her. These insights would form the basis of the community empowerment workshop Lori developed—a multiday training geared toward educating community leaders about how to reframe marriage in ways that would resonate with migrant communities. Lori also drew from the insights she recalled from a woman she met in Afghanistan while working in humanitarian aid prior to her job in Australia. The woman had recently been granted asylum in Australia and had also been victim to coercion into marriage, but rejected the idea of criminalization. Yet Lori felt disappointed that she could not talk to people her organization was directly helping. The amalgam of information she was putting together was formed through her encounters with caseworkers and her emergent relationships with recently arrived Afghan refugees in Australia.[8]

When I asked why it was so difficult to get victims'/survivors' stories, Lori noted that she could not pinpoint one reason but that isolating them from advocacy discussions was not, in and of itself, a kind of protection. Lori vehemently expressed that victims/survivors need emotional and trauma support but that the opportunity to tell their stories in a careful and ethical way was automatically deemed too dangerous by the sector.[9] Lori mentioned that, at one point, she was told that there were no mechanisms in place to get in touch with victims/survivors to get proper approvals to use their stories. Lori and Bridget brought up the need to get victims/survivors to share their stories in a protected, structured, and safe way so that the sector would not continue to develop service responses without their input. However, there was often a hesitation in the sector to take the conversation further, and during my fieldwork, this was never seriously pursued. The idea of having victims/survivors at meetings to discuss their experience of Victoria's direct-service response program was often met with reluctance. This was due to a desire to avoid retraumatizing victims/survivors and not wanting to reveal their identities for fear that other local family members would discover what refuge or shelter they were housed in. While these concerns are fair and important, they are not necessarily universally applicable to all victims/survivors. For Lori, the reluctance was less a case-specific response and more of a standardized approach the sector took. It assumed that no victims/survivors would want to tell their stories and share their experiences for the purposes of improving services.

As anthropologist Erin Debenport (2015, 7) has pointed out in her study of Indigenous language literacy and the politics of secrecy, secrecy itself "depends on a certain measure of shared knowledge to communicate the significance of limited information." It represents a form of information control in which the owners of the information declare greater control over its value and circulation. The forced marriage prevention apparatus is similarly animated by these narrative asymmetries—certain narratives are deemed more digestible for the purposes of intervention and prevention than others, which creates a self-reinforcing cycle of rendering certain stories invisible for reasons that go well beyond safety. Ochs and Capps's (1996, 34) explanation of narrative asymmetries and how they are part of the community-building technologies of a particular set of practitioners is helpful here: "Adherence to a dominant narrative is also community-building in that it presumes that each member ascribes to a common story.... Narrative asymmetries lie in the values assigned not only to different versions of experience but also to different ways of recounting experience.... Yet another manifestation of narrative asymmetry involves entitlement to narrate. Who can tell a story? What role can one play in the course of a storytelling interaction?" In the forced marriage sector, who can tell a story also conditions which stories can be told, which in turn informs what becomes a "standardized approach." Which narratives gain currency in the moral economy of stories created in the forced marriage sector is part of the sector's "bureaucratic rationality."

The sentiment that stories of victimhood were often cited but rarely engaged with as complex experiences of violence was felt among certain migrant community leaders. After a September VFMN meeting, a Muslim Australian community advocate named Amina, who works in Narre Warren, Geelong, and Shepparton on behalf of an organization serving Muslim immigrant women, expressed that while members of the network were pointing out the lack of research, there was no concentrated effort to include victims/survivors within meetings, planned workshops, or conferences. At the same time, practitioners were quick to, if even subconsciously, focus on forced marriage as a Muslim issue. She saw this as deeply racialized and that the focus on culture and religion was obscuring larger problems:

> Oftentimes I feel like the lone person in the room and I have to defend where we [the community organization she works with] are coming from and our approach, which people seem uncomfortable with because it is not interventionist enough—it is more preventative. Yeah, it sucks that a 15 year old gets married, but why does it happen in the first place. Let's work on changing the sense of choice, aspiration, and options that these girls feel they have or don't have. Let's tackle the issues that are important to them. For many of the young girls, they were concerned about their families' inability to meet the new 457 requirements and the new citizenship requirements. They are worried about racism and scrutiny.... Why do people wanna know the numbers [of cases]? These are families being torn apart and people being criminalized.... There is no space to think critically about race and power.

For Amina, the sector not only ignored victim/survivor stories—they also had not adequately considered the impact of other issues on their lived experience, including racialization and the precarities introduced by new immigration policies. The 457 visa changes that Amina referred to put many temporary migrants into vulnerable positions in the spring of 2017. In April, former Prime Minister Malcolm Turnbull announced that 457 visas, which foreign temporary workers used, would be significantly overhauled and replaced with a new temporary work visa available only for two or four years. There would be a reduction in the occupations available to skilled foreign workers, and the threshold to qualify would be raised, including having to prove that they have previous work experience, English language proficiency, and high labor market testing. Turnbull noted that doing so would allow "Australians priority for Australian jobs.... We'll no longer let 457 visas be passports to jobs that could and should go to Australians" (Karp 2017). For the communities Amina worked with, such a reform was deeply troubling to those who were relying on extended family members to migrate to Australia to provide further economic support. Amina's insights speak to how the prevention system was focused on disrupting the immediate events preceding a marriage (which Amina describes as more "interventionist") but not on understanding the structural factors that made marriage a viable option in the first place. Moreover, the prevention system's preoccupation with constructing forced marriage as a social problem diverted attention from making sense of the true social problem at hand—racialized border regimes that made migrant entry and citizenship conditional on labor power. For Amina, while migrants were rendered visible as objects of intervention, they were less visible as subjects of exclusionary border regimes.

Phantom Figures

For practitioners in the VFMN, the preoccupation with stories of victimhood is also one with how to create institutions that are effective, work cohesively, and tackle a distinct problem. Victim stories are used as heuristic devices to render cohesive institutional logics and expectations that feel disjointed. While the story of the sisters functioned as objects of reflection for practitioners, in the everyday workings of the prevention system, stories were often guarded from those who were not directly involved in the case. The story of the sisters was treated as an exemplary case the system could learn from, and this may have partially explained why it was circulated so ubiquitously. It reflected a rare moment when victim/survivor stories were made visible but in a very curated form.

Lori came to realize that in prevention work, victims/survivors only existed as curated stories and never as people with complex subjectivities who could be part of a community-led conversation on redefining the role of marriage in crafting more viable individual and community futures. The sequestering of stories from those who sought to facilitate such conversations rendered victims/survivors as phantom-like figures—always present in neat narratives of criminality but absent in their full experiences as intersectional subjects.

I borrow the frame of the "phantom" from anthropological analyses concerned with the enduring power of that which goes unseen. I propose phantom figures as an analytical frame that describes how the subjects of social welfare are rendered visible as heuristic devices through which social welfare can reflect on its own institutional logics but invisible as complex subjects who can meaningfully participate in that system. I am inspired by Suzana Sawyer's (2001, 159) conceptualization of the phantom as encompassing "conditions of invisibility." Writing in the context of subaltern groups, such as Indigenous peoples living in Ecuador, Sawyer's concept of phantom citizens looks at what happens when marginalized groups get formal rights as citizens but no substantive rights in practice (160). While this chapter addresses a differently marginalized group, the phantom concept resonates because victim/survivor experiences are frequently evoked in the sector as important yet are rarely part of advocacy conversations. Victims/survivors in the forced marriage prevention system are also treated as forms, illusory subjects who are never present to express their own realities but whose existence is critical to validating and creating institutional logics and memory. The phantom in other anthropological analyses has been defined as that which has a form but no substance. Diane Nelson (2001, 306) discusses phantoms through the frame of the phantom limb and embodiment. Inspired by Elizabeth Grosz, phantom limbs "take the place of what is corporeally missing," which allows for a "new way of maneuvering the world." For Grosz (1994), the subject always exceeds the phantom limb and "makes its own any prosthetic brought into use."[10]

While the phantom figure in this example is not a stand-in for the corporeal, it is, for practitioners, a stand-in figure. Marilyn Ivy's (1995, 20) conception of the phantom as "something passing away but not quite, suspended between presence and absence" captures the faint traces of victim/survivor subjectivity that find their way into this biopolitical regime. This figure is a stand-in that helps practitioners work through their epistemic anxieties and remains guarded from view by those who see it as fragile and incapacious. In proposing the phantom figure to understand the curation and suppression of victim/survivor narratives in prevention work, I do not mean to imply that "phantomness" is a kind of existential state in which subjects exist. Victims/survivors are never overdetermined by their institutional erasure and always engage in practices of self-making that defy erasure (Lazzari 2003, 60). While their complex subjectivities do not matter to the institutional logics of forced marriage prevention, people affected by coercion around marriage continue to question, redefine, and transform community with each other.

Beyond Biopolitical Narratives

About one month after meeting the refuge director, I was told that I could meet the sisters in person. The sisters were currently attending a school that aimed to help victims of family violence, mostly of immigrant and refugee backgrounds. Their school was in a secret location, so the address could only be disclosed through a phone call with the principal. I walked cautiously to the building's entrance and went to the floor where the school was located. When I finally arrived, I was greeted by the principal and taken to a meeting room, a small common area with a kitchenette surrounded by glass windows that looked into the hallway. I was told that the sisters would arrive shortly and that I could sit in the room and talk to them for about an hour until their next class activity. We met during the month of Ramadan which Homaira and Simin were observing by undertaking the day-long fast. This resulted in our conversation being slightly shorter than it may have been otherwise, given the need to preserve one's energy during this time. I was struck by how easily we were able to talk about their everyday lives attending school back in Australia as they attempted to re-establish a sense of place in Melbourne. I decided not to ask questions about what happened to the sisters during their travels to Pakistan to avoid making them repeat a narrative that they had already told to multiple agencies. My conversation with Homaira and Simin focused less on this experience and its aftermath and more on their aspirations for the future—educationally, professionally, and personally. Simin expressed that she was fasting and felt quite weak because it was in the dead heat of summer, but her laugh was infectious. I talked to them about how, as a self-identifying Muslim and Afghan, I was delinquent with fasting. Simin replied that she was also exhausted because they both had stayed up until three or four in the morning watching the India-Pakistan cricket match and were excited that Pakistan had won. I asked them about their everyday routine since starting their studies at this new school. They said they go to school five days per week but have to travel a long way to get there from an outer suburb of Melbourne.

We quickly transitioned to their love of South Asian films and they asked me if I knew Urdu because I mentioned that I enjoyed Bollywood films. I replied that I didn't but attempted to follow the film plots through the song and dance numbers. Homaira added that she speaks Urdu, Hindi, Pashto, and a bit of Farsi. While her family is from Afghanistan, she spent much of her childhood in Pakistan and adolescence in Australia, so her knowledge of Farsi was a work in progress. She started listing the phrases she remembered as we laughed, "*Chetowri?*" (How are you?); "*Koja budi?*" (Where were you?); and "*Tashakor*" (Thank you). Simin interjected and talked about the community of friends she had made from Iranian, Afghan, and Pakistani backgrounds since returning to Australia. Homaira added that she did not have as many friends, but she did enjoy talking to her boyfriend on video chat on WhatsApp. I added that it must have been difficult to spend so much time away from him. She said it was incredibly hard but that it was good to have a strong support system and someone she could rely on as they tried to rebuild their lives in Australia. There was an awkward silence, and I asked them if they had any questions about my research. It was at this point that I realized I could not completely shed the perception that I was yet another person who wanted to get "their story." Homaira replied with a sigh and slight smile, aware that perhaps she was breaking the fourth wall, "Just ask the questions you came here to ask." I smiled and laughed nervously, becoming aware of how my avoidance of their experience in Pakistan gave a false impression that I as an anthropologist was not participating in the assemblage of people and institutions who sought "their story" to validate their own sense of purpose and identity. Due to the fact that I had been referred to them by multiple agencies (Bridget's organization, the refuge, and the AFP) to whom they had already told their story, I, too, was implicated in an emerging lineage of biopolitical forms of storytelling that saw their story as valuable. However, it was the case that the story I was interested in was different than that of the prevention sector. Rather than ask about the events that led up to their trip to Pakistan and the unfolding of their rescue, I wanted to understand more about how they were feeling in this moment as they navigated the pressures of school, relationships, and rebuilding a new life without their parents. I responded to Homaira that I would be interested to hear whatever they wanted to share about their recent experience in Pakistan, their relationships with their families, and their aspirations for the future.

Simin began by saying that they missed their mother who was still in Pakistan because their father had told her that she could not return to Australia and have a relationship with her daughters after the incident. Homaira added more details about their experience being taken to Pakistan but not in the way that service providers narrated it. I noticed that their narrative was much more open about their own role in coordinating their leaving of Islamabad than had been suggested by agency narratives. In their version, it was Homaira and Simin who set the groundwork for leaving the house they were being kept in well before the embassy and AFP got involved. Simin mentioned that part of her fear of leaving Australia was losing the friends she had made. She added that while they were in Pakistan, her boyfriend there helped them escape to the Australian embassy and was now being threatened by her uncle's family. They said that their father was a good man who was easily influenced by their uncle (his brother). Homaira and Simin mentioned that they were living together in an apartment but were scared to travel too far out of their current neighborhood. They usually just went from school to home, because their brother—who was invested in them getting married and was concerned about the fallout of their escape on his family's reputation—lived in a nearby suburb and they were not yet ready to interact with him. Simin discussed how difficult it was for them to be away from their mother and family friends, noting, "Family is the most important thing. I can't imagine a life without my family in my life." I also learned that their mother did not rejoin them in Australia because of both immigration restrictions put on her family members and pressure from her husband (their father) and in-laws, who told her to cut all relations with her own children—something their father had already done. The conversation was illuminating; the sisters had suffered these traumas yet still longed for the connection with their mother and other family friends. The new layers Homaira and Simin added to existing biopolitical stories illustrated that they felt attached to family members and that emotional attachments endured across transnational divides. At the same time, it was not clear how much accountability their parents had taken for putting them in this situation in the first place; at some level, their mother felt beholden to her husband and in-laws in ways that resulted in a geographic separation from her daughters. However, because they did not bring up accountability, I decided to not probe into this question further. They also wanted me to focus my writing on their lives in Australia, which is partly why the focus on what happened in Pakistan is not as present. This decision to not probe further is also a decision to disconnect this research from the kinds of questions that are relevant to colonial social welfare.

In thinking about the conditions that led up to our conversation and the awkward yet mundane encounters during it, I try to take seriously Johannes Fabian's (1986, 42) call to avoid the use of the ethnographic present. The ethnographic present is a mode of written analysis that gives the impression that subjects simply were or are the way the anthropologist describes them; it is a snapshot approach to writing that willfully leaves out the other happenings and subtexts of a conversation, encounter, or social interaction that may offer a more complicated picture. By refusing the ethnographic present, I am able to see the conversation with Homaira and Simin as illuminating in ways that go beyond their subjectivities in the forced marriage prevention apparatus. When I spoke with them, they were very much in the process of trying to rebuild their lives, their sense of place in the world, and their routine, and to develop some type of everyday normalcy. This desire to build a sense of normalcy coexisted with the disorientation that came from being separated from one's beloved parent. This side of the sisters' story had not been of interest to practitioners. It was the side where the enduring effects of trauma existed in simultaneity with the mundane struggles of maintaining a sibling relationship, and getting through the everyday challenges of school. Their experience could not be characterized by a distinct moment of coercion by their parents—rather, the experience of being coerced unfolded over several years and was interspersed with moments and periods of love, care, and respect for and from their parents. With despair in their voices, they expressed how they longed to see their mother who was caught up in a patriarchal system of familial pressure of her own, not able to contradict her husband's choices about where she could travel. This was a different kind of story—one that was not premised on discrete moments of betrayal, infraction, or familial breakdown. It was the kind that exceeded the narrative forms privileged in the juridical and social welfare domains.

Homaira and Simin's stories transcended institutional narratives of victimhood. They were not simply discussing how the system failed to prevent them from being coerced into a marriage; instead, they made sense of their experience of violence through the lens of interconnected pressures within a family. They expressed surprise and outrage that their uncle could have manipulated their father to the point that he would have exercised so much power over their futures. They situated their own father as pressured, as part of a broader and more expansive situation of family trauma that led him to convince their mother to approve the marriage. As legal scholar Richard Sherwin (2017, 42) writes, legal stories hardly allow for ambivalence and complexity but "it is also worth thinking about what a more complex and messy form of storytelling would allow." While Sherwin is discussing integrating a more complex form of narrative within criminal justice procedure itself, it is important to recognize how biopolitics forms the enclosures within which stories get told in the social welfare space.

Studies have shown how victim-centered epistemologies of suffering get erased through institutional logics that paint victims as either suffering subjects whose futures are inevitably doomed or deviant subjects who have failed to be resilient enough to overcome their suffering. Angela García (2010, 71–80) has shown how the narrative forms privileged in rehabilitation and juridical discourses of the "patient-prisoner" rely upon a linear narration of one's addiction—one that has a clear beginning and distinct turning points that ultimately lead to either full rehabilitation or eternal addiction. This narration demands a re-inscription of traumatic events into a teleological narrative. This inadvertently sets the subject up for failure because it implicitly expects an end, marked by either the individual pulling themselves into full recovery or being subjected to death. For García's interlocutors who were struggling with heroin addiction in New Mexico's Española Valley, narrating one's lived experience with addiction is a different kind of storytelling—one that brings together seemingly disconnected utterances about the past and the present, about deep histories of loss and dispossession (of land, family, inheritances, and a sense of the future), and the precarity of everyday life (2010, 79). For those who live it, addiction cannot be captured through discrete events—it is, rather, narrated through connecting the present back to the past in often unexpected ways, which differs from chronological storytelling. As Ochs and Capps (1996, 24) state, "The chronological dimension offers narrators a vehicle for imposing order on otherwise disconnected experiences. That is, chronology provides a coherence that is reassuring." Alessandra Gribaldo (2014) has discussed the ways that the juridical system limits the testimonies of the victim-subject in Italy's domestic violence hearings. She writes: "The testimony of female victims of abuse is trapped between the normativity of justice system requirements and the confessional device, rendering it legally insignificant and thus essentially inadequate." I, too, felt that Homaira and Simin were refusing to engage in a teleological and event-centered narrative of violence. While I was not interviewing their experiences within a medical, juridical, or rehabilitative institution, it was clear that their narratives did not neatly fit into the narrative structures that emerged in forced marriage prevention spaces. The sisters did not talk about the immediate events that led up to the trip. They did not frame their escape as a rescue effort resulting from their collaboration with the AFP and DFAT. They also did not discuss how, exactly, they were coerced. The tone I walked away with after our conversation was that they were hopeful yet uncertain about the future. I could sense the loss that they carried with them—family relations fragmented yet still tethered to memories of a past sense of trust that was broken. This was not a narrative designed to render one's coercion as distinctly identifiable. There was the coercion into marriage, and then there was the pressure of continuing with everyday life while knowing their mother was excluded by the interlocking violences of borders and patriarchy.

The privileging of an event-based narrative brings up a larger point around the logic of forced marriage prevention. Preventing forced marriage is, in some ways, essentially about preventing one's entry into the union of marriage. Entry into marriage is the fact or event where the work of social service and law enforcement intersects. The focus on this event is indicative of how stories in the sector are shaped by criminal justice narratives. Stories that are linked to a criminal justice approach are marked by events and actors that are traceable and can be easily referenced by other practitioners. To create a story rooted in a criminal justice approach is to create a story marked by linear events—pointed actions that have an origin, a clear vector of power, and can be retrospectively referred to as sources of evidence.[11]

As I left the conversation, I felt that I had gained insights that could provide a new dimension to practitioner understandings of coercion into marriage. However, I would soon discover that the sector valued particular kinds of narratives, ones that had clear trajectories of violence framed by the binaries of autonomy and subjugation, which made it difficult to capture the emotional complexity and family dynamics Homaira and Simin had talked about.

Initially, I thought that focusing on Homaira and Simin's hopes for the future and how they were remaking the everyday (Das 2006) could be valuable in showing the different familial demands victims were caught up in, which goes beyond the victim-perpetrator model. However, I realized that the sector saw my meeting with the sisters as important but not exactly for the reasons I had imagined. Here, there emerged a dissonance between how I thought about the "new information" I held as an anthropologist and how the sector viewed it.

I met with Bridget a few weeks after my interview. She had invited me to a caseworkers meeting at a local library in Carleton to observe the work of forced marriage caseworkers. Afterward, we walked outside the library to quickly catch up. As we were about to part ways, she told me she wanted to know how the interview with the sisters went. She asked a few questions, including what my take on them was. I immediately felt a sense of disappointment because I had not addressed these questions in my conversation with the sisters. Some questions included: Which sister was more outspoken and which more reserved? What was it that made the younger sister change her mind and not want to go through with the wedding? Was the boyfriend involved in their escape? Was it the uncle who had orchestrated this whole situation? I felt that I had very little insight into any of these questions—we had only discussed their escape for a small portion of the conversation. Even then, I had simply asked them to tell whatever narrative they wanted, rather than prompt with overly specific questions. The consequences of my refusal to ask certain questions were beginning to show. My answers, for the most part, dodged Bridget's questions and rerouted the conversation to what I thought were telling moments about how the sisters were creating a new normal—an everyday that was oriented toward their career aspirations, their desire to get a good education, and their desire to support each other through a time of continuing transition. Bridget listened, but I could sense that something was missing. She repeated some of her previous questions in a gentle, yet deliberate way. I felt that I had let Bridget down; even though I was not working on behalf of her organization, I did feel that, as an ethnographer, I should offer some valuable insight. I did not, however, feel that I could tell her a story that would adhere to the type of narrative demanded by direct service agencies. The story that Bridget had hoped for was marked by a discrete set of events, turning points, "aha" moments, committed decisions, traceable injuries, bounded moments, and key people who did the coercing that led to the imminent forced marriage. She expressed how disappointing it was that more people did not have access to these sisters and that even I only had one hour to "get information." She continued that if I had more time, perhaps the sisters could have revealed where social service agencies let them fall through the cracks, where various government departments could have made their return more seamless and less clandestine, or how airport security officials could have prevented them from getting on a plane. While Bridget wanted to understand their experience of the prevention and direct-response system, she also wanted to understand what allowed them to escape and, by extension, what prevented other people who had been in a similar situation from doing it. It was clear that Bridget and others who narrated their story saw the two sisters as both quintessential and exceptional—their circumstances mapped on to how the sectors thought victim stories typically unfolded, yet in their escape, they were exceptional, resilient, and illustrative of institutional failures. For direct service practitioners like Bridget, the goal was to prevent the girls from being taken abroad ever again. My conversation with Homaira and Simin could not fill in the gaps for service providers. It could not reveal who the vectors of coercion were and what exactly drove the sisters to escape. Part of this was due to the fact that I did not know how the sisters thought about the consequences of such an escape—did they do a cost-benefit analysis to determine the best course of action, or did they plan the escape knowing and accepting the uncertainty of it all? Did they experience themselves as subversive people, violating familial and cultural codes? Or was their escape something they had already threatened to do previously when their parents had told them they were going to Pakistan?

Bridget is part of an apparatus that generates knowledge about victims. In trying to excavate the sisters' narrative, she not only hoped for facts to fill in the "gaps" but for facts to fill in particular gaps that would create a particularly oriented narrative. This narrative would have clear victims, perpetrators, and moments of coercion that could be used as blueprints for further prevention models, programs, and efforts (factual gaps were epistemic gaps). She said, "If we could see where these girls had to rely on themselves, we could use that as part of a new strengths-based approach. We could also use those moments of manipulation and coercion as moments of entry and potential 'disruption' of forced marriage—those are the moments where the rationale of parents need to be targeted." In other words, these stories, the stories of Homaira and Simin, were seen as potential sites of knowledge production around victimhood. They were subjects through whom the prevention sector could examine its own limitations and continue to refine its understanding of who victims were.

Conclusion

Storytelling is as much a governing technology as it is an epistemic practice—it is a mode by which this biopolitical project (forced marriage prevention) defines how the experiences of victims/survivors come to matter to social policy. As Lisa Stevenson (2014) has described in her ethnography of the Inuit-targeted suicide prevention apparatus in the Canadian Arctic, it is precisely care-based projects that not only aim to intervene in people's well-being but also define how they are deemed of value to the state. The way stories about people are told in biopolitical projects also functions to guard what exactly about people's lived experiences matter for the purposes of colonial welfare. As a mode of determining how to make which facts and details visible, it produces a regime of narration, in which certain narratives about victims gain traction over others. In the end, I too have curated their stories in particular ways that perhaps function to fulfill the ethnographic imagination. But in doing so, I hope to have provided an alternative underexplored dimension of a broader narrative of coercion that can further humanize the people the sector seeks to help.

5

Beyond Criminality

Narratives of Familial Duress in Times of Displacement

Thus far, I have examined how familial coercion becomes an object of concern for the Australian state and for social service and policing institutions and how practitioners resist such objectifications. While the forced marriage policy sees migrant familial relations as objects of concern, less explored in policy discussions has been how Muslim women from migrant families think about their familial relations. This chapter turns to how a group of Muslim Australian women thinks about familial duress when it comes to intimate partner relationships. In focusing on their stories, I do not seek to show that Muslim Australian women's perspectives on family, gender, and violence are wholly incommensurable with state and public discourse. Rather, I seek to highlight how narratives of familial duress (with a focus on marital and intimate partner relations) that are shaped by experiences of displacement think about kin relations and accountability in ways that transcend the language of state policy. Specifically, the women whose stories constitute this chapter see their family members not as perpetrators of criminal acts. They see them as subjects whose decisions are shaped by a dense nexus of power relations and structural violence (related to migration, resettlement, and displacement). In doing so, these women do not trivialize the violence of these coercive acts. Rather, they see themselves as subjects with the capacity to negotiate these decisions and use it as a starting point for collective transformation. I also show that, for some, forced marriage was an apt way to describe their experiences, and intervention was needed. However, these stories do show that culture and family separation prove to be inadequate lenses to make sense of the breakdown of familial relations and fundamentally ignore why marriage becomes a site of familial strife in the first place. Two of the four narratives presented here are not reflections of an individual's encounter with the forced marriage prevention system. However, I have included them because they can clarify both what the sector misses about family life and what other frameworks exist for making sense of duress in times of precarity and uncertainty. In that sense, this chapter takes seriously Saida

Hodžić's (2009, 332) concern that "culture" need not be understood as a "native form of resistance" to the concept of "rights," thereby making "culture" immune from critical analyses of power.[1]

In what follows, I do not mean to situate these narratives as representative expressions of cultural resistance or understandings of culture that are absolved of problematic understandings of "community" or "obligation." In fact, I hesitate to treat them as culturally specific narratives in the first place that are somehow more qualitatively "accurate" than those that appear in prevention literature because they are articulated by Muslim women, the sector's intended audience. Rather, I treat these narratives as renderings of family violence that exceed the sector's idea that there are culturally distinct forms of violence that require specific kinds of cultural knowledge. On the contrary, my interlocutors' very narrations question this key pillar of family violence prevention, some more intentionally and consciously than others. Thus, rather than viewing these narrations as culturally authentic or genuine, I view them as politically and culturally situated analyses, rooted in specific times and places, that offer new layers to the understanding of familial duress. What my interlocutors have in common is that they do not frame their experiences as symptoms of their families' cultures. Grasping their narratives requires provincializing the idea of "culture" in the first place and questioning how it has been mobilized to reproduce the hierarchy between what have been judged as "liberal" and "illiberal" cultural forms (Abu-Lughod 1991).

The narratives here are also not "native forms of resistance" against liberal notions of rights and multiculturalism. This idea assumes that there is a homogeneous group that considers itself distinct from monolithic discourses of liberalism. Rather, my interlocutors are rethinking family violence, not as a way to assert their cultural difference against the dominant discourse of human rights and multiculturalism. Rather, these narratives show alternative ways in which people think about their familial relationships in the wake of experiencing violence at their hands. These ways do not have to mean the full erasure or full acceptance of family. They see the importance of agency over one's life while considering the consequences for one's family members. They see the promise of autonomy over one's relationship choices but not in ways that have to mean refusing the role of their communities in helping them understand what it means to live a meaningful life. I remove culture from the equation as a guiding analytic to understand the significance of these renarrations and reapprehensions.[2] These alternative approaches resituate family violence outside the lens of penality. Perhaps these narrations could, to borrow from Silvana Tapia's analysis of violence against women in Ecuador (2016, 152), "invite us to rethink women's rights and VAW outside a positivistic, punishment-centered lens." The alternative narratives laid out here are not invested in a carceral approach to punishing family members. Rather, they develop alternative explanations around what it means to be at the hands of violence and the conditions of possibility that produce it. In that sense, my interlocutors also do not situate their narrations as representative or reflective of a monolithic or distinctly identifiable Islamic ethos around family, violence, or gender.[3] They are, rather, situated within the aftermath of resettlement, the demands of assimilation, and the ongoing expectations of transnational networks of obligation.

This chapter shows how women see the constellation of family, autonomy, duress, and desire operating in their daily lives in comparison to state and prevention discourse. I focus on Muslim Australian women's narratives of violence not because family violence is intrinsic to the Muslim Australian community (which is not a monolithic social entity), but because first and second generation Muslim migrant communities are disproportionately targeted by Australia's family violence policies. The discussion around family violence has brought the Muslim Australian community into its fold, producing a spectrum of reactions and conversations about race, citizenship, belonging, and violence at the hands of family and the state. One of the key themes that structure the stories of the four women whose narratives I spotlight here is that family violence cannot be explained by cultural tradition nor reduced to the perpetrator-victim framework. In short, it cannot be abstracted from the pressures of broader domestic and transnational familial obligations nor from the enduring impact of war, displacement, and resettlement. Their insights reflect the ways in which familial care and violence can and do coexist. This coupling of care and violence is unsettling for social service workers and even for me as an anthropologist, and perhaps for the reader as well. However, the coexistence of both too often gets ignored in social welfare settings. In making this claim, I do not mean to imply that women and their families function through their own internal and insular operative logics. As Saida Hodžić (2013) has written, "community" cannot be seen as the site of ontological difference; rather, the focus should be on how difference actually matters to everyday experiences of violence.

In this chapter, then, I would like to return to the phrase which began this book: Lori's call to "get closer to the violence." I have posited that getting closer to the violence means attending to how duress is actually understood by those who have experienced its varied expressions. My interlocutors' renderings of familial deception and duress show that familial relations are marked by enduring patterns of violence and care. In that sense, my interlocutors do not glorify their families as simply defending their cultural traditions, nor do they indict them for blindly reproducing patriarchal systems of power (though that is one part of how some hold them accountable). They see their familial experiences as an amalgam of multiple violations of autonomy, trust, and mutual accountability. While for some this marked the end of any viable relationship, for others, there remained the possibility of a collective path forward.

In what follows, I draw from my conversations with four women who had experienced familial pressures around their intimate partner relationships and in one case, those of their siblings. They all identify as Muslim Australian and their parents are first generation migrants from Afghanistan (3) and the Gulf region (1).

Anthropologist Madelaine Adelman (2004, 135) has pointed to the need for domestic violence research to focus not only on how violence is conceptualized but also on how the space of the domestic is constructed. In this chapter, I echo Adelman's call and underline the importance of understanding familial relations as structured by other kinds of violences that do not have a place in family violence discussions—the structural violence of border control regimes, detention, displacement, and war. How does such structural violence manifest in everyday life as families try to pick up the pieces and make a life in an unfamiliar place that makes it increasingly difficult for migrants to feel accepted?

Rethinking the Domestic as a Space Where Care Breaks Down

In social welfare approaches to family violence, the domestic space has, over time, been constructed as always potentially rife with threat, danger, and violation. In this framework, returning to the domestic to rebuild social relations to reorganize everyday life (Das, Ellen, and Leonard 2008) becomes impossible. Such a framework also leaves little room to consider the multiplicity of relations that may have constituted social dynamics in a given domestic context—including care and forms of violence conditioned by other kinds of structural violences. What would it mean to treat the home as a site where structural violence coalesces with fragmented subjects who are entangled in the afterlife of such violence?[4] In this chapter, I treat the domestic as a site where both duress and care, stability and unpredictability, and the unmaking and remaking of familial relations coexist. While not always, it is to the domestic space that some people return to begin to reorientate to the everyday (Das, Kleinman, et al. 2001).[5]

This chapter takes inspiration from ethnographic analyses that have peeled back the layers of how intimate social relations fragment people's lives but also reconstruct them amid ongoing precarity and uncertainty. As many ethnographic studies have shown, the push and pull of kinship relations in domestic spaces or arrangements are not always antithetical to relations of care. Such relations of mutual care and interdependence can refuse the judgment and moral valuations of biomedical and therapeutic settings of care while continuing to inflict harm (García 2010; Stevenson 2014; Wool and Messinger 2012).[6] As anthropologist Angela García (2010, 357) writes, care-based policies that hinge on criminalization obscure the complexities of family relationships, making it difficult to understand the flawed decisions people make. I apply García's point to how forced marriage prevention policies' use of the victim-perpetrator binary obscures the complexities of family relationships in the aftermath of war and displacement. The victim-perpetrator binary is a framework that animates how criminal justice views intimate partner and family violence. Such a framework sees those who are subject to violence as only victims and those who carried it out as only perpetrators (Larance et al. 2022, 466). It leaves no room for situations in which the "perpetrator" is also a victim within other structures or relations of power, nor does it recognize situations in which violence is carried out by multiple parties. Deborah Weissman (2019, 46) has written that the depiction of victims and perpetrators through domestic violence frameworks has largely been shaped by its reliance on the criminal justice model, which required the construction of a model of victimhood that assumes numerous things about the victim. This includes the idea that when a "victim" refuses to use legal remedies to address the violence she experiences, she is seen as a less than worthy victim who does not "have the capacity to act on her own behalf," thereby denying her agency and how she views her own experience, which may not view a carceral response as desirable.[7] The victim-perpetrator binary also renders impossible an understanding of the conditions that produce people who enact violence (47). Weissman notes that "Proponents of victim rights deride those who engage in an analysis of perpetrator conduct outside of the premise of patriarchy and individual choice; to do otherwise implies a dangerous form of justification" (2019, 47). In sum, the victim-perpetrator binary corners different parties who are affected by and who enact violence into limiting scripts. This censors what can and cannot be said about why someone enacts violence and how those who are subject to it think about their own power and survival. Weissman (2019, 47) quotes scholar of domestic violence and intimate partner violence studies Leigh Goodmark: "The law disadvantages women who, by virtue of their subordinated status as victims of a patriarchal system, are rarely able to exercise the sort of autonomy contemplated by philosophers."

In this chapter, I attend to how those subjected to coercive behavior on the part of their family members narrate their lived experience of violence in ways that exceed the victim-perpetrator binary. While these individuals were not all systematically disadvantaged by the forced marriage law, they each have experiences that have been dismissed in some way by law enforcement, social welfare, and popular misconceptions about women who are subject to coercion around their marital choices. These individuals do not see their family members as simply and only perpetrators of violent behavior. They do not view the family unit, full stop, as the site where violence began and transpired and where relations of care are impossible. To be clear, I am not making the argument that parental pressure around marriage is an act of care as much as it is an act of coercion. These women would certainly not represent it that way and, in most cases, I do not believe it should be framed that way. Rather, I show that in the aftermath of violence, family relations do not necessarily map on to the victim-perpetrator binary, and that the possibility to reestablish relations of care does exist. Unlike what family violence prevention models imply, the reconciliation of family members does not mean an acceptance, sanctioning of, or return to violent relations. Rather, such reconciliations can imply a much more sober set of mutual recognitions that differ with each case. The domestic can become a space where family relations get rebuilt after these acts of duress and the broader structural violences that have shaped them.

By putting this forth, I do not prescribe this as an alternative to family violence prevention models or a "better way of handling" relationships that might be categorized as abusive. I am, rather, presenting this approach as one that some people take. It is born out of shared experiences with family members in other situations of structural violence and precarity that do not get considered in prevention discourse. By pointing to the interplay of care, duress, and structural violence within these familial relationships, I do not wish to suggest that the pressures parents put their children under are to be interpreted or romanticized as part of a cultural attitude that values a collectivist worldview that believes the subject must subsume herself within interdependent social relations. There is no one worldview that operates in these cases, and interdependent relations differ under different circumstances of displacement, war, and resettlement. Rather, I wish to show that: a) there are multiple ways to know something as violent; b) it is worth considering how violence exists both in interpersonal relations and within the broader structures that produce particular choices as seemingly more sensical but end up harming others; and c) relations can and do endure, albeit in different ways, in the aftermath of such violence. I use the phrase "enduring present" to signal that pressures around one's choice of relationships are not bounded events that simply begin and end. Rather, their effects continue in the lives of all parties involved to different extents and intensities. Forced marriage prevention discourse forecloses the possibility that there are multiple ways to identify the violence of duress into and around marriage and how to understand the fragmentation of familial relations. Through these women's narratives, I present alternative ways of knowing violence that continue to remain illegible to Australian policymaking and family violence prevention discourses and structures.

My interlocutors move beyond an understanding of family violence as a problem of "culture" that does not respond to a human rights framework. While taking a human rights framework seriously, they also see their family dynamics as shaped by the structural conditions of war and displacement. These explanations are not meant to imply that intervention should not take place. Rather, they take discussions about intervention outside the realm of criminality. They also recognize that people operate with more hybrid frameworks that combine notions of personhood and subjectivity. In other words, my interlocutors take what is deemed "cultural" and place it within the realm of the political and a more dynamic notion of the social.[8] This chapter seriously entertains the possibility that what gets defined as "culture" is actually an amalgam of structural and historical conditions of possibility and the responses that people generate in relation to them based on available responses in a given historical moment.

Tracing Transformed Relations

Layla is in her mid-twenties and living in New South Wales. She experienced a tumultuous childhood and was eventually separated from her family and placed in state-sponsored care along with her siblings when she was fifteen. I first learned about Layla's story after reading a news feature on forced marriage on an Australian news outlet. We initially spoke on the phone and then met in person. I was surprised by how forthright and willing she was to share her experience publicly, not only with me but with the news outlet. Eventually, her story was the central focus of a thirty-minute news feature on forced marriage in Australia. What was particularly striking about my conversations with Layla was how little she focused on the actual details of the marriages her parents had been organizing. Instead, she focused on the abuse that occurred between her parents and the abuse she and her siblings suffered at the hands of their mother. In focusing on Layla's story, I realized that her experience of almost being forcibly married was not the only thing that drove her current advocacy for reforms in the forced marriage prevention sector. What also drove her advocacy was the many experiences of family violence across multiple people in her immediate family. Yet Layla's representation of this violence was not pathological. She expressly rejected a cultural explanation in place of one that was attuned to her parents' life histories, marked by displacement, disenfranchisement, and the complexities of resettlement within Australia, rather than simply individual moral failure. Layla narrated her parents' experience not to excuse or apologize for them but to highlight the elements of victims'/survivors' life stories that are missed in intervention efforts and to help reshape some of the rapidly solidifying forms of common sense guiding forced marriage prevention today. Layla had become an advocate for the shortcomings of forced marriage interventions. To her, while they attempted to be culturally sensitive, they relied too heavily on cultural explanations. This led to a refusal to intervene in situations where the victim would have benefited from being separated from her family members and access to counseling (both individual and family).

Layla's parents, both from Iraq, had resettled in Australia but had a tumultuous relationship. Her father had left their family while they were living in New South Wales and had an affair for two years. During the period of his absence, she described her mother as not particularly nurturing. When her father returned home and ended the affair, Layla described him as quite nurturing and dedicated to his kids, which was his way of making up for his absence. However, according to Layla, upon his return, Layla's mother had begun to verbally abuse him. As a way to compensate for the two years he spent away, Layla's father gave in to all of her mother's demands, including agreeing to have Layla's two sisters married to older men at fifteen—marriages that took place before the 2013 law was passed. Layla herself was also almost married to another man during this period. Layla escaped the house at fifteen and has been living on her own since. She was recently diagnosed with complex PTSD and goes to regular counselling. When we spoke, she was able to describe her experience with fluidity and clarity. The following is an excerpt from our conversation that speaks to the ways in which Layla herself experienced the decisions of her parents as a violation that members of the community she grew up with were attempting to stop:

We are fairly isolated with family members here in Australia. We are the only family from our extended family who ended up in Australia—we don't have uncles or cousins, no outsider or native influence. Even in Iraq, I visited my family there, and even they, it [her mother coercing her to get married] was an isolated thing with my own mother being that way. Even when I was there, I met my cousins. They were way older than any of us. They weren't married and it was not an issue. It was just something to do with my own parents. Not so much a [generational] cycle thing [either]. My mom was fairly young herself, about fifteen, a lot older than when my sisters were married. I found it was something exclusive to her, it was not extended family. It was the opposite—we had people who came and told them, your daughters are very young. They didn't think it was a good idea but my mom was very adamant. Nobody picks fights with each other [in their community], you just have to respect what the person of that household thinks. Back off from my daughter, so everyone followed suit. Nobody exposes each other. I found out, all the cases I know . . . the ones who have done it, are the ones who do it on their own, it's their own ideology. People did support it, obviously. My sister had hundreds of guests at her wedding. People aren't against it if they show up to the wedding. I definitely believed that my mother succumbed to a certain type of pressure—[but] it was not that your daughter has to get married right now. She was a proud woman, and [she thought] people are gonna think something is wrong with them, if they don't get married, but everybody else . . . did wait a bit. She definitely had a lot of concerns about reputation and what people say about us, but [with regard to] marriage, that was just her own initiative.

Here, Layla situates her mother's decision as both shaped by and resistant to community norms around marriage; while she accepted that her daughters needed to get married, she resisted the idea that it should happen at a later age. She describes her mom as different from other members of the Iraqi community in the suburb of Sydney where Layla grew up. Layla understands her mother as feeling beholden to the norm to get her daughters married, but also as deviating from the advice that her friends gave her around age of marriage. Layla's explanation also explicitly resists the narrative tropes that are typically used to explain parents' decisions to forcibly marry their children. From the beginning, she notes that her mother's actions are not just a symptom of a generational behavior pattern, given that her mother's family had a different approach to marriage, but rather the product of an "individual ideology." She situates her mother as part of a community that does have particular ideas about familial reputation, but decisions around marriage are not always tied to those ideas. They could be rooted in concerns outside of reputation. I wondered what Layla meant by "individual ideology." As she continued explaining, I learned that Layla did not think of "ideology" in the sense of a static cultural belief system that is intrinsic to the individual. Rather, Layla framed her parents' approach and views on marriage as produced by formative experiences they experienced after being displaced from their home countries:

> [Growing up] everything that was not strictly religious, was not acceptable; they were crazy even if we had the TV on, anything normal was not okay. [My family was] completely closed toward the outside world in Australia. I've met before the extended family in Iraq. On my dad's side, [they were] strict and holier than thou—my dad was the one who said this [marriage] was a bad [idea]; on my mom's side, her family was the relaxed progressive type, she was the religious fanatic, it was really weird. I put it down to maybe she wasn't like that until . . . during the Kuwait invasion [of Iraq]. My parents went to Saudi Arabia—they were refugees, they crossed the border to Saudi Arabia, and the Saudis detained them there, and kept them there in the detention camp, and I was born there. . . . But I think being from where she was, Iraq was laid back, more than Afghanistan and Iran. I found the Iraqis were more laid back religiously, yeah so I think maybe it was two extremes. She went from a religiously relaxed state in Iraq, to this detention camp in Saudi Arabia where they were just completely. . . . They [her parents] are Shi'a. The Saudis were charged with war crimes because they tortured them for being Shi'a. That might've changed her values and ideas. Women were covered head to toe, weren't allowed to leave the tents. The freedoms [she had] in Iraq were stripped from her. Getting to Australia, [she saw that] women have rights, [and it was a] culture shock. [There was] no one holding a gun to her head, you can be whatever. [Getting us married] was a way to preserve her religion and values. . . . My dad's family was not liberal but he was and my mom's family was liberal but she was more extreme. So it was like they were both the different ones from their family.

Layla's mother's experience as a refugee subject to Saudi Arabia's detention regime marked the beginning of a shift in her attitude toward women's public and private comportment. Layla sees her mother's attachment to religious values as stemming from multiple stages of displacement during the Persian Gulf War. Layla makes legible the effects of displacement, specifically the violent detention regime that restricted her mother's mobility, dress, and sense of the future, as well as the abrupt transition to Australian life. Living a life of constant transition meant that the security of certain values was never ensured. For Layla, her mother's approach to her daughters' futures was haunted by the lingering sense that certain values were precarious and the sense of certainty of the future itself was always subject to being unmade. Layla situates her father not as the typical male perpetrator figure highlighted in forced marriage scenarios or as a menacing figure deeply invested in conservative religious values. Instead, he was seen as adopting more liberal values in relation to his family.[9]

Family violence prevention explanations focusing on the moment that consent is to be given or is at risk obscures longer legacies of abuse and violence that

Layla experienced at the hands of her parents whose belief systems were disoriented in the wake of displacement and detention. It was not only Layla and her siblings' capacity to consent to marriage that was violated but also the sense that kin have ethical obligations to one another. The relationship between Layla and her mother remains corroded. She mentioned that she had spoken with her mother on the phone a few weeks back and was scolded. "She told me, 'God cursed me with children like you.' . . . I don't think it's ever something I'll forgive her for. My older sister spoke to her, and she has not changed her stance. She doesn't feel in any way she has done anything wrong. She still firmly believes in this." Layla's sister also suffers from severe psychological problems as a result of the emotional abuse that preceded her forced marriage. Layla and her sisters had experienced neglect prior to the forced marriage when their father left the family for two years. At this time, they experienced emotional abuse at the hands of their mother:

> I left because it reached the point where it was my turn to get married. There was massive pressure. I couldn't even leave my bedroom without being yelled at, spat at, or having something thrown at me. There was constant verbal and emotional abuse, and physical abuse—all because I was not cooperating with them. After I realized that, I couldn't fight it anymore. They already had the groom, the dress, and everything else.
>
> She [her mother] was very abusive but the marriage was the last straw. Well, you ruined our childhood . . . and you determined who we are going to be with. It was the biggest realization I've ever had that we are going to end up with these men. And our adulthood is gonna be crap. It was a big realization for that age—I got up and took my stuff and left. Fifteen years old. I'd fought for years. I'm the oldest one, and for years I've fought, one guy after the next. My mother tried everything. Even when they took me to Iraq, that was a trick, and if my dad hadn't come back at the time, I would have definitely been married and never come back to Australia.
>
> My dad got a lot of pressure from her, and he always buckled to her. I think it's worth saying when we were really young, he was the abusive one, and my mother was the nurturing one, but this all changed when I turned five. We were terrified of my dad coming home, ran to our rooms, and we were scared of him. I think something changed. I'm not sure—it was my mother, she had health complications or something. Then he became nurturing and nice and then she became psycho. It just completely changed. I think he couldn't deal with her. I don't know—he had a lot of pressure himself. Looking at it as an adult, I see a man who had a partner that he couldn't deal with anymore. He had a relationship with another woman. We didn't see him for two years, and then he broke it off with her. . . . And then he came back to start the marriage again, and then parent us. And when he came back, he felt guilt for leaving, so he did everything and anything to please her [her mother]. So when he came back, my older sister turned thirteen

and for those two years my mom was not there for us and she was like 'My husband left me.' So we lived in a house on our own. So when he came back and she came back, she said 'oh yeah I have kids, and I don't wanna' deal with them.' I think during her absence, what started the whole thing, she was gone for close to two years. And we had to fend for ourselves, and we had my older sister who was talking to a boy in school, an Islamic school. . . . She talked to a boy and when my mother came back, [she said], 'Oh in my absence you girls have become whores, you girls have let loose a bit, and you need to be taught lessons.' So she said 'You're getting married' to the older one and my dad who was against it tried to say no and there was massive fights over it but because of the guilt, she held that against him [and said] 'You left me for another lady,' and he said 'You didn't even care about your daughters. I raised the girls. You're worrying about the boys and finances?' Even though there was a lot of cultural stuff [at play] there, there was a whole lot to do with that relationship.

Here, Layla's attempt to stop the marriage was part of a multiyear struggle to navigate the complexities of her mother and father's relationship. The neglect of her father coupled with her mother's inability to cope with such abandonment and her abusive responses. The idea of her own prospective marriage rendered the future impossible. The hope that things could be different no longer sustained her. Layla sees her parents' relationship to their children as shaped through their neglect toward each other and as undergoing drastic transformations through escape and return. This led to judgments between her parents about who bears the burden of guilt and innocence and who deserves to do the labor of childrearing. Following this, their mother perceived her absence in their lives as a gap in proper disciplining. These absences and reappearances of their parents and what they felt they had to do as a result produced a range of manipulative and coercive practices that unfolded between her mother and father and were imposed on their children.

Before her mother declared that Layla had to get married following her two younger sisters, Layla felt scared but knew the marriage would be inevitable. However, when she saw that her sisters had been physically abused by their husbands without her parents' intervention, she realized that a similar fate might await her. For Layla, her parents' ignoring this abuse was the culmination of multiple years of coercive practices undertaken by her mother in the absence of her father. Layla saw forced marriage as potentially leading to further abuse and intimate partner violence—an indicator of the future yet to come—yet also an ongoing legacy of her mother's abusive tendencies. Layla proceeded to run away from home and appeared at a refuge (a housing shelter for teenage women) a few years prior to the 2013 passage of the law and prior to forced marriage being seen as a legally codified category of violence. She reported her parents' neglect and abuse of their children.

Layla noted in our interview that she called the local police so they could remove Layla and her siblings from her mother. This, she noted, was useful because it introduced an external institution that could disrupt her mother's ongoing pattern of organizing marriages for her children due to a lack of support with childrearing. However, Layla mentioned that while the 2013 law was an important step, it was highly focused on addressing the immediate events leading up to entry into marriage which failed to account for other periods of time in which coercion and abuse is experienced and relations of trust, care, and mutual reliance are broken. In Layla's case, coercion cannot be thought of as a linear spectrum with forced marriage lying as the culmination of such abuse. Layla and her sisters were subject to emotional abuse before their mother had introduced the idea of marriage and afterward. Layla was then transferred to three different refuges that were less than ideal environments for her rehabilitation for several reasons, one of which included frequent drug use in the common areas. One refuge attempted to get Layla to speak with her family despite her pleading that she did not want to reconnect with them:

> I refused to give them details because they would send me back; they asked me my parents' name, home address. I didn't tell them that; I didn't want them to send me back. They wanted me to talk to my parents and work it out. Do you not understand, both my sisters are married with kids and they both are under 15—a stand-off for 2 hours. I didn't want to give them details. Finally, they decided to call a social worker and I had bruises and everything and I showed them. They still wanted to mediate with the families. I think if you're a kid who doesn't have that fight in you, more often than not, you're in twice the amount of trouble for leaving them.

Layla continued that the idea of facilitating familial reconciliation was a result of social welfare using "culture" to explain what happened to her. To use culture is to say that violence is part of an insular cultural logic that does not require any outside intervention. The same steps that would be taken to keep someone who is not of a CALD background safe would not be taken in the name of culture. Layla continued that, due to her cultural background, social service workers and police felt they could not get involved and provide any kind of support to avoid being thought of as culturally insensitive. This conclusion was short-sighted; Layla describes her family's abuse as born out of a complicated amalgam of variables, and refuses to explain it through the lens of culture as a set of stagnant values, traditions, and worldviews that sanction this kind of behavior.

Layla's reapprehension of her family's story was part of an ongoing endeavor on her part to reorient social services' attention toward specific victims' family circumstances rather than their cultural background and the narratives of violence they recruit. For her story to be legible to law enforcement upon running away, she needed to prove that certain familial dynamics were not intrinsic to her culture and thus were a violation of her rights. Layla felt that the script around forced marriage prevention had already been set and was too culture-centered. She noted that a lot of journalists already know what they want to write and have an agenda around forced marriage, so victims/survivors do not feel like they have control over what they say. For example, when she recently spoke about her experience on a radio show, she tried to make the point that the AFP had refused to investigate her case due to viewing this as a cultural issue. The radio host responded that the government had indeed been comprehensively approaching all reported cases. The culturalization of forced marriage (in this case, as a pretext not to act), contributed to Layla's view that prevention already saw victims from certain communities as doomed by their cultures.

Another key theme that emerged in Layla's narration was that the violence she and her sisters suffered could also be traced to multiple people in addition to her parents. This violence was felt in the lack of support from her specific community and in the lack of response by social services:

> My intuition is to say that it is hard to pinpoint one person who is responsible for what happened. . . . I think it is systemic—it was a lot of people who contributed to what happened to me and my sisters. It was the community, the people at the weddings who didn't stand up and say this is a child getting married, this is wrong. The police, the social service people. . . . I blame the social service sector, the police, and the law. It was the whole community. Yes, it was my parents and my mom, but the whole thing could have been stopped if someone had stepped up and spoke out against it. It didn't have to happen.

Layla saw forced marriage as a systemic failure of multiple institutions. There was a failure of her parents' family friends, the social service sector, and her family. While on paper, Layla may have been seen as someone who, cumulatively, was at risk of a forced marriage because of how her parents treated her, the role that other actors played in her and her parents' lives was not accounted for in the "cumulative risk" model. In addition, she did not see her parents' choices as overdetermined by their cultural backgrounds. She saw their decisions as on the one hand shaped by their experiences of war and displacement, and at the same time, needing to be held accountable by the state. Here, Layla's recounting of her parents' decisions and simultaneous attempts to report her situation is an example of what Mulla (2014, 174) calls "a reworking of kin relations as [victims] leverage the potential of institutional intervention against the modalities of being related in everyday life." While calling state police did not actually result in the provision of tangible services, Layla did feel that it marked a new chapter for her and her sisters to strengthen their relationships with each other, separate from their mother and father. Layla's decision to get authorities involved was not a disavowal of her cultural background or a move to completely separate from kin. Rather, it was a way to regenerate a new context from which to resume and reimagine kin relations with her sisters and to recomprehend the structures and events that shaped her parents' actions.

Intersecting Systems of Violence

In 2017, I spoke with a young adult Afghan woman named Gulnaz, who is based in New South Wales. Gulnaz's family had fled from Afghanistan to Pakistan in the late 1990s, and she had grown up there before her parents were resettled in Australia when she was nine years old in 2004. Gulnaz described her experience with marriage as one of force. When she was seventeen, her parents increasingly pressured her to get married to her cousin who was experiencing threats to his life and had recently fled Afghanistan to Pakistan. Her parents expected her to apply for a spousal visa for him upon her return to Australia after the religious marital ceremony. She said she agreed to the marriage, but when she arrived in Pakistan, she realized she did not know the man well enough and was not as ready as she thought to enter into a marriage. She still went through with a *nikah* (Islamic wedding ceremony). After the ceremony, her parents told her that the man she married was ten years older than they had initially noted, which made Gulnaz feel deceived. When she returned to Australia in 2013, she demanded a divorce, and eventually her family agreed. However, shortly thereafter, after their local community of family friends heard about the divorce, her father and brother became physically violent toward her. Gulnaz fled to her friend's house about a year later and found herself homeless because she could not afford to pay rent. She noted, "I had gone through financial abuse and wasn't allowed to work while living at home. I was eighteen years old, and it was very hard for me to find a job." Years later, Gulnaz took on a new role as a social worker and focuses on conducting forced marriage prevention programs.

In her new role, Gulnaz has felt hopeful about the 2013 forced marriage law. However, she expressed concern that the social welfare sector has many limitations and disempowering aspects about how it treats migrant women. Specifically, she has observed that the sector victimizes women as passive subjects while also essentializing their cultures to avoid intervening when it would actually help. She noted: "There are people who feel extremely sorry about people who have gone through forced marriage, in a way that is demeaning, not empowering. And not optimistic.... They wanna help in an unhelpful way. I'm an example. People see me as this poor little thing. They look down upon me as that. I don't like feeling sorry for myself. I know I've gone through shitty things and people going through domestic violence or family violence are in a shitty situation. This doesn't mean we are completely helpless." As a victim/survivor of forced marriage and someone who has been navigating the family violence and domestic violence system since 2012, Gulnaz has witnessed how multiple institutions, from refuges to state police to counselors, view her as helpless. This perspective has translated into a one-size-fits-all approach, especially because proposed solutions often ignored that not all individuals found the same set of services helpful:

> And there are those people who are trying to enforce their own perspective about how they should go about it.... They literally force people to seek

those services. Psychologists and counselors. They don't understand that people can go about things their own way and at their own pace. . . . I'm sitting with people and I'm telling them my perspective, and they don't agree, but then I think for example when I say we should have more focus on accommodation services that are more sustainable, more long-term, instead of putting people in hotel rooms their first night out after they've left their family, they don't agree with me. But I'm coming from the perspective that they grow up in a family and community-oriented environment. Once they've made the biggest decisions of their lives, it's scary to be in a room alone.

Gulnaz often referred to the need to more seriously consider the social milieu in which victims/survivors came of age. To do so would be to take seriously the multiple layers and stages of violence and uprooting that animated migrant women's lives. Many women could not identify with the idea that trauma relief could be an individual endeavor rather than a collectively produced experience. In our conversation, I was also struck by Gulnaz's point that the sector should be more aware of how women's experiences in war and displacement shaped their experience of this trauma and their parents' decisions. This is important to mention because Gulnaz also noted several times that she believes in the consent and coercion binary and is in support of forced marriage criminal legislation. At other times, she also seemed to subscribe to the idea that migrants do bring in customs and beliefs from their home countries. However, at the same time, she felt that there had to be a more serious consideration of the specific kinds of traumas that refugees and migrants experience. It is important to consider the complexities in beliefs that can coexist among people who have experienced various versions of marital coercion: "With every migrant community when they come here, especially when they are old, they sort of try to hold on to everything that is familiar to them because in some sense it's about power. All of a sudden, you have been uprooted from your family and community. You're in a foreign land and you have to start all over. You lose all your power. But you're still someone in your community." While there are generalizations present in her assessment that I would contest, it is valuable to think about how, for Gulnaz, a given story of "forced marriage" could also be one about war, asylum, and uprooting. It could be a story of people trying to rebuild social relations and maintain their social standing in their communities. But Gulnaz does not romanticize this as an attempt to reassert "local" or community-oriented ways of seeing the world. She disputes the idea that this is a part of the Afghan Australian community's identity. Gulnaz saw forced marriage as a tool of power for parents to control their own futures. For many Afghan Australians, being held in offshore detention between 2012 and 2019, or seeing their loved ones held there, was defined by prolonged social isolation and a sense that community was always precarious. Rebuilding community in Australia sometimes meant that parents felt like they had to preserve their social reputation within their community by turning to problematic modes of control. For Gulnaz, trying to cope with the effects of war produces various responses that prevention was systematically ignoring. It was surprising to hear Gulnaz incorporate this complexity in relation to her father from whom she was estranged: "What I'm really saying is that when you talk about refugees, you need to give them the support they need, the help they need. Otherwise, they can become violent. My father came here when he was sixty by boat by himself. He has been through a lot. He has bullet wounds on his body. He started working when he was nine, ten to support his family. In Afghan families, you don't just support your immediate family. You support your uncle, aunt, grandmother, extended family. Being so young and supporting so many people. He grew up not in a very nice environment." While it is important not to generalize about Afghan refugee experiences, Gulnaz's framing of her father as growing up in an environment that expected a great deal from him financially and professionally in a time of ongoing war (his father was in Afghanistan during the Civil War and prior to the rise of the Taliban in 1996) illustrates the layered traumas that many refugees confront. Her father was also detained by the Australian government upon arriving by boat and it took several years for her family members to be reunified with him and resettled in Australia. To find community and belonging in the aftermath of such experiences was something Gulnaz mentioned her parents were dedicated to holding on to, even at the cost of fragmenting their children's futures.

Following Gulnaz's divorce, her relationship with her mother, father, and siblings is now fragmented. She sometimes visits her siblings, and only occasionally speaks with her father. After she moved away from her family, her mother and father were no longer welcome to other families' gatherings and Gulnaz has had to weather the blame for it. She noted, "Sometimes, survivors, they go through so much but at the end of the day, everyone looks at them as the issue or the problem. Survivors are the outcasts—they are the ones who lose everything and are uprooted." Gulnaz expressed regret that her siblings have to live in what she calls a toxic environment. However, she has observed some changes in her parents' views and approaches to marriage in recent years, during which her father's income had increased. Since then, they have not put as much pressure on her siblings to get married as young adults. I point to Gulnaz's story because it shows the coexistence of the interlocking emotional responses in intimate familial relationships that, in this case, intensified during a period of marital coercion. Gulnaz views her parents as having developed a set of mechanisms to feel a sense of community belonging and to deal with the lack of community after her father's detention and their family's reunification and resettlement in Australia. Gulnaz also does not see herself as a passive victim of culturalized violence. She views her experience as one that she was able to harness toward supporting others who find themselves in untenable situations. My conversation with Gulnaz was illuminating. I learned from her that while one may subscribe to the idea that forced marriage is an accurate descriptor of certain forms of coercion into marriage, this does not mean that one subscribes to the idea that migrants simply import static notions of culturally sanctioned forms of violence. Gulnaz says she made a choice to be separated from her family, but this separation does not mean abandoning a sense of love and care for the people who matter to her.

Undoing the "Domestic"

I first met Sofia through my friend Fereshta in 2016, after interviewing the latter about her family's views on marriage, life partners, and social pressures around both. Fereshta and Sofia are Afghan Australian and living in the Narre Warren suburb of Melbourne, where many Afghan migrants resettled in the late 1980s after the beginning of the Afghan-Soviet War (1979–1989) and in the early 2000s following the beginning of the US/NATO intervention into Afghanistan. Fereshta and I had met at a shopping center in Narre Warren. As we sat down with our coffee, I told Sofia about my project and my interest in understanding how young adults were navigating their families' expectations about their intimate partner relationships in the wake of the forced marriage law. Sofia responded, "I probably have a lot to share about that." Fereshta echoed her sentiment, noting, "Yeah, she has gone through a lot with her relationship." Sofia mentioned briefly that her immediate family members, who lived in Adelaide, South Australia had only recently come to support her relationship with her now husband. I was interested to know how her relationship with her family had changed since her relationship began and how she experienced their disapproval. I wanted to know why she made the choice to reconcile with them and how this reconciliation was experienced as a choice. I reached out to Sofia soon thereafter and asked if she would be willing to share her experience with me.

We met in Narre Warren a few weeks later at a coffee shop. Sofia's narration of her family's reluctance to accept her relationship with AJ, her now husband, began with her family's escape from Afghanistan in the early 2000s. Sofia herself was born to an Hazara family living in Iran a few years after her family fled their home in Herat, Afghanistan because of Taliban-led violence toward the local Hazara community in response to the ongoing US/NATO-led war. Sofia's mother died when she was a child, so her immediate family unit consisted of her father, older sister, and younger brother. Sofia and her family experienced routine discrimination in Iran, which has a troubled history with integrating Afghan refugees, as documented by several anthropologists (Khosravi 2017; Olszewksa 2015; Rostami-Povey 2007). As part of the Hazara community in Afghanistan, Sofia and her family have historically been discriminated against by the Taliban and prior government regimes. While in Iran, Sofia, along with her father and two siblings, confronted intense discrimination and found it difficult to find employment and establish an economically secure life.

After being granted asylum in Australia, Sofia's family resettled in South Australia. Her father struggled to hold a job, forcing Sofia to begin working while attending university. Her family managed to build a tight-knit sense of community with other recently resettled Afghan migrants in Adelaide. They would spend the weekends attending parties or hosting friends at their house, rebuilding old connections with friends they knew in Afghanistan and creating new ones with migrants who had recently resettled in Adelaide. Sofia mentioned that they had finally started to feel a sense of belonging and that the future seemed more hopeful. Sofia said her life consisted of work, school, and family. At the same time, Sofia's mother's death in Afghanistan was a haunting absence in her mind.

Financially, Sofia's family was struggling to make ends meet. While attending college, she began to work part time at Qantas Airlines' catering division and spent the weekends hanging out with friends at restaurants and nightclubs in the city, which is where she met AJ. Soon thereafter, they began a relationship over the course of six months. AJ came from a half-Bosnian, half-Filipino migrant family. However, Sofia knew his non-Muslim and non-Afghan background would not be looked upon well by her father. Sofia began to lie to her father that she had to start work early, so she could sneak in meetings with AJ. She also began to include her friends in her clandestine plans, asking them to lie to her family about where she was going during the evenings. The constant lying to her father made her feel distress and as though she was "living a double life," marked by constantly having to reacquaint herself with the lies she had told, what she kept as the truth, and the lies yet to come. The domestic space transformed from a place of security and a sense that Sofia, her siblings, and her father were all on the same page, trying to move toward a future where they were united in purpose, to a place of surveillance, alienation, and secrecy, and uncertainty about where Sofia's individual desires would fit within those of the family. This began the breakdown of her relationship with her father. Sofia reflected that she felt, at the time, that she "had to be selfish" to pursue her relationship through lying and keeping secrets from her father and siblings. For Sofia, spending time with AJ was not simply an act of transgression of cultural and social norms; it was an act of choosing not to orient all of her time toward work and school in the name of working toward her family's financial security and a future in which they could hold on to the same set of worldviews and belong in a community in the way they knew how. AJ's potential presence in her family and the community they we rebuilding in Adelaide was going to be seen as a dent in this emergent sense of a cohesive future. Sofia chose to lie to her father in the wake of feeling controlled by him and by the financial and social pressures of being newly resettled refugees. In describing this choice as selfish, Sofia describes it as a reluctant choice made under conditions of duress.

The stress of living a dual life that relied on constant lying compelled Sofia to decide to move away from Adelaide and in with AJ. In the process, and after telling her father, she knew that she would have to give up a future in which she and her husband would be part of her immediate family's everyday lives and those of their local Afghan community. As their relationship progressed, Sofia's father began to get suspicious that she was seeing someone, and he began to give her curfews and asked her brother to monitor the state of her relationship:

All of a sudden, things changed. I couldn't go out at night—during the day I was either at work or uni [university], so there was no other choice [than to consider leaving Adelaide entirely]. I think it was about a month or two that were really stressful and really hard for us. Then I just told him [AJ]—I said 'Look, the only way for us is to leave [from] here.' I was getting a lot of pressure from my brother. He was saying all these things because I think he had seen a photo of us somewhere on Facebook or whatever. It was basically a lot of pressure and then I said, 'AJ, look, the easiest thing for us to prove to them is to just pack up and leave.' We decided to come down to Melbourne for a day, looked for a place. We didn't have our jobs lined up or anything. We knew some people but not people we would rely on in that way or someone to stay with. And we were both kind of independent and we didn't want to rely on people to have hope for something. . . . I was having my uni exams. So, we decided as soon as my exams were over, we would go. And we didn't tell anyone except for his really close friends—his circle—and just about three of my really close friends and one of them who was also an Afghan—she is like kind of our family friend. When we first came to Australia, our families were friends. So the whole time she had to pretend she didn't know as well [that we left].

Sofia and AJ's decision to leave Adelaide for Melbourne was marked by both hope and a sense of guilt that she would be leaving a whole community behind. At the same time, leaving was a way to avoid confronting her family's inability to reconcile her partner's identity with their sense of what the future should look like—one in which Sofia and her siblings would be the gateway to ensuring the economic and social stability of the family through marrying into Afghans in the local community. The decision to relocate to Melbourne also caused a rift in her relationship with AJ. She felt withdrawn, and AJ would constantly apologize for "taking her away from her family."

After living in Melbourne for about a year, Sofia began to enter a depressive state. She had been communicating with her sister sporadically via email. Otherwise, she had not been in touch with her father, brother, or older sister and had begun to miss being a part of an Afghan community in Melbourne. Sofia had met Fereshta and Shabnam (Fereshta's friend) only a few months prior to our first interview. Sofia said meeting them helped her feel reconnected to people who could understand her struggles with her father and how torn she felt about running away and the reluctant desire to reconcile with her father and siblings. After about a year, Sofia learned that her sister was pregnant and found it hard to come to terms with the possibility that she would not be a part of her niece's life. AJ noticed that Sofia was becoming more withdrawn. He suggested that they set up a meeting with her father and tell him that they did want him to be part of their lives. Her father agreed to meet with them. The meeting, Sofia noted, was quite awkward. Her father was angry and refused to look at AJ. A few weeks after the meeting, AJ made the decision to convert to Islam to convince her father to entertain the possibility that they could be in each other's lives. AJ's offer to convert was strategic in that he knew it could open doors for familial reconciliation. It was not based on a desire to undertake a deep study of the religion or engage in religious and spiritual rituals, at least on any consistent basis. Sofia mentioned that, for AJ, converting to Islam would be a starting point to get her family and community to recognize the legitimacy of their union and serve as an entry point into reconciling. Such a reconciliation, while not necessarily based on a deeper understanding of each other's struggles, was at the very least a way for Sofia and her natal family and community to be in each other's lives that was consistent and reliable. Converting to Islam was a familiar enough possibility and idea for AJ because his father's side of the family was Muslim, so the ideas of Islam were already prevalent within AJ's upbringing. AJ decided to convert, and they eventually took part in an Islamic marriage ceremony, after which they traveled back to Adelaide to tell her father. Sofia explained that her father's disposition was already quite cold, and he did not seem any different from the previous time. She told her father at the tense meeting that AJ had converted to Islam and that all they wanted to do was have a good life and a sense of connection to the community in South Australia. She expanded that making this decision catalyzed her family's acceptance of their union and activated a desire on their part to get to know AJ in new ways: "And so, after two long awkward meetings . . . I guess we all just needed the time to heal. So I guess after that, things just moved pretty quickly. We went a few times back and forth to Adelaide and we had another *nikah* and then it became official within our close circle. And ever since then, they [her family] love him [AJ]. They just gave him a chance. They got to know him for who he really is, and things changed really quickly. It does surprise me sometimes." Sofia continued that her father and uncles (whom he had unexpectedly invited to Sofia and AJ's second meeting with him) then asked that Sofia and AJ do a second *nikah* in the presence of her extended family members and family friends living in Adelaide. Sofia's father's acceptance yet simultaneous expectation that they conduct a second *nikah* was something Sofia was reluctant about. At the same time, she framed it as a pathway toward familial reconciliation that offered the possibility of resuming relations with her father and the rest of her family friends she had become close to in Adelaide. Time was needed to heal or, at the very least, provide a pathway to work through the resentment that brewed between her and her father and brother. Sofia spoke about wanting her future children to meet their grandfather and aunt (her sister) and wanting to be a part of her nieces' lives (her sister's children). While she felt that living at a distance from them allowed her and AJ to conduct their lives with more freedom, she could not imagine a future in which those same people would be completely removed. Rather than frame Sofia and AJ's return to Adelaide as a kind of blind acquiescence to her father's desires, I interpret this as a desire to participate in forms of community building that helped to anchor her sense of who she was.

There are multiple forms of violence and manipulation happening in Sofia's reconciliation with her father and AJ's first meeting with him: her father's invitation of other extended family members to a discussion about Sofia and AJ's *nikah* without Sofia's consent; his demand that they get married a second time; the refusal to recognize AJ's conversion or to acknowledge the past modes of duress that led Sofia and AJ to flee Adelaide; and there may be other moments that are not reflected in Sofia's conversations with me. Sofia's experience as a whole does not neatly fit within the victim-perpetrator binary nor does it reflect a parent becoming more caring and accepting of his child's choices. Sofia has reconciled the fact that her father has accepted a certain version of her relationship with AJ (the one where AJ, on paper, can be categorized as Muslim and in which they are part of regular social gatherings). Even though her father recognizes AJ as part of Sofia's life, the shift that Sofia noticed in her father's attitude toward AJ was not a complete reversal of their approach to their relationship:

> I mean he's still very—I get that feeling where he is not ever going to be 100 percent with us. Like, you know, I still get that feeling where he is still a little bit . . . but that's just my dad. . . . At first I used to think it's his English—like the barrier between us to be able to talk and now I know he speaks English. But when I'm there he's not really appreciating the fact that I'm there or making any effort. And I say to him he doesn't even make an effort with me, and I'm his daughter so [I tell myself] don't get upset over it. And I feel like, even if we have kids one day, he will still have that sense of hate for me not following what he wanted.

Sofia went on to talk about how her father openly praises her older sister because she married a man from Afghanistan, even though her sister's relationship has been quite volatile. However, it remains more morally sound in the eyes of her father. At the same time, Sofia expressed that she feels revitalized that she can now have a relationship with her sister and be part of her niece's life.

Reconciling with her father did not mean the creation of a relationship that was free from lies. Sofia discussed how the experience of living a "double life" has not subsided even in the wake of her father and extended family members' approval of her marriage and their continued role in their lives: "I still think like that. I still feel like sometimes I have this—it's funny, AJ calls it a 'double life.' I still think that in front of my family I have to be a certain way. I have to be saying certain things—like I can't be myself. When they are not around me . . . it's easier because I don't have that restriction of 'okay I can't say this, I can't say that.' I sometimes wear shorts or little things like that if I'm on holiday. It's just little things and it's so funny because I still think that, you know, I feel like I'm stuck in this two-way street or whatever." Reconstituting her relationship with her family produced a set of new challenges for Sofia—namely the need to perform modesty and to restrict her speech in her family's presence. Despite her being open about the existence of her relationship with AJ and his background, this did not translate into feeling that she could be open to her family about other facets of her life. While Sofia could now determine when she could see her father, thus rendering the domestic a site of renewed possibility, the domestic space was still one where Sofia felt she had to control her comportment. To reconcile with one's family members does not necessarily correlate to a situation where duress is absent. Sofia is still living in a situation of duress, and her escape did not mark the beginning of it nor did her father's acceptance of her relationship mark the end of it. Yet it is important to underscore that Sofia does not see her family as encompassed or dictated by her father, though her marrying AJ through an Islamic ceremony was key to opening up the possibility that she could have a relationship with family members outside of Australia too, including in Iran, where many of her extended family members live. The legitimizing of their marriage in the eyes of her father also allowed Sofia to feel like she herself could begin to visit her extended family in Iran and bring AJ with her.

A few months after I returned to the United States, Sofia and AJ welcomed a child, whom they excitedly introduced to her immediate family in South Australia and to her extended family in Iran. Here, the return to the domestic (and the constraints that conditioned such a return) was an entry point into the reconstitution of intimate kin relations. Sofia was excited at the prospect of getting to know her extended family in ways that she did not before. In her ethnography of kin-based rehabilitative care for veterans of the Iraq and Afghanistan wars at Walter Reed Medical Center, Zoë Wool (2015, 158) writes that "the problem of intimacy is thus a problem of the attachments that make and sustain forms of life . . . being attached and being intimate have multiple implications in this rehabilitative context, as various kinds of attachments enable, constrain, and threaten modes of life in the making." Reuniting with family members after periods of violence are moments when people participate in acts of "securing life within intimate relations of a normative domestic present," in which people feel "obligated to others" (2015, 169).[10] Wool's analysis is resonant in situations where kin try to reimagine and rebuild their version of normal domestic life in the wake of fragmented social relations. Here, it is important to note that the domestic is not limited to what occurs within the home. Das, Ellen, and Leonard (2008, 351) describe how the domestic exceeds the house and the material possessions through which social relations are created. Rather, the domestic is an idea that can connect people to historically specific understandings of sentimentality that are themselves the products of global circulations of artifacts, stories, and other ideas (Berlant 1991). Sentimental domesticity comes to organize how kinship relations and domesticity become so intertwined among those who are experiencing multiple regimes of governance. Sentimental domesticity constitutes "forms of doing that connect possibility with actuality, the subjunctive with the indicative, [and] are enacted over [multiple] spaces. . . . The domestic combines intimacy and alienation, proximity and distance as modes of caring, loving, and grieving come into being or are brought into being" (1991, 352). It is this relationship to the domestic as both a physical space and an ideology that now undergirds Sofia's relationship with her father and her family.

Free and fully consensual choices do not constitute Sofia and her father's relationship. There is an unstated understanding between them that certain things about the past cannot be talked about or made issues of—those are key conditions for the relationship to work. In my reading, Sofia is continuing to come to terms with the fact that, as a daughter and a family member, one could be refused, rejected, loved, and cared for at the same time. While Sofia herself never framed her experience using the words "abuse," "emotional violence," or "family violence," the criteria for being subjected to a potential forced marriage could have easily been applied to her, given that she has been subject to her father's manipulation, pressure to leave the home, and undue duress in her marriage choices. While this is true, it is misleading to conclude that, upon deciding to reconcile with her father and having a wedding on his terms, Sofia was simply returning to a domestic space filled with familial breakdown and seamless oppression. Rather, Sofia's experiences might also be understood as a return to consistency, toward a more stable orientation to the world that entails returning to community dynamics that are familiar yet continue to exert their weight on her and AJ, compelling them to perform as good religious and cultural subjects. In order to live their lives away in Melbourne with a sense of contentment, they needed to know there was a community they could return to—living freely meant surrendering oneself to power in other ways and in other spaces.

In Sofia's case, we also see a reconstitution of the lines along which kinship relations are structured themselves. The control over one's marriage choices is no longer something upon which her relationship with her father can be based. However, how Sofia and AJ comport themselves in front of her father and with her siblings is a new basis for kinship to sustain itself (Wool 2015). Kinship relations are reconstructed through the renewed understanding that genealogical ties provide consistency and help to assuage the enduring trauma of the precarity of displacement which in the context of Australia, increasingly brings with it the risk of family separation. The regeneration of one's world can be considered what Veena Das (Das, Kleinman, et al. 2001, 6) calls the remaking of a world or the everyday: "Finding one's voice in the making of one's history, the remaking of a world . . . is also a matter of being able to recontextualize the narratives of devastation and generate new contexts through which everyday life may become possible."[11]

The Renewal of Familial Bonds

Sitara is a twenty-five-year-old prolific writer living in Narre Warren who comes from an Afghan Muslim background. She and her parents initially resettled in New Zealand and moved to Australia in 2011, in part because of racial and religious discrimination she and her family faced. Sitara explained that her sister was almost coerced into a marriage. I was intrigued by Sitara's story because I had seen, through her Facebook page, that she was a well-respected advocate of women's rights and was already in the process of publishing her memoir. She also had won several awards at the local and state level for her advocacy and organizing of community workshops for the local Afghan community.

When we first met, Sitara was energetic and much more open about her experiences with marriage than I had expected. A few minutes into our conversation, she brought up her sister's almost-marriage and her own almost-engagement as an example of the types of familial pressures they both had to negotiate as they attempted to carve out their own professional and educational aspirations. In her narratives, Sitara conveyed that these instances could not be understood through a perpetrator-victim model, but they marked the starting point for a reconfiguration of her family relations while keeping the love and care she had for them alive.

Sitara explained that a few years ago, her family had heard about a man living in Kabul who was well educated and whom they thought would be a good fit for marriage to her sister. Coordinating a marriage with an individual one had never met who was based in Afghanistan was common for Afghan families in the diaspora. Now an adult, Sitara's sister agreed to it and traveled with her family to Kabul to meet the man with the hopes of leaving the trip engaged. Sitara explained that she and her family were quite impressed with her sister's would-be fiancé, noting, "He was good looking, educated, and really seemed like an angel" because of how kind and generous he was. After getting engaged in Kabul, Sitara's family returned to Australia while her sister's fiancé remained in Kabul. After about two weeks, Sitara's sister confided that she no longer wanted to pursue the engagement.

She had realized that her fiancé's religious beliefs and practices were not in line with her own. For example, she did not believe that his requests that she "cover herself from head to toe," as she put it, and that she live with his family once they were married, were either religiously sanctioned or steps she was comfortable taking. While their father refused to end the engagement, Sitara advocated for her sister and told her father on multiple occasions that he needed to learn to respect her sister's wishes, despite the consequences of breaking it off—namely backlash from their local Afghan community and from family back in Kabul. Eventually, after much hesitation, Sitara's father obliged and agreed to breaking off her sister's engagement. He was prompted to reflect on the situation and realized that the request that Sitara's sister cover for religious reasons was a violation of her freedom to dress as she wished. For her father, a prospective partner requesting that his fiancée cover herself was a sign that he would be controlling of her behavior in other ways in the future. While this conclusion was also mired in its own problematic assumptions about veiling as necessarily meaning submission to patriarchal control, Sitara's point was that what happened to her sister was not deserving of being labeled a crime, as the forced marriage prevention risk assessment would have framed it. During our conversation, Sitara would pause her narrative and bring up instances in which she, her father, and her brother would go out to restaurants and parks and discuss women's rights issues and gender-based violence, around which Sitara did a great deal of advocacy work in Narre Warren. While Sitara's sister was subject to coercive control, she was not ready to end the relationship with her parents. During this period, Sitara took steps to convince her father that deviating from community-held norms, while risky, could mark the beginning of a more understanding relationship with his daughters. Through a series of conversations, the three family members were able to critically reflect on long-held beliefs. Her father eventually expressed that he would support the ending of the engagement. Following the end of her sister's engagement, Sitara's father, sister, and brother embarked on a months-long period wherein they would regularly discuss passages from the Qur'an, specifically surahs relating to women's rights and marriage and what it would mean to apply that to their own lives. Here, Sitara and her sister used feminist interpretations of the Qur'an as a starting point to expand the horizon of issues they could discuss with their family members. While they were not looking for consensus, they discussed the rights of women in marriage, interfaith marriages, and the role each partner plays in marriage. Through their weekly discussions, Sitara felt more comfortable voicing her preferences about a potential spouse to her father. Through dialogue that emerged from Sitara's sister's experience, Sitara felt able to communicate her preferences more openly without the same kind of response from her father.

Sitara's own journey into finding a spouse revealed new tensions and possibilities with her father. Sitara explained other instances in which she was approached with a marriage proposal. Sitara was particularly excited about the prospect of getting engaged to one young man who had approached her with a proposal. This person was actually someone to whom they had initially introduced her. Sitara decided to have coffee with the man a few times before informing her father about what she wanted to do. On a few occasions, he had asked her if she would be okay with covering her face and body in public after they got married. She said that she would do it because she liked this person's character and felt it was worth the sacrifice of being in the relationship. Sitara informed her parents that she wanted to go through with the engagement. However, this time, her father and brother warned her against it. They would send her text messages saying that she could go through with the engagement but that she should be aware her whole life would be controlled by this man. It turns out they had discovered the man had been imprisoned in an offshore detention center on the island of Nauru for several years and was suffering from complex trauma that was manifesting in the way he treated Sitara. After several text messages and conversations with her family, Sitara finally decided not to go through with the engagement. Sitara's father, reminded of her sister's experience with her fiancé's viewpoints on the headscarf, had dissuaded Sitara from entering further into relations of control.

Sitara's father's response illustrates the complex relationships that parents have with their children and that one instance of controlling behavior does not point to a coherent ideology around gender, womanhood, or Islamic comportment.

This is not captured in the forced marriage warning signs that view control over children's relationships as indicative of a broader value system around gender, religion, and comportment. For example, one warning sign states: the person is unable to make significant decisions about their future, including without consultation or agreement from their parents" (Attorney-General's Department n.d.). Though a parent may control the orchestration of an engagement and the location of a potential spouse, it does not always mean that they control and dominate all aspects of their children's lives. Even more importantly, a parent's approach to marriage is not an effective indicator of how their children experience them as parents and caregivers. In relation to the prevention sector, this observation shows that the warning sign that someone is at risk of a forced marriage if "the person's family has a lot of control over the person's life which doesn't seem normal or necessary" (Attorney-General's Department n.d.) cannot be universally applied given the variety of spheres in which parents might enact control and relinquish it.

Even though Sitara and her sister did not have full control over their options for spouses (i.e., they were not permitted to find a suitor on their own—the suitor had to approach their father first), this did not mean that their ability to weigh in and assert their desires vis-à-vis other points in the engagement process were compromised. In fact, Sitara was ready to make the choice to change her dress to be married to a man she liked. She was also ready to advocate on behalf of her sister, who was not ready to change her dress. This can be read as enacting agency in a way that is not premised on the subversion of a social norm but rather a decision to adhere to certain aspects of such norms (Mahmood 2005). Following this decision, Sitara expressed that she, her father, and her brothers were able to discuss their disagreements more openly about what their cultural and religious traditions required of them in ways they had not done before. This led all of them to reconsider what expectations around marriage they were and were not willing to entertain. As Qureshi, Charsley, and Shaw (2012) have commented in their analysis of British South Asian marriages, "Marriage emerges as an important means of producing and transforming transnational networks, while marriage practices and dynamics are themselves transformed in the process."

In Sitara's case, family dynamics are incredibly complicated, and the lines between familial control and love are blurry. Sitara did not see her father and brother as perpetrators of coercion. In fact, she talked about her family with a critical and caring disposition, emphasizing how encouraged she was by how often they would now openly discuss certain passages of the Qur'an, debating different verses around gender and relationships—conversations that are ongoing. While Sitara did indict her brother and father's actions, she also chose to bring them back into the fold of her life and reimagine how their viewpoints on culture and religion could matter to her life. This brushes up against the prism of perpetrator-victim, which assumes that victims do not actively try to change the terms of a given relationship because they know that the current terms are unfair and unjust.

This narrative also defies the idea that, as Patton (2018, 36) writes, "liberation lies in distancing oneself from one's culture, and . . . marginalizes more complicated experiences that cannot be understood within simplistic cultural terms."

Thus, Sitara's love of her family cannot be reduced to the idea that, through understanding the forced marriage prevention warning signs, potential victims will see that they are more oppressed or controlled than they think they are. Rather, Sitara is engaged in an ongoing effort to find spaces where she can pursue her aspirations both within and against the grain of a patriarchal family dynamic, which several scholars have written about in the context of first and second-generation immigrant women (Alamri 2013; Naber 2012). Sitara's story is an example of family relations that, on the surface, may appear to index an imminent forced marriage crisis, but upon deeper analysis, reflect changing and enduring bonds marked by love, care, as well as control and duress. Yet Sitara's story reveals that she approached decision making through the lens of her larger social orbit, always considering how her decisions might affect not only other individual family members but the relationships between them and others. It was only through viewing each other as valued kin members (Karim 2001) who were beginning from a place of care, even if misguided initially, that Sitara, her sister, her father, and her brother could entertain the possibility of deviating from certain social norms and transforming their relationship based on ongoing critical dialogue.[12]

Conclusion: Reapprehending Violence

"At the level of the ordinary, the everyday social realities, the state of rebuilding and accommodation are as complex as are the networks of individual lives of victims, perpetrators, victim-perpetrators, internal resisters, and critics and witnesses. There usually is no clear-cut victory, no definitive crossing over to safety and renewal. But if that sounds too bleak a conclusion, think of it the other way around: there usually is no complete defeat, no ultimate breakdown and dissolution" (Das, Kleinman, et al. 2001, 24). Veena Das's analysis of violence deeply resonates with the themes of this chapter. Her understanding of rebuilding after violence is applicable to the aforementioned examples, both in terms of how families try to rebuild social relations in the aftermath of structural violence and interpersonal violence. There is no "definitive crossing over to safety and renewal" in each case. As such, the attempt to address and cope with different kinds of violence usually produces new kinds of violence that family members must reconcile with and readdress.

What does it mean to reapprehend violence? Apprehension refers to capturing something and keeping it in its constraints. There are multiple apprehensions happening across these stories. Parents apprehend their children—see them as particular subjects and sometimes literally apprehend them or their futures for their own desires. Parents' futures have also been apprehended by refugee and migration policies and the violence of war that make it difficult to feel any sense of stability or safety. The Australian state apprehends people's lives by making it difficult for them to feel a sense of stability even after a harrowing escape journey. Marriage is a way for parents to apprehend women's sexualities and their futures. It is a way to tie one's own future as a parent with that of one's children in order to build a life where the future is stitched together in a way that feels solid. These are not wholly good choices, but they are what some people felt were available. And now, these women find themselves trying to apprehend what has been taken away from them and why, and what new futures are possible. Sometimes, this means letting go of their parents entirely. Other times, they seek to transform their relationships with their parents and create a horizon for something new to bloom—something imperfect and filled with the enduring presence of duress. Duress is multi-scalar here—duress from the state, duress from interpersonal relations, and the everyday forms of duress of building a new life in an unfamiliar environment. Relationships are filled with all kinds of duress. These kinds of duress are not reflected in the language of the law or the bureaucratic language of forced marriage prevention. In these narratives, women seek accountability, but not just that—they seek to build something else from the ruins of familial relationships that are anchored in a shared experience of displacement and migration rather than simply shared genealogical ties. These reapprehensions, then, are reframings of the past and the future. They reject the temporal horizons of family violence prevention discourse because they are not focused on just the immediate past and present (the moments that led up to the acts of violence and the present danger the victim is confronting). These stories also show that the past continues to exert its weight in producing the subject who experiences duress, the weight of her individual past with those of her parents and larger social network. The subject also conceives of herself as in and of the future—these are individuals whose actions vis-à-vis their family members are rooted in reimagining the possibilities for the future which is, in and of itself, an act of self-making.

These narratives complicate the binaries of perpetrator and victim; rights and culture; and agency and structure. They show how the subject gets reconstituted and how her social world comes to be done and undone multiple times over. The subject here is being constituted and reconstituted in relation to other constituted and reconstituted subjects (Throop 2010). These narrations are not invested in a carceral, punitive, or juridical logic that sees the people in their lives as criminals or socially deviant people. They are, rather, interested in understanding the violence done to them as choices structured by intergenerational violence, displacement, and systemic failures. My interlocutors see the choices their parents made as wrong and having had the potential to be different choices, indeed. In that sense, they are not seen as inevitable.

It is important to recognize that Layla's, Gulnaz's, Sofia's, and Sitara's experiences with family violence and how they rechanneled the fallout are, for me, and perhaps for the reader as well, at some visceral level, unsatisfying. They are not stories in which leaving situations of violence result in lives free from other types of violence, intimate or structural. We might read Layla's and Sofia's accountings of their experiences as reapprehensions of state family violence prevention discourses. Their reapprehensions are not necessarily geared toward changing family violence prevention policies or discourse. Neither are they meant to change the dynamics within each of their families. In each case, my interlocutors have come to terms with the state of their familial relations. They illustrate alternative ways of thinking about the nature of the domestic space, how family relations transform over time, and new entry points into understanding what the culture of a family is like.

Elizabeth Povinelli (2006) writes about the "intimate event" as central to the politicization of love in liberal settler colonial states. Povinelli writes that, in late liberal settler states, "the moment the liberal subject of love, the liberal subject in love, experiences her inability to author the event of love, she insists there is a vast and insurmountable difference between societies of freedom and societies of social constraint." This "difference" is the divide between the autological subject and the genealogical society. Maintaining the illusion of this divide is key to how liberal societies preserve the logic of liberal forms of recognition—otherwise, "liberals experience themselves as facing an instance of a so-called morally repugnant form of life" (2006). Sofia's narrative does not maintain this divide. When she sees the constraints on her relationship with AJ, she does not immediately view her own community and the one in which her father and siblings make life as wholly and essentially marked by constraint. She finds new kinds of freedom and possibility in being part of this community, albeit in newly configured ways. Sofia felt weighed down when she was away from this community and now manages the duress she is willing to bear from their worldviews. Sitara's narrative also questions this divide. To be subject to her father's controlling behavior did not result in a breakdown of relations or a separation, but it did require a recalibration and a new way of collectively reapprehending the politics of gender and relationships together. These are stories of people who seek to build, keep what sense of community they have made, and reimagine what connection can look like among the loosened social threads brought on by war and displacement. To get closer to the violence, then, is a matter of uncovering the multiple subjectivities within intimate entanglements that are historically and structurally located.

Conclusion

Reflections on the Coercive State

"What is particularly interesting about the medieval French origins of the word 'policy' in the sense of governing and management are its close semantic associations with 'policing' (*policie*) and 'polishing.' Although now obsolete, the sixteenth-century use of policy as a verb meaning to police or, more precisely, 'to organize and regulate the internal order of,' is suggestive of what are, perhaps, some of the less conspicuous but no less unimportant functions" (Wedel et al. 2005, 35). The etymology of "policy" reveals that its original social functions went hand in hand with governing the social order. In practice, though, policies always produce unanticipated effects and generate new questions, dilemmas, and contestations. This is true of the forced marriage prevention policy—while it sought to create a cadre of practitioners who could easily identify at-risk people, it created new dilemmas for how to know violence and the assumptions intrinsic to such knowledge. Through the process, practitioners came to contest and, at times, refuse the demands of the prevention system and begin to reimagine what the "internal order" of this system would look like.

Through analyzing practitioner experiences of forced marriage prevention and migrant women's narratives of familial duress, this book has sought to illustrate how knowledge about a social problem is produced and contested in the domain of social policy. It aimed to ethnographically depict the institutional and discursive processes through which social welfare practitioners learned to recognize and make knowable coercive violence. Such modes of making violence knowable are undergirded by racialized and colonial histories that endure through the ways in which migrant mobility and social relations are governed today. Yet an ethnographic perspective reveals that such histories are not overdetermining; practitioners do not uncritically submit to colonial social welfare. Rather, practitioners attempt, if imperfectly, to reflect on the typologies the work of risk assessment and prevention demand. Yet the ideological foundations of the law remain outside the control of practitioners. The foundations of the forced marriage law hold that

Muslim migrant communities are already socially deviant "figures." Such figures, if identified properly by practitioners, are seen to prognosticate, in their suffering, a threat to the future of Australian values around freedom, "healthy families," and free and full consent in all things love and marriage.

By examining the perspectives of young adult first and second generation migrant women who experienced the push and pull of familial expectations, I show that migrant women are both sensitive to but not completely defined by their family members' decisions. Furthermore, their narratives show that familial duress is not always framed through the binary of coercion and consent. As Anitha and Gill (2009, 266) have written about the United Kingdom, "A binary understanding of consent and coercion in marriage, involving a criminal justice response aimed at preventing such marriages through injunctions and/or criminal proceedings, cannot hope to embrace the range of constraints that women face in matters of marriage." My interlocutors show that sometimes kinship relations become redefined, thereby reimagining the domestic not only as a space of coercive social pressures but as one where new negotiations are had around the obligations of kinship in the wake of structural violence. For people displaced as a result of the ongoing Global War on Terror, there is no clear-cut victory or linear trajectory to safety or security. Upon arriving to Australia, familial relations are already fragmented due to the structural violence of displacement (sometimes more than once), living as refugees in transit countries, and the enduring economic precarities of displacement. By acknowledging this and the violence of coercive familial practices around marriage, some women are living in the unsettling and ongoing discomfort of familial life—where connections to one's family members do not easily come undone, but are re-established along new lines. Renewed hope can emerge out of fragmented family relations, sometimes alongside those very same family members and sometimes without them.

My hope is that the reader can see that the oppositions underlying forced marriage prevention—victims and perpetrators, coercion and consent, familial constraint and individual freedom—obscure more than they reveal about people's actual lives. Pressures around marriage are, by contrast, entangled with other trajectories of violence, including that of displacement, war, detention, and resettlement.

Forced marriage prevention maintains that the power dynamics of families are understandable through the discursive framework of scenarios and risk profiles. Through certain epistemic tools, migrant family dynamics are rendered apprehensible objects of biopolitical epistemologies and metrics of consent. The struggles of social welfare to conceptualize the relationship between culture and family violence reveals the enduring effects of coloniality in Australian social welfare and social policy. Migrants, then, must always prove their worthiness of colonial standards of citizenship by demonstrating that they can be the ideal type of person imagined by the colonial state, and this goes for their intimate kin relations as well. Coloniality in modern Australia comes in the form of managing the familial relations of migrant populations and rendering them as participants in illegalizable forms of sociality. The call to become good citizens via demonstrating one's capacity to be part of a healthy family dynamic produces social welfare as a frontier for assimilation and migrant governance.

Logics of Border Control and Difference in Social Welfare

The Australian case is one of many nation-states in which the creation of new laws criminalizing migrant behavior correlates with increased state anxiety around migration from contexts of war, civil conflict, and political instability. This especially applies to those who attempt entry via maritime routes. While those migrant families targeted by the law are not always the same asylum seekers who have attempted to reach Australia via boat, the two are often conflated in policy debates. As a result, forced marriage is seen as a symptom of recent maritime migration. It affects the way both first-generation resettled families and asylum seekers awaiting permanent residence are perceived in society, including their transnational ties to family abroad. Those who have not yet been resettled in Australia are now scrutinized through the lens of the forced marriage law in that they are seen as people who are already prone to importing strange cultural practices. The law, then, functions as an interiorized form of border control that uses the juridical system to pre-emptively criminalize Muslim migrants who encompass multiple legal statuses and are at different stages of the migration journey.

Political philosopher Wendy Brown (1995, 70) argues that a politics of recognition cannot exceed the conditions of a group's oppression—the conditions that produced their positions in society as marginalized (and which gets read as simply "different" or "deviant"). Because it ignores the conditions that produced such marginalization, the language of recognition can become antithetical to freedom, even as it attempts to achieve liberation (66). At times, recognition demands that people speak from a place of culture and that culture is the place from which individual voices should be recovered (Das 2013). This book has extended the critique of a politics of recognition by attending to how culturally competent social welfare, event when it wants to understand people's realities better, can still reproduce a politics of difference that continues to "other" them. Cultural competence, when invested in reproducing long-held tropes, sees culture as intrinsic, immutable, and, more importantly, incommensurable with the dominant social order.

Forced Marriage Prevention Today

Since I completed fieldwork, certain notable events have unfolded that reflect the ongoing preoccupations of prevention work. The concern with overseas marriages culminated in a campaign co-organized by the AFP and Anti-Slavery Australia to put a stop to the practice at Melbourne and Sydney's international airport. Known as Project Skywarp, the campaign's stated objectives were to make travelers in the airport aware of the signs of a forced marriage so they could identify it in their communities or seek support for themselves. Posters were hung across bathrooms in international terminals given that bathrooms are the only places that passengers at risk of being taken overseas may access information, and digital screens were used in common areas. The posters also inform passengers on how they can report information to the AFP and provide contact information about direct services, including the My Blue Sky website. A key part of the messaging was that the practice was illegal in Australia. In a report on the results of the pilot program, no information was provided on how many people had been stopped from getting on planes at the airport itself as a result of these posters. One report noted that a school counselor was contacted by a person concerned that her friend was being forced into marriage. In response, the AFP put out a PACE alert for her and her male companion at the airport. After being questioned by the AFP, she said that she did not want to travel and was then provided support under the STPP. The officer reporting on this incident noted in the same article, "This puts into context some of the work we do. It doesn't always have to include lights, sirens, and handcuffs" (Worthing 2020). Yet the posters clearly emphasize the illegality of the practice as a deterrent. Forced marriage's illegality is emphasized over the fact that it is a form of gender-based violence and a human rights abuse. One poster illustrates the responses a victim might get through visuals of text message bubbles from the people in their community if they expressed that "forcing someone to marry is illegal." Interestingly here, the victim is not saying "I don't want to marry this person"—rather, their declaration that the practice is illegal is met with responses like "You'll bring shame to our family" and "The marriage has been decided." The senders of these messages include "Big Bro," "Mum," "Cuz M," "Dad," and "Aunty A," indicating a familial pattern in which multiple immediate and extended family members are involved in the decision. The term "Aunty" also indicates that the example in the poster may be of a South Asian family, who would use it to refer to both biologically and non-biologically related females who are respected members of the individual's social world. But beyond this ethnically specific suggestion, it is telling that the responses are in relation to the declaration that the practice is illegal. In doing so, the AFP poster gives the impression that migrant communities exist, relate, and communicate in states of illegality and social deviance.

In addition to the implications about migrant criminality embedded in the posters, the actual results of the poster campaign are dubious. According to an AFP report on the project, while traffic to My Blue Sky's website increased from 5704 users in 2019–2020 to 6842 users in 2020–2021, the rise in reports of human trafficking in general (including forced marriage, among other recognized categories of trafficking) increased from 61 in 2018 to 91 in 2019 and to 92 in 2020. Given that Project Skywarp launched in October 2019, it is hard to say if the jump from 2018 to 2019 was due to the campaign or other factors (Australian Federal Police

2021b). All in all, it is not clear if the poster campaign was effective in getting people to report themselves to the AFP at the airport itself or even outside of it. The campaign is a telling example of how the airport gets used as a space of "policing lite," (one that is not invested in spectacle but still invested in managing and judging deviance) where the whole population is being called upon to practice a more watchful form of care and participate in such risk assessment practices.

Since my fieldwork ended in 2017, a few cases have made national news that are testing the efficacy of the 2013 law. This includes the case of Ruqia Haidari, an Afghan woman in Shepparton who was killed by Mohammad Halimi a year after allegedly being coerced into marrying him by her mother. Her mother, Sakina Mohammad Jan, has been charged under the forced marriage law, has pled not guilty, and is awaiting trial at the time this is being written. Mohammad Halimi was sentenced to twenty-one years in prison for murdering Haidari. I have chosen not to analyze this case because I cannot provide any additional ethnographic insight given that it occurred following my fieldwork. I did not speak with people investigating the case or members of the immediate family. However, in the many news articles that have covered the story, I have gleaned that Ruqia Haidari was someone who had large aspirations for herself and was promised that this marriage would afford her multiple kinds of freedom, including financial security and the opportunity to attend university. She wanted to attend school and had dreams of becoming a social worker with the local Afghan community. Ruqia fled Afghanistan at the age of 16 with her family members. When she was 21, she was forced to marry Halimi (25 at the time). It was not too long after that her life was taken away. Halimi arrived to Australia via boat, after which he was kept in a detention center until 2011. He had fled Afghanistan, where his father was brutally killed by the Taliban (Juanola 2021).

Rather than explain this horrific act of violence primarily through a cultural framework, we might consider how an individual's already misogynistic beliefs and understandings of intimate partner relationships become further entrenched and magnified when coupled with such structural violence. As one report stated, Halimi already had mental health issues that may have been exacerbated through the detention process (Raphael 2021). Haidari did call the AFP reporting that she was being coerced into a marriage. The AFP had offered Haidari assistance to leave the family home. However, according to reports, she concluded that she would face increased violence due to outside intervention and decided not to proceed (Zana 2021). Here, while the AFP may have been following protocol, how does criminalization as a system of interventions, judgments, and carceral responses generate additional environments of violence that make it difficult for victims to see a horizon of care and support in their short and long-term future? Furthermore, what does an analysis of the Australian state (its policing and immigration arms) as another actor in the web of violence that produced Ruqia's death look like? Perhaps the answer to this question goes beyond the training and methodologies of cultural anthropology, but it is a question worth asking and requires sustained reflection.

In the wake of Haidari's death, AFP recently put out a statement noting that it will support newly resettled migrants by making them aware that forced marriage is illegal in Australia. In a media statement about Afghan refugees being newly resettled since the 2021 Taliban takeover, AFP Commander Dametto recently stated: "We will prevent any attempts to take people overseas against their will to be married. If we can build trusted relationships, community members will be willing to seek our help. . . . I believe we all want the same thing in the end; for all Australians to feel safe in their community, and this means protecting Australia from extremist violence in all its forms" (Australian Federal Police 2021a). This quote illustrates that forced marriage is associated with refugees, and that they continue to be seen as security problems to be managed. It shows that their belief systems about marriage are yet another thing added to the litmus test of how insecure migrants make the nation-state. The singling out of forced marriage in this quote reflects the ways in which migrants are converted into vectors of threat that need to be properly governed.

Invitations for Reflection

The goal of this book is not to reify the distinction between a community-led way of knowing violence and a state-led one. Furthermore, it does not subscribe to the idea that community definitions of violence are either universal or qualitatively better than, or less immune to, blind spots than state-sanctioned definitions. That stance would be guilty of what Fabian (1986, 34) calls the "protective walls of cultural relativism." Such a stance would also fetishize what counts as community. Critical reflection is needed on who gets to speak for a community and what power dynamics and conditions allow certain stances to be publicly expressed and others marginalized. Another key premise of this analysis is that social welfare practitioners are not direct messengers of state-sanctioned definitions of violence. By contrast, practitioners are often caught in uneasy positions where they must negotiate definitions handed to them by policy language with what they witness in their everyday work, as well as their own ethical commitments to human rights. In making this clear, I wish to respond to what will be an inevitable question—how is this analysis helpful for those who work within forced marriage prevention?

I believe that anthropologists of social policy can orient practitioners to think in more pointed ways about the issues they care about. Those tasked with caring for others need to have a framework in place to determine when and how someone is suffering and what constitute the best ways to support them. Any framework that requires one to intervene in the lives of others is not immune from the push and pull of power. Care is not immune from violence, and a politics of care has to be willing to confront its produced effects, some of which can be harmful, either intentionally or not. However, there are things that can be done, in my view, that lessen the violences of social policies whose foundations are fundamentally flawed and based on an anti-immigrant politics.

As Winifred Tate (2020, 87) has written, policy narratives tend to situate "specific programs within broader spheres of political value, as well as erasing and obscuring alternatives. . . . An anthropology of policy can also reveal the unrealized possibilities of foreclosed futures" and according to Wedel and Feldman (2005, 2) can "destabilize the assumptions and conceptual metaphors that underpin the formulation of policy problems and thereby help create room for alternative policy options." If we take seriously the possibility that alternative paradigms exist for understanding and supporting those who experience coercion into all kinds of intimate relational situations (not just marriage), then I believe that practitioners are well positioned to reflect on the systems in which they work. They are willing to think more deeply about the consequences of prevention's assumptions when they have the time and space. In my observations, what allows for certain assumptions to go unquestioned is lack of time, lack of energy from being burned out by the work, and the large caseload that presents practitioners with "fires" they are constantly putting out, as one caseworker put it. Many of the practitioners I spoke with mentioned that our conversations were the first time they ever dedicated any focused time to reflect on the consequences of their approaches.

I agree with the claim that "announcing the relevance" of one's study can impose constraints on interpretation because it takes for granted claims about what things mean and who people are rather than leaving them open to examination (Tate 2020, 92). However, I also believe that recommendations do not need to be immediately actionable items. Recommendations can also be calls for deeper, slowed-down, and long-term reflection and engagement. As Charles Hale (2008) has written, ethnographies of policy can be one of many existing ways that social transformation could be brought about, including mutual aid, protest, activism, and policy advocacy. For practitioners and policymakers who have taken the time and energy to engage with this book, I hope to offer insight into some of prevention's blind spots and potential areas where prevention can be reframed. Here, I offer some recommendations around what practitioners can think more deeply about as they figure out which part of the prevention sector they are in a position to reform or, perhaps, transform. These recommendations exist at multiple scales. Some rest on the assumption that the encounter between a direct service provider and the individual is a desirable one. There is important work being done across critical Indigenous studies to imagine more radical and decolonial futures of social welfare in the settler colonial nation-state paradigm. Some argue that the Australian social welfare system and professionalization must be decolonized (Briskman 2016; Dittfeld 2020; Hollinsworth 2012; Motta 2016). However, I cannot in good conscience, based on the specific ethnographic project I have done, propose this without any semblance of a proposed path forward. Thus, I have admittedly kept my recommendations limited to a world in which such systems are being rethought and transformed rather than dismantled:

a. For those invested in questioning the assumptions anchoring the forced marriage law, tracing the connections between such a law and settler colonialism is worth pursuing. This means asking: what notions of citizenship and family is the forced marriage law invested in reinforcing and how are they informed by a colonial worldview and technologies of power?
b. For those who think there is room to reform the law rather than repeal it, removing it from the federal criminal justice framework and treating it as a civil issue presents many positives. Doing so could alleviate the fear that reporting coercion into marriage would involve state and federal police and a juridical process that could jeopardize people's immigration and citizenship statuses. However, even if forced marriage is treated under a civil framework, this does not resolve the problem of its racialized foundations (Patton 2018) and its view of certain communities as sites of coercive practices. However, treating coercion into marriage as a civil issue could, over time, destigmatize it as an issue of national security, vulnerable borders, or immigration. By refusing to see forced marriage as an issue of national security or vulnerable borders, more imaginative possibilities for support pathways could be opened up (Hussein 2017).
c. When practitioners are asked to think about the role of culture in shaping views on marriage, culture is best treated less as a set of static beliefs and traditions and more as a set of produced worldviews and practices shaped by people's lived experiences. These experiences are always in flux and include migration, resettlement, and life before migration. Here, practitioners might think about subjectivity rather than culture. Thinking about produced subjectivities would mean considering how people experience themselves as conscious beings whose choices are conditioned by systems and relations of power that change over time. This is different from predominant conceptions of culture as a repository of rules and codes that remain static no matter the circumstances and to which people blindly submit. In recent years, advocates such as Jennifer Burn have called for a more deculturalizing approach (Siagian 2018). Others, including Fauzia Shariff, an advocate for forced marriage victims in the United Kingdom, have called for a deeper understanding of how individuals as subjects engage in the making of choice. Shariff's work proposes the framework of "consensus" rather than a liberal notion of choice to understand how marital decisions are made in communities (Shariff 2012). While one must be careful about applying this across all Muslim migrant communities, the notion of consensus invites important questions, because it accounts for decisions as accumulations of "long processes of negotiation and critique; attempts to negotiate competing claims to legitimacy, authority and power and young people testing out how much they can push back against authority" (Shariff 2012, 13). For Shariff, consensus is not the only way to understand marital choices, because it does not fully capture situations involving children, differently abled adults, or LGBTQ people whose subjectivities are

marginalized to the point where a premise for consensus cannot be established. However, it does offer one alternative framework for understanding the complexities of family dynamics. Helen Sowey (2014), an Australia-based scholar, has argued for a more "emic perspective" that foregrounds migrant women's experiences as the basis for understanding the nature of choice. And even after considering the ways that neoliberal paradigms of autonomy do not capture how women themselves understand choice, Sowey writes that for all of us, "Any choice must be made within certain constraints" (2014, 10).

d. In considering subjectivity over culture, practitioners could also more intentionally integrate reflections on these questions: What does it mean for people (whether they seek support around marriage issues or other kinds of interpersonal relationships) to think about themselves as coerced and pressured? What are the different scales at which violence exists for such individuals? Is it just at the level of intimate and familial relationships or also in their interactions with state institutions, including the immigration system and the resettlement system? Considering these questions is key to ensuring that individuals can come forward, especially in the wake of recent reports that this has not been the case (Tuohy 2017). If family separation has been an issue, forced marriage prevention should reconsider it as an immediate go-to method and, instead, take seriously the ways in which individuals frame the power dynamics within their families. A study by Aisha Gill (2011) notes that "For many victims it is crucial that seeking help does not prevent future reconciliation with their families, especially their parents. In this regard, criminalization may actively discourage many victims from speaking out about the abuse/coercion they are facing." I would invite practitioners to think about both the advantages and pitfalls of standardized risk assessment that plug into a criminal justice model. As an advocate and I have written previously, implementing change does not have to mean giving up standardized models of care. However, it does mean being open to rethinking when standardized risk assessment is and is not useful, and what the objective of linking it to a carceral and criminal justice system actually is (Zeweri and Shinkfield 2021, 13).

Having said this, it is also up to practitioners to decide for themselves what these insights could mean for their daily practice. Not all practitioners are in the same position professionally or personally. As intersectional subjects, they face different vulnerabilities depending on their own subjectivities, especially migrant community leaders who work in prevention and some of whom need to be careful about how much they can critique Australian government institutions due to their immigration statuses. Not all practitioners can question the systems in which they work in the same way—differently situated people will face different consequences for doing so. Beyond systemic barriers, many direct service workers and advocates are already suffering from vicarious trauma and the ongoing emotional fallout of feeling like they are not doing enough all the time. Thus, these recommendations may not feel satisfactorily tangible, because what constitute "next steps" is largely shaped by the conditions under which practitioners work, live, and the freedom they have to express dissent in the workplace.

Expanding the Scope of "Coercion"

Here, I would like to return to the title of the first section of the introductory chapter, "Configuring Violence." To configure is to arrange to produce a certain outcome. This verb reflects how the forced marriage prevention apparatus created the contours and details of the problem it sought to prevent. In its attempts to construct the various actors, stories, and relationships that constituted coercive violence, other forms of coercion remained obscured from view. In the stories that practitioners learned about and told each other, coercion unfolded at multiple levels and at multiple stages in all parties' lives. There exist the coercive pressures parents exert on their children around marriage and building a family. There is the coercion parents feel from their extended family members. They include economic pressures (i.e., the need to pay back someone for help securing a visa to Australia) and resettlement pressures (i.e., the fear of being alone in a place where one rarely finds moments of true acceptance). Interwoven with all these interpersonal coercions is the coercive state. As a settler colonial state, Australian legal and political institutions are not built on genuine consent from Indigenous communities. Their origins are built on what anthropologist Audra Simpson (2017) has called "the ruse of consent." More research that carefully tells the history of settler colonial violence as part of a history of anti-immigrant policies needs to be done. However, it is clear that many of the coercive logics of colonial social welfare, such as the self-other binary, rescue, and the preoccupation with "non-normative" intimate social relations play out in contemporary migrant-targeted social welfare. More ethnographic research is also needed on the contemporary coercive nature of marriage itself in settler colonial states. What do aspirations around marriage and family look like for White Anglo settler descendants? How do such aspirations exert their own forms of duress, and shape people's ideas of to whom they should or should not tether themselves?

The Australian state also enacts its coercive power to securitize its borders and assert its sovereignty in increasingly extraterritorial ways (Dastyari and Hirsch 2019; Hirsch 2017; Mountz 2011). It outsources its violence to offshore resource-poor islands, as was the case with Australia's detention centers in Manus and Nauru. Its global campaigns deter maritime migration and have reached refugee camps in Pakistan and Iran, refugee transit points in Indonesia, and billboards in Kabul, Afghanistan. Beyond offshore detention, the Australian state has made people's citizenship hinge on their public and private comportment. Looming over these layers of coercion is the coercion of war and empire. This study provided a cursory overview of the effects of the Global War on Terror (which Australia has participated in through sending ground troops to Afghanistan and Iraq) on recently resettled migrants in Australia. One is hard-pressed to find something as coercive as the impossible choice to leave home or to stay that military occupation and imperial wars force people to make as they attempt to find some semblance of orientation and sense of the future. And finally, through focusing on the work of social welfare itself, it becomes clear that practitioners are also working under conditions of duress in which there is little flexibility to help clients outside the confines of a criminal justice and colonial framework.

This ethnography was about how people invested in an ethics of care learn to build narratives about violence. As a knowledge producing apparatus, forced marriage prevention participates in the creation of litmus tests around the potential for migrants to be good citizens based on their belief systems and intimate familial relations. It reflects an emerging trend in migrant-targeted social welfare in which being a good citizen means having "healthy family relationships." At the same time, practitioners are trying to reconcile this social policy's assumptions with their own understandings of their clients' lives. The world continues to see the fallout of war in the form of human displacement. As people find themselves marginalized at staggering levels globally, marriage will continue to be used as a tool for mobility, economic security, and ensuring a sense of community. Many of the practitioners I met valued the idea of understanding the complex realities in which their clients lived, but did not have the tools, space, or time, to put this into practice. Perhaps it is time to create spaces where social welfare can take the time to better understand the impossible choices that borders, war, and colonialism force people to make and the many forms of coercion that shape our contemporary world.

ACKNOWLEDGMENTS

This book is the product of several years of engagement with the question of *what it means to intervene in the life of another.* The people I recognize below helped me to think about this question in different ways. They are people whose orientations to the world I admire, have learned from, and who continue to teach me about what it means to care for, about, and alongside the many people who make up the communities we inhabit.

First, I wish to thank my interlocutors in Australia who took the time and energy to welcome me into their everyday work and who saw the value in critically reflecting on social welfare's practices and intentions. There are too many people to list, but I would like to extend a special thanks to the individuals and organizations who were part of the Victorian Forced Marriage Network, as well as select individuals including Sara Shinkfield and Bernadette Marantelli. I am grateful to the many direct service workers, advocates, government workers, and policy researchers who generously offered their time and energy across participating organizations in the VFMN. To critically reflect on their own work and the moral ambiguities associated with it was a lesson in how practitioners, given the space and time, can theorize and analyze the gravity and impact of their work and the systems that confront them with difficult choices.

I am grateful to Monash University's Gender, Leadership, and Social Sustainability Institute (GLASS), which provided me with an academic community during my fieldwork. I'm particularly grateful to Margaret Alston and Kerry Ward, who very generously offered their time and feedback to the project's questions and were encouraging from the beginning. Other faculty who were thoughtful interlocutors to this research include: Deborah Weston, Zoe Robertson, Sandra Gifford, Raelene Wilding, Margarita Windisch, and Kaye Queck. Zhaoen (Penny) Pan was a constant source of intellectual and emotional support and I am lucky to have found a lifelong friend. Uma Kothari at the University of Melbourne prompted me to think about migrant relations beyond the realm of the pragmatic and has become a lifelong friend and collaborator. Friends at the Refugee Council of Australia, including Laura Maya Stacey, also probed me to think about Australia's history of offshore detention in shaping the lives of newly resettled migrant communities. I am grateful to the members of Action on Disability within Ethnic Communities, with whom I volunteered during my preliminary fieldwork in Melbourne in 2015, including Peehu Gupta and Shaima Shahbaz. The wonderful group of people I met through Muslims for Progressive Values and their Qur'an Reading Group in Melbourne helped me to see that religious texts are rich sources of social justice and revolutionary ideas, including when it comes to marriage and gender. I'm especially grateful to Tahera, Irma, and Reem for creating such a welcoming and open space. I was lucky to meet the members of the Moroccan Delicacy in Brunswick, Victoria who welcomed me to their seminars. The Delicacy's commitment to understanding Islamophobia through Australia's settler colonial history opened up my thinking in many ways. They showed that it is in spaces of community building that we can transcend the limits of multiculturalism as the only language for equality and social justice. I have left out the names of victims/survivors of gender-based violence and select migrant community leaders to protect their anonymity, but they all played a crucial role in shedding light on the political and ethical questions that matter in undertaking culturally sensitive social welfare. They taught me that to recognize violence is not to relinquish relations and obligations of care.

I am deeply indebted to those who introduced me to Afghan Australian community leaders who are tirelessly working to create fairer social welfare and immigration policies. My conversations with these individuals have deeply impacted the way I see social policy as shaped by longer histories of displacement and war. Thank you to Shaima jan, Hosi, Farkhonda, Kobra, Shabnam, Fatema, Abuzar, Temur, Shaheen, Aquilla, Wida, and Fatima.

I was lucky to be able to communicate the findings of this research with a range of public-facing organizations working to better services for victims/survivors of gender-based violence and advocate for the rights of immigrant and refugee communities. I workshopped the findings of this paper through a report I submitted to the Victorian Forced Marriage Network and the Houston branch of the Tahirih Justice Center. I participated in an interdisciplinary panel with lawyers, advocates, and social workers at the 2019 American Immigration Lawyers Association Conference alongside Jae Lee, Brandon Roché, and Desirée Salinas.

This book was born out of my doctoral dissertation, which I could not have completed without the encouragement and support of my dissertation committee at Rice University's anthropology department. Thank you to James Faubion for always being a generous listener and prompting me to think about the broader genealogies of this book's anchoring concepts. I am deeply grateful to Cymene Howe, whose thoughtful and consistent engagement with this project and the many steps leading up to it inspired my own approach to supporting students today. Her commitment to ethnographic methods and analysis have and will continue to stay with me. I am indebted to Zoë Wool whose ability to render valuable the everyday through writing has been empowering for my own writing practice. Elora Shehabuddin's support was critical to this project. Her work's commitment to transcending the limiting analytical scripts and theoretical paradigms around Muslim women has inspired me from the beginning. Other faculty at Rice anthropology who allowed me to think through the political and conceptual stakes of this project include: Andrea Ballestero, Eugenia Georges, Dominic Boyer, and, in more recent years, Kamala Visweswaran. Faculty at Rice's Center for the Study of Women, Gender, and Sexuality (CSWGS) were thoughtful voices on this project at various symposia and seminars, including Rosemary Hennessey and Brian Riedel. The administrators in both the anthropology departments (Altha Rodgers and Addison Verger) and CSWGS (Angela Wren-Wall) made the dissertation process much more seamless and filled with compassion. I am also grateful to the faculty at Rice's Center for Academic and Professional Communication who gave me some of my first teaching opportunities, which allowed me to take seriously the importance of accessibly communicating one's research to a student audience: Jennifer Wilson, Elizabeth Festa, David Messmer, and Kyung-Hee Bae.

Conceptualizing this project happened in the intermittent periods between teaching, office visits in the basement of Rice anthropology, and drinks and food with a cohort of PhD students I am lucky to call lifelong friends. Thank you to Svetlana Borodina and Baird Campbell for always living the ethics and politics you write about so beautifully in your work and for always being there to listen and exchange when life felt uncertain. I am grateful to Sólveig Ásta Sigurðardóttir and Eliza Williamson for reminding me about the power of friendship and the simple pleasure of exchanging an article or book recommendation and checking in amidst the solitude of academic life. Thank you to the following people for their feedback, encouragement, and engagement with this research over the years: Lupe Flores, Jing Wang, Magnús Örn Sigurðsson, Yifan Wang, Ellie Vainker, Victor Giménez, Nathanael Vlachos, and Drew Winter.

In between the dissertation and book, I have been lucky to workshop parts of this research with two institutions where I have had the pleasure of teaching students whose commitment to a more just and equitable world have been inspiring (the University of Virginia's global studies program and the University of British Columbia's anthropology program, where I have been based since 2022). I am grateful to UVA's global studies program (both faculty and students) for creating a space where, as a new faculty member, I had the freedom to develop courses on migration, refugees, and borders where I could think through many of the book's key conceptual questions. In particular, I would like to recognize the following people: Tessa Farmer, thank you for your genuine friendship, collaboration, and for exemplifying what it means to practice the values and commitments you write about. Thank you to Sylvia Chong, whose scholarship, public-facing work, and aspirations to change the way we think about migrants and borders today empowered me to feel like my work could do the same. I am deeply grateful to the following people at UVA who created such a warm and collaborative environment: Phoebe Crisman, Jim Igoe, David Edmunds, Pete Furia, Sylvia Tidey, Steve Parks, Mauricio Herrera, Spencer Phillips, Richard Handler, Ingrid Hakala, Caterina

Eubanks, Kathryn Quissell, Samhita Sunya, Hanadi Al-Samman, and Penny Von Eschen. I would also like to thank Morgan Chung, a student who provided invaluable research assistance on global histories of violence prevention for this book.

I am grateful for the many opportunities to workshop early versions of chapters of this book at various conferences, including the 2018 Society for Applied Anthropology Conference, where I benefited from feedback from April Petillo and Amalia Mora, and the 2019 American Anthropological Association Conference, where I benefited from feedback from Virginia Dominguez. My fieldwork in Australia also prompted an ongoing project on the history of offshore detention, which I was able to present at the UC-Irvine Emerging Global Studies Scholars Conference. Thank you to Eve Darian-Smith and Vibhuti Ramachandran for their insightful comments and resources. I also presented on offshore detention at the Boston University Migration Matters Symposium in April 2021 and am grateful to Ayşe Parla, Miriam Ticktin, and Nooria Lori for their invaluable feedback on my paper and research. My time as a digital editorial fellow at the *Political and Legal Anthropology Review* shaped my thinking on the history of Australian border control policy, and I appreciate getting to collaborate with Kate Henne and Nadja Eisenberg-Guyot.

At the University of British Columbia, I am grateful to my colleagues for providing support and encouragement as I embarked on the last stages of this book and began a new position in the anthropology department. I am genuinely looking forward to continuing to collaborate with them. A sincere thank you to my fellow colleagues with whom I began the journey to UBC in tandem and who are deeply generous with their time, feedback, and support: Elif Sari, Zahra Hayat, Maya Wind, Kristen Barnett, and Aleksa Alaica. Thank you to Amir Shiva and Sima Sajjadiani for creating a warm community of friendship and support as I began the journey in Vancouver. Thank you to Alexia Bloch for providing positive encouragement as I navigated through the last stages of this manuscript, as well as Shaylih Muehlmann's ongoing mentorship. I am thankful to the UBC Centre for Migration Studies—an ideal intellectual home to think about the afterlife of this research and new dimensions to explore in Australia and beyond, specifically Antje Ellermann and everyone in the Borders Research Group. I have also benefited by being in dialogue with a writing collective alongside Greg Feldman, Hugh Gusterson, Kalyani Menon, Cris Shore, Raghu Trichur, Lynda Dematteo, and Nancy Ries, which has allowed me to think about state power across different colonial contexts.

The fieldwork for this research was made possible by the following research institutions: The Wenner-Gren Foundation for Anthropological Research; the American Institute for Afghanistan Studies; and various research institutes at Rice University, including: the James F. Wagoner Foreign Study Scholarship; the Social Science Research Institute; the Center for the Study of Women, Gender, and Sexuality; and the Center for the Middle East. I am also grateful to Péter Berta, the editor of this series, for taking the time to review and consider this book proposal in its early stages. Thank you to Carah Naseem and Jasper Chang at Rutgers University Press for their ongoing support for a first time book author. I am also grateful to the anonymous reviewers of this manuscript for their thoughtful feedback and positive encouragement. Chapter 3 of this book originally appeared in a slightly altered version in *Ethnos: Journal of Anthropology* (https://www.tandfonline.com/).

I also could not have experienced this journey without the life-giving conversations with friends outside of academia who have helped me to see how other spaces (art, activism, and public service) are thinking about more equitable futures for migrants, refugees, and marginalized peoples. My friendship with these individuals always reminded me of the many spaces where liberation is being thought about and reimagined within and beyond academia: Angela Jackson, Ann Garcia, Arash Azizzada, Victor Ancheta, Ayesha Hassan, Gerard Lynch, Adhemir Romero, Bárbara Pinto, Guadalupe Fernández, Oscar Lopez, Arielle Milkman, Effrosyni Rantou, Grace Tran, Omid Tofighian, Elahe Zivardar, Alex Schank, Yalda Afif, and Morwari Zafar. Thank you to my lifelong friends for being that familiar place one could turn to celebrate the joys of life: Marilyn Meza, Fernando Rojas, and René Serulle,

I am deeply grateful to have found friendship, community, and a sense of purpose outside of research within the Afghan American Artists and Writers Association, a collective of artists and writers that formed in 2011 and has since grown into something none of us could have imagined. Both founding and current members of AAAWA are people who truly believe in the idea that life can be lived multiple ways and that building a more just future begins with learning to truly value each other's differences. These members include Zohra Saed, Laimah Osman, and Madina Tabesh. Thank you to Gazelle Samizay for bringing me back down to earth during times of uncertainty and for your unwavering commitment to using art as a tool for change. Wazhmah Osman has been the kind of collaborator one could only wish for and whose courage and resilience within academia was precedent-setting for Afghan scholars in the U.S. diaspora. Thank you to Sahar Muradi, Seelai Karzai, and Katayoun Bahrami for always being such generous interlocutors and for using art and writing to change the narrative about migrant life.

While writing about questions of family and connection, I have become attentive to my own familial relations in new ways. I realized that, growing up, many of my family members had always been thinking anthropologically—consistently putting themselves in other people's shoes, trying to understand them on their own terms, and refusing to pass immediate judgment on others' decisions. Perhaps what initially began as a survival skill for a family experiencing displacement turned into a powerful way to forge community, empathy, and solidarity with others. I would like to thank members of my family who not only made it possible for me to complete this book but whose encouragement has allowed me to pursue academia as a profession. The economic and social sacrifices of supporting this pursuit are real, not to mention lost time and memories that I wish I could go back and remake. Thank you to my grandmother, Samia Mirzad. Throughout her life, whether as a creative coming of age in Kabul, Afghanistan or as a migrant trying to rebuild her life in the United States, she has pushed the boundaries of what it means to be a strong woman with a sense of empathy, grace, and fun. I like to think it was through learning about her life and the difficult yet empowering choices she made that inspired my interest in questions of agency and power. I am grateful to my aunt Mariam, whose capacity to care and love so consistently is always an anchor for me. I can't thank my brother Edrees and my cousin Helai enough for their unconditional support and love, even as I missed so many birthdays, celebrations, and school events. I am forever indebted to my mother for her open-mindedness to anthropology's ways of knowing the world and for always being there to take phone calls as I tried to bounce off ideas and hold on to connection amidst the uprooting involved with academic life. I am grateful to my father for his consistent belief in the power of sciences, natural and social, to reveal new dimensions of the human condition and for always supporting my aspirations, and always helping me to ask the right questions. Thank you to my life partner, Eloy—it has been life's joy to navigate new places with you while realizing that home is any place where we are together. I am inspired by your humility, commitment to supporting migrants in their struggles, and your own capacity to activate joy with whomever you meet. Thank you to Mali, Rocío, Héctor, Lily, Daniel, Trino, Gael, Danielito, Elly, Julissa, Tiffany, Romie, Chris, Erika, and the many other beautiful people in the Rodriguez and Gardea families for teaching me the power of community. Señor Gardea, you left us too soon, but your passion for living in the present and searching for the spark in human connection stays with me. Your presence runs throughout these pages that explore what it would mean to value the connections that make us who we are.

It is difficult to properly credit all of the people one encounters in the course of a project's conception to its published form. It is inevitable that certain people will have been missed in this, but they have shaped the research that follows and I know they will continue to inspire its afterlife.

NOTES

INTRODUCTION

1. While I present this term in the initial section of the introduction, I will explain later in the introduction why it is controversial and how I am using it throughout the book.
2. Secondary school is the Australian equivalent to high school in the United States.
3. The names of all my interlocuters in this book have been changed.
4. I use the term "victim/survivor" to signal that people who have experienced duress around marriage and do identify with how the law would categorize them may not think about their experiences as simply one of victimhood but also one of survival. Having said that, this binary is imperfect and still obscures a great deal about people's lived experiences (Boyle and Rodgers 2020) and runs the risk of portraying their life experiences as tied to their experience of trauma.
5. I put these terms in quotes to connote that such labels, while they have a long history that cannot be done justice here, have their roots in modernization theory, which ranks societies based on how "closely" their economies mirror those of industrialized societies. Sally Engle Merry (2016) has shown how such metrics are created through Euro-centric metrics of advancement.
6. The main way that a forced marriage was distinguished from an arranged marriage, according to the Australian government's official information packet on forced marriage, was that the former is entered into with the "free and full consent" of the parties, whereas the latter is not entered into with free and full consent (Australian Department of Home Affairs 2017). As I have written elsewhere (Zeweri 2023), multiple actors in the forced marriage prevention and response apparatus see this distinction as important for their respective audiences to know about. More importantly, state discourse situates arranged marriage as a central reference point from which to make sense of the violence of forced marriage. While arranged marriage has been commonly referred to within Australian media and public discourse, it is now increasingly being talked about in relation to forced marriage. One of the key ways that the practices are distinguished from each other is through the groups that are associated with them. Through popular media and prevention trainings, "forced marriages" are typically associated with Muslim immigrant communities from the Middle East and South Asia, whereas those stories that are called "arranged marriages" typically involved South Asian non-Muslim immigrant communities. The language of state policy, coupled with media discourse, demonstrate that arranged marriage emerges as a foil to forced marriage and as less socially deviant to affirm the state's commitment to multiculturalism while also implying a ceiling to the forms of sociality it will tolerate (Zeweri 2023).
7. I cite Clifford's term here because there is something similar between how classic anthropology has produced partial truths about its objects of study and how forced

marriage prevention produces knowledge about communities it seeks to help. What is similar between both is how they see communities as static, bounded societies that live in isolation and engage in cultural practices that have their own internal logic that are not shaped by any outside forces. Both forms of knowledge production also engage in what Johannes Fabian has called the denial of coevalness in the sense that they treat the people they are studying or helping as living in the past or as backward (Fabian 1986).

8. This is an important caveat, because this figure does not reflect refugees settled through the onshore program. This refers to people who had entered Australia, were in the country, and then applied for and were granted asylum. It is likely this number may be close to double if the statistics on onshore resettlement during this period were available.

9. This was pronounced in the wake of the global emergence of the Islamic State (ISIS), which recruited Muslim men and women citizens of global North countries to join its project and often used marriage with fighters as a tool to get Muslim women to travel overseas. The Australian Parliament's proposal of a bill to criminalize forced marriage emerged during this period, in which migrant connections and travel to their home countries was being increasingly scrutinized.

10. While coercion into marriage may involve Australian-based Islamic religious leaders, they are often not the same entities that are advocating for Islamic religious institutions' right to lead different social practices. Another key foundation of the "knowledge-building" that occurred around forced marriage was set up by policymakers who had begun defining it as a moral crisis beginning in 2011 for not only individual victims, but for the Australian nation as a whole. It is no coincidence that such claims of crisis coincided with state level inquiries into the limits of religious freedom in Australia, including the extent to which shari'a law councils should be permitted to officially mediate family matters such as divorce for Australia's Muslim communities. This produced several debates under the Rudd and Turnbull administrations, including the 2018 Government Inquiry into Religious Freedom (Attorney-General's Department 2018). In that sense, forced marriage emerges in a climate that sees Muslim life as threatening to the values of the nation-state.

11. The AFP received seventy referrals of forced marriage in 2016–2017, forty-nine between July 1, 2017 and April 30, 2018, and ninety in fiscal year (FY) 2018–2019 (Mottram 2019), bringing the total to 313 between 2013 (the year the law was passed) and October 2019. Some have offered a slightly different statistic at 325 (Vidal 2018, 4). Organizations continue to repeat the phrase, "This prevalence of forced marriage in Australia is believed to be only the tip of the iceberg" (Good Shepherd Australia/New Zealand 2018). It is unclear what happened to the rest of the referrals.

12. According to a recent *ABC News* report, from 2021 to 2022, there had been more than eighty reports nationwide to the AFP of forced marriages, but in recent years, the number of reports has plateaued. As of February 2023, there have been zero convictions under the law, though an individual named Sakina Muhammad Jan is currently awaiting trial and will be prosecuted under the legislation for coercing her daughter, Ruqia Haidari, who was murdered by her husband, into a marriage in 2019 (Hildebrandt 2022).

13. See the following news stories: "Forced Marriage Is Happening in Australia and We Need to Do Something about It" (Vidal 2016); "Putting an End to Forced Marriage in Australia" (Burn 2013); "The Slave Trade in Our Own Backyard" (Burke 2016); "Most Girls at Risk of Being Married Against Their Will Are Falling through the Gaps" (Tuohy 2017); "Experts Warn Child Bride Cases Tip of the Iceberg" (Deery 2017); "Forced Marriage Cases Increasing" (2017); "More than 50 Australian Girls as Young as Nine Married Off

as Child Brides to Older Men—Often Leaving the Country before Police Can Stop Them" (Duncan and Margan 2017); "It Happens Here: Underage Forced Marriage in Suburban Australia" (Potaka and Costello 2017); "Labour Vows to Crack Down on Child Brides and Forced Marriage" (Koziol 2018); and "Report Details Abuse of Forced Marriage Victims Living in Australia" (Baker 2018).

14. Lisa Stevenson (2014, 95) discusses how the creation of statistics around Inuit rates of suicide in the Canadian arctic make it real for bureaucrats and social welfare practitioners. Citing S. Lochlann Jain (2007, 78), Stevenson points to the ways in which statistics conflate the "*you* who either will or will not die and the *you* that has a 5 percent chance of survival" (2014, 95).

15. In this book, I find Stephen Collier and Andrew Lakoff's (2008a, 22) notion of "regimes of living" resonant. Regimes of living refer to the ways in which one lives one's life, and what counts as virtuous conduct in different contexts becomes problematized as an object of governance. A regime of living is, they add, "a tentative and situated configuration of normative, technical, and political elements that are brought into alignment in situations that present ethical problems—that is, situations in which the question of how to live is at stake" (2008, 23). Forced marriage prevention, in its configuration of assimilationist discourses, policy infrastructure, and multiple infrastructures of governance, represents a regime of living that is also distinctly biopolitical—in that sense, it is a regime of living imposed and generated by the state at the level of the population, even though it disproportionately focuses on certain communities within it.

16. Veena Das and others (2001, 5) write that certain genres "mold the articulation of suffering, assigning a subject position as the place from which suffering may be voiced." She notes that institutions are implicated in "allowing or disallowing voice" at the nexus point where questions of representation meet questions of the actual lived world of survivors or victims.

17. Policies are different from laws in that the latter are created by state officials and enforced through juridical bodies and police, whereas the former are created through private institutional mechanisms and are enforced by bureaucrats and decision-making by individuals (Tate 2020, 84).

18. Interestingly, this report uses E. B. Tylor's definition of culture. Tylor was a social scientist who was key to bringing evolutionary theory to anthropology, which served as the foundation for the discipline's earlier premise that certain societies as more or less advanced than others and its concern with finding "laws of cultural progress." Tylor's definition uses the presence of certain institutions in his own society as the reference point for judging other cultures in remote places in terms of how advanced they are, and believes cultures exist as static wholes.

19. Zoë Wool and Seth Messinger's (2012, 45) analysis of the kinship configurations that are counted as legible and illegible in the Non-Medical Attendant (NMA) program at Walter Reed Rehabilitation Clinic also shows the ways that certain kinds of intimacies escape biomedical logics of rehabilitation and therapy. The kinship of the NMA program is "full of specific histories of intimacy" as well as attendant limits and expectations. While I am not looking at a biomedical space, the illegibility of certain child-parent configurations as relationships of care is a resonant theme in this book. These kin relations are also intimate in that they represent intersubjective relations in which desire itself is worked upon and reshaped between kin members, which anthropologist Cymene Howe (2013) has called "intimate pedagogies" in her exploration of gender rights activists in Nicaragua.

20. The 2015 amendment expanded the definition of forced marriage to "include circumstances in which a victim does not freely and fully consent because he or she 'was

incapable of understanding the nature and effect of the marriage ceremony'. This could be, for example, because of age or mental capacity" (Australian Human Rights Commission 2015). This was seen as an important protection for people with cognitive disabilities.

21. Claudia Castañeda's (2002, 4) conceptualization of the child is a particularly helpful starting point for understanding how the prevention sector thinks about its role in securing children's futures: "Just as the child's potential for physical growth must be ensured by specific means, so too must the child's socialization and enculturation be secured." The vast range of psychological theories, government policies, and social welfare programs directed at procuring the child's proper development indicate the pervasiveness of this teleological model of the child across biological, social, and cultural domains.

CHAPTER 1 A GENEALOGY OF FORCED MARRIAGE PREVENTION

1. While the UDHR was an important step in directly addressing marriage, Article 16's formation is historically and geopolitically situated. It was drafted in the aftermath of World War II, partly in response to the repressive laws of Nazi Germany that explicitly outlawed interracial marriage (Brueggemann and Newman 1998, 56). The protection of consent into marriage in the UDHR was, in part, a reaction to eugenics policies that saw marriage as the ideal institution to ensure that reproduction would produce biological forms of racial purity at the national level. Article 16 is also a way to ensure that the family is the entry point into accessing other rights, resources, and recognitions.

2. According to Ruth Gaffney-Rhys (2011, 364), in 1975, the UN adopted CEDAW's Article 16(2), which states that "the betrothal and marriage of a child shall have no legal effect." The caveat is that CEDAW does not define what constitutes a child and what kinds of marriages are prohibited. The UN Convention on Consent to Marriage, Minimum Age of Marriage and Registration of Marriages (United Nations General Assembly 1962) also notes that states must "take legislative action to specify a minimum age for marriage" but does not suggest a minimum age. However, in 1965, the UN General Assembly recommended that the minimum age for marriage should not be less than fifteen, which most countries and states tend to subscribe to.

3. While these treaties do not unequivocally privilege a particular age, other institutions, such as the United Nations Population Fund (UNFPA) and the United Nations Children's Fund (UNICEF) have noted that child marriage involves a person under the age of eighteen (Gaffney-Rhys 2011, 360).

4. In addition to these blindspots, critics have questioned why less advocacy has been undertaken at a systemic level around protecting the right to enter into same-sex marriage. This includes the right to marry without having to abide by heteronormative social institutions (Samar 2007; Gerber, Tay, and Sifris 2014; Brown 2016), such as being able to create different kinds of kinship configurations. Such critics claim that if consent and autonomy of both parties were to be truly protected, then such documents would protect the ability to choose partners across the board. These documents also reinforce the idea that the purpose of marriage is to create a family, a social unit that functions as the building block of society itself.

5. As studies of social contract theory and liberal law and personhood have written, the liberal subject of rights is one that allows people to make choices about their destiny, uninhibited by other subjects, collectives, or institutions (Collier, Maurer, and Suárez-Návaz 1995; Mehta 1990).

6. Only recently has violence against women become measured through the development of various indicators and metrics by global institutions, such as the UN Statistical Commission (UNSC). However, as Merry (2016, 44) points out, as the UNSC decided how to measure VAW and what counted as data, it defined the very nature of the problem itself. The definition ended up being a conglomerate of definitions from different experts. Whereas statisticians aimed for an objective "neutral" definition, feminist and human rights organizations called for one rooted in gender inequality and structural violence. Thus, VAW became "a site of technical knowledge" (2016, 45) and in becoming a more globally recognizable category that requires intervention and prevention, "there are increasing demands to classify, measure, and count it" (2016, 45).

7. Mohammad Shakir was charged with marrying someone of an unmarriageable age, a violation of Section 95, Subsection S-1 of the 1961 Marriage Act. It was determined that Shakir knew the victim was fifteen or under. Ultimately, the imam and Shakir were convicted of violating provisions of the 1961 Marriage Act and were sentenced to two months and eighteen months in prison, respectively. Discussion of the case emerged in almost every forced marriage forum I attended from late 2016 until the end of my fieldwork in late 2017. Practitioners were taken aback that, even with video evidence, the imam had not been prosecuted under the law, but they nevertheless saw the case as a key moment in that the option of prosecuting under the 2013 law was entertained. This sent a public message that forced and early marriage were not acceptable in Australia.

8. Statistics are then cited from the National Children's and Youth Law Centre (NCYLC), which has located 250 cases of underage marriage from 2012 to 2014, while others cite that at least sixty child wives live in southwestern Sydney (2014). However, the actual reported cases of the NCYLC in 2013 were referred and investigated much less.

9. The law goes on to state that a marriage is defined as either a registered relationship in Australia under the Acts Interpretation Act of 1901, a marriage recognized under a foreign country's law, or a marriage that normally would not be recognized under Australia's Marriage Act. This invalidity could be due to a lack of consent; natural, induced, or age-related incapacity; or a party to the marriage already being married (Section 270.7A, subsections 1–2).

10. "Underage Forced Marriage."

11. All in all, forced marriage's inclusion within the FVPA of Victoria was a significant win for advocates. The inclusion has now allowed people to apply for family violence intervention orders in court to put a stop to contact with their family members rather than reporting the crime to AFP. This provides an alternative route to those who do not want to pursue the criminalization framework. However, because this change occurred after fieldwork, I was not able to do an in-depth study of its effects. According to the family violence prevention initiative South Safe, there is little empirical research on the impacts of this inclusion on individual filings of Family Violence Protection Orders.

12. It is important to acknowledge that forced marriage has also been considered a child protection issue by several advocates and legal practitioners; however, its place within existing plans to combat child abuse remains uncertain and not particularly robust. Because child protection agencies squarely focus on people under eighteen and, in some states, sixteen and under, many individuals who are seventeen and over have had trouble availing themselves of child protection agencies' help. According to Vidal, those over sixteen are "considered independent and, for example, can self-place outside of their homes without the involvement of a statutory agency. Child protection systems are not designed to be responsive to this issue or cohort of young people unless they are very young in age" (Vidal 2018, 10). While forced marriage prevention, in general, does focus

on the threats of such violence on one's childhood and the importance of empowering adolescents and young adults in migrant communities, the actual child protection intervention structure does not map on to this discourse.

It is worth pointing out that, because forced marriage can sometimes involve a minor, it gets exclusively framed as a child exploitation issue. For example, in a 2020 Women's Forum article ("Forced Marriages in Australia a Bigger Problem Than We Think" 2020), AFP Commissioner Reece Kershaw discussed the underreported nature of forced marriages. He went on to discuss child exploitation and abuse crimes, including child pornography and the thousands of referrals his office has received about child exploitation. The conflation of forced marriage with the same kinds of coercion and violence as other kinds of child exploitation has raised questions for advocates around what it means to assume that a child marriage is coercion and a violation of consent, as with an adult.

13. The logic behind the act was that people of full Aboriginal descent were destined to die out because they were an inferior race. On the other hand, those of mixed descent were increasing in numbers and should strategically be deprived of government support by removing them from reserves and ceasing food rations, while pure Aboriginals should be kept on reserves and continue receiving government support (Ellinghaus 2003, 194).

14. According to historian Katherine Ellinghaus (2003, 186),

> Biological absorption was to be a two stage process: firstly, the "doomed race" theory posited that people of full descent would soon "die out"; and secondly, it was believed that Aboriginal physical characteristics, and it was hoped, Aboriginality itself, would disappear altogether through biological absorption. The latter theory relied on the dubious scientific idea that Aboriginal genes would not create any "throw-backs," or children who physically resembled stereotypes of "the Aboriginal", after a few generations of "inter-breeding". Ideas about who was or was not "fit" to "breed" were closely related to the rhetoric of eugenics which had been filtering into Australia since the 1890s and which gained in popularity during the inter-war years.

15. The prevention of forced marriage, then, is one of many instances in which the state has decided to assert its monopoly over the familial relations of communities already seen as incommensurable with the values of the nation-state. While, in the case of Indigenous communities, the outlawing of miscegenation was a way to manage the population's racial purity and to ensure the non-proliferation of non-White life, the 2013 law and policy is focused on policing how familial relations translate into a violation of national borders and their integrity.

16. See Samia Khatun's (2019; 2017) work on Indigenous people's relationships with Muslim migrants in *Australianama: The South Asian Odyssey in Australia* and "The Book of Marriage: Histories of Muslim Women in Twentieth Century Australia" published in *Gender & History*.

17. The fear of losing one's children to the justice system given the history of the "Stolen Generations" (1909–1969) in which the Australian government forcibly removed children from their Indigenous parents also contributes to this ongoing mistrust between Indigenous communities and social services (Cooper and Morris 2005).

18. Historically, sexual abuse and family violence have been used interchangeably when referring to social ills in Indigenous communities. It is through the realm of sexual relations that deviant family behavior has been identified and then reinscribed within the policy language of family violence. However, in the case of recent migrant communities, family violence has been used more frequently than sexual abuse to refer to acts of both emotional abuse and sexual abuse.

19. Lisa Stevenson (2014, 29, 96, 7) writes that "statistics and constructing a 'case' is a form of 'tracking' and covering the migratory Inuit that reimagines them as 'cases' and 'vectors' of a devastating disease—so many muskrats dying." In doing so, there is also a "sense of expectancy" around the death of those who are already living as suicidal or afflicted with some other condition. "Thus it happens that the death of the tubercular or the suicidal Inuk comes as no surprise."

20. She writes, "As in other Aboriginal communities, life in this region is also characterized by high levels of violence and child neglect and abuse and by recurring and often paralyzing loss and grief through high rates of premature deaths, chronic diseases and rising mental illnesses. The ubiquitous presence of alcohol and cannabis and the omnipresent threat of suicide add to the adversity and trauma in people's lives" (2014, 101).

21. As Howard-Wagner (2013, 227) writes: "Anecdotal reports of the child 'promised wife' being sexually assaulted by old men with the consent of the family dominated the media causing a 'ripple of outrage across the country.' In that same interview [Mel] Brough [the then Minister for Families, Community Services, and Indigenous Affairs] declared that 'paedophile rings were working behind a veil of customary law' in the Northern Territory and that 'everybody who lives in those communities knows who runs the pedophile rings.'"

22. According to Madiha Tahir (2019, 410, 409), the military and the police have increasingly converged to police "the enemy within" in liberal democratic states. Once can trace contemporary family violence prevention services for Indigenous communities to settler colonialism itself as undergirded by this type of policing: "Colonial wars were often conceived as 'small wars' . . . where overwhelming bouts of militarist violence worked in tandem with colonial civil administration to construct a colonial social order (Neocleous 2014; Moyn 2013; Khalili 2012)."

23. Colonialism in Australia stems from the British occupation of what was initially referred to as "terra nullius incognita Australis" or (unknown land of the South), which automatically erased Indigenous people as inhabitants (Porter 2006, 383). British occupation in the eighteenth century drove Indigenous communities further inland on reserves. In 1992, the concept of terra nullius was overturned in the *Mabo v. Queensland* case in the High Court of Australia. The High Court held that the doctrine of terra nullius, which imported all laws of England to a new land, did not apply in circumstances where there were already inhabitants present—even if they had been regarded at the time as "uncivilized," and that existing law included Indigenous land title. As such, any indigenous land rights that had not been extinguished by subsequent grants by the Crown continued to exist in Australia. The ruling also stated that the Crown acquired sovereignty and radical title upon settlement, that acquisition cannot be questioned in a municipal court, and that grants of land inconsistent with native title extinguish the native title. Ultimately, *Mabo v. Queensland*'s decision ushered in a new era of the recognition of Indigenous rights and the potentiality for a treaty between the Australian commonwealth government and indigenous communities over land control. However, a treaty is yet to be reached and Indigenous peoples still suffer from the consequences of having their histories, practices, ways of life, and communities routinely discounted and eliminated through government-sanctioned interventions, profiling, and imprisonment.

CHAPTER 2 THE THREAT OF SUFFERING

1. Just a month before, I had met with Bridget who worked with young adult migrants for a direct service organization. I had gotten the sense that, while she was still trying to figure out how to know what consent and coercion looked like, treating forced marriage

as a cultural issue was off the table for her. She adamantly explained that doing so really took away from its gravity as a human rights and gender-based violence issue. I wondered if this training was also going to avoid treating it as a cultural issue, especially because her organization was supposed to be coordinating the training alongside another anti-trafficking organization. I point this out to show that there were critical perspectives present in these trainings as well.

2. Legal scholar Leti Volpp (2011, 92) has written about how the construction of violence in Muslim immigrant communities relies on the curation of facts that depict violence in immigrant families as directly linked to cultural pathologies.

3. There was a moment when Alice explained that "forced marriage does happen across a range of ethnic communities, including White Anglo immigrants." She proceeded to give an example of marriage occurring within Irish Catholic families in the 1950s if someone had a child out of wedlock. In doing so, Alice signals that pressures around marriage in White Anglo communities happened but were mostly relegated to the historical past and no longer pose an issue of concern.

4. While the AFP had statistics about the number of reports it received nationally and statewide, there were no statistics on which reports were actually investigated.

5. Hannah Arendt (1958, 181) addresses the difficulties of distinguishing between "who" people are versus "what" they are—the challenges of developing a grammar that adequately captures the complexities and essences of individuals. This can certainly be said to apply to the space of family violence prevention and its practitioners, who often had difficulty expressing who their clients were. She writes in the chapter on "Action" in *The Human Condition*:

> The manifestation of who the speaker and doer unexchangeably is, though it is plainly visible, retains a curious intangibility that confounds all efforts toward unequivocal verbal expression. The moment we want to say *who* somebody is, our very vocabulary leads us astray into saying *what* he is; we get entangled in a description of qualities he necessarily shares with others like him; we begin to describe a type or a "character" in the old meaning of the word, with the result that his specific uniqueness escapes us. This frustration has the closest affinity with the well-known philosophic impossibility to arrive at a definition of man, all definitions being determinations or interpretations of *what* man is, of qualities, therefore, which he could possibly share with other living beings, whereas his specific difference would be found in a determination of what kind of a "who" he is (Arendt 1958, 181).

6. Lila Abu Lughod writes:

> To a great extent, the construction of the honor crime gives legitimacy and resilience not just to all the mechanisms of regulation, surveillance, discipline, and punishment that Foucault and others have taught us to understand as intrinsic to modern state power but to the specific forms and forums of transnational governance, whether neoliberal, humanitarian, or military, that are so characteristic of the contemporary global world. Blaming culture means not just flattening and fixing cultures, stripping moral systems of their complexity, homogenizing human experiences within communities, and occluding political and social interventions of the most modern kind, but ignoring the dynamism of historical and political transformations of women, families, and everyday social and cultural life and experience (2011, 44).

7. According to the National Children's Youth and Law Centre's 2013 report on forced marriage in Australia, between 2011 and 2013, eight cases were identified by criminal investigators out of 103 referrals made to the AFP, whereas according to the AFP, only eleven cases were referred in 2013 (Hildebrandt 2022).

CHAPTER 3   RELUCTANT DISCLOSURE

1. Other pieces have looked at how assimilationist programs function in the workplace in relation to Muslim women (Aziz 2014; 2015), within social welfare (Ahmad and Sheriff 2001; Husain and O'Brien 1999), and in projects tied to economic inclusion (Fozdar 2014). Taking these studies as an important basis for this research, I extend this literature by examining what happens when the demand to rescue through risk assessment brushes up against practitioner ethics and their everyday understandings of student realities.

2. School staff operated with a sense of themselves as practitioners of culturally competent social welfare and as what Ghassan Hage (2000, 23) has termed "multiculturalists." In Hage's study, the multiculturalists deploy a "more sophisticated fantasy of White supremacy" to maintain their position in the politically and culturally dominant social group. They do so by excluding from public discourse and spaces other cultural realities that are not explicitly recognized within public spaces and discourses. However, I posit that the school staff I observed, while they would identify as aligned with multiculturalism as a social and political ideal, oftentimes do not neatly fit within this paradigm because they are not interested in looking at whether the "cultural other" fits within the hegemonic norms of the nation, nor are they particularly invested in keeping the realities of their students away from public discourse.

3. Cristiana Giordano's ethnography, *Migrants in Translation*, is particularly inspiring. Her analysis focuses on how different social welfare actors reimagine what begins as the Italian state's explicitly dehumanizing approach to asylum seeker and refugee rights, rooted in a misrecognition of migrant narratives. Giordano (2014, 11) shows how Catholic nuns and state bureaucrats try to develop "alternative forms of translation to mitigate the violent effects of misrecognition," resulting in a turn to imperfect forms of culturally competent approaches to social welfare that produce other reductive categories of recognition.

4. This includes the person demonstrating anxiety, suicidal thoughts, depressive tendencies, and self-harm.

CHAPTER 4   PHANTOM FIGURES

1. As of early 2016, a policy advisor for the ARC's STPP had reported that the agency was housing thirty-five people, up from fourteen in 2015. However, the number of those who were forced marriage victims was not disclosed.

2. Engseng Ho (2006, 117) uses the concept of present absences to describe the ways in which the mobile diaspora thinks about the absence of the dead as a life-giving force—a potent presence around which a strong sociality forms. Those who are absent create sociality and their being is marked through their stories' silent presences. I do not want to draw an analogous situation here between the analytic significance of Ho's interlocutors—the Hadrami diaspora—with those circulated about the sisters. However, I do evoke the concept to connote how the omission of victims/survivors from particular social welfare domains, especially spaces of advocacy, rendered them present in the stories but absent from the crafting of these stories.

3. The case as an amalgam of institutional logics is an important premise for this chapter. In the forced marriage sector, I see "the case" as constructed through the logic of culturally competent social welfare (tracing those family relations) and criminality (identifying the moment when someone was coerced for the purpose of developing a case for potential prosecution).

4. By this, I mean that unlike family violence prevention, the criminal justice arm is not always viewed as a means to get a victim or at-risk person the support they need. However, because forced marriage is a criminal act, the federal police need to be involved in investigating any reports of an imminent forced marriage or one that is alleged to have taken place.
5. It is not clear that these were the sisters' actual ages. It was reported by practitioners that they may have been older than eighteen.
6. When I conducted fieldwork, CPS was hesitant to intervene in the situation of anyone over the age of sixteen, because they were no longer considered a minor.
7. While they were from Afghanistan, Greg had misidentified them as Pakistani.
8. For example, at a VFMN meeting, a senior researcher with a national advocacy and research organization focusing on human trafficking, brought up the organization's research proposal to gather more evidence around forced marriage, namely victim experiences of support services and what led to their coercion into marriage. She noted that their proposal hit a stumbling block in that it did not receive funding from Australia's National Research Organization for Women's Safety (ANROWS). She mentioned that ANROWS did not understand that doing research with the actual victims would be impossible because they needed to rely on organizations to talk to them, and it was not safe to talk to them directly. At a prior meeting, the researcher had introduced the project as an exploration of social service direct response and seemed disappointed that the research could not engage with victims themselves, even though that is where the research gaps were.
9. The only research report that has included victim narratives is published by the Australian Muslim Women's Centre for Human Rights (Prattis and Matrah 2017), titled "Marrying Young: An Exploratory Study of Young Muslim Women's Decision-Making around Early Marriage."
10. Nelson (2001, 307) also sees the phantom limb as encompassed by transnational bodies like corporations, empires, and nation-states that "reach out and inhabit prosthetics in violent ways." Thus, that which is a supposed phantom is shaped by enduring histories and structures of violence.
11. Legal scholar Richard Sherwin writes about the demands of legal narratives in their relation to the complexity of real lives:

> Law's demand for truth and justice can clash with the modern mind's demand for closure and certainty. When truth defies certainty and becomes complex, justice requires difficult decisions on the basis of that doubt. The struggle between shifting cognitive needs and legal duty is commonplace, and without a way to question how a given narrative shapes and informs our desire for certain and tidy justice, that desire, and competing ones, cannot be adequately understood. As a result, the kind of justice operating in a particular case at a given cultural juncture may remain confused or hidden from view. (1994, 41)

CHAPTER 5 BEYOND CRIMINALITY

1. James Clifford's critique of culture as a primordialist construction notes the following: "Cultures are not scientific 'objects' (assuming such things exist, even in the natural sciences). Culture, and our view of 'it,' are produced historically and are actively contested (1986, 18)." And "If culture is not an object to be described, neither is it a unified corpus of symbols and meanings that can be definitively interpreted. Culture is contested, temporal, and emergent. Representation and explanation—both by insiders and outsiders—is implicated in this emergence" (1986, 19).

2. In her analysis of the criminalization of violence against women in Ecuador's constitution, Silvana Tapia Tapia (2016) explains that there are ongoing discontinuities with how gender norms, women's family roles, and the lived realities of women trying to access justice through the courts are dismissed. This is due to the privileging of a penalization logic, thereby obscuring alternative approaches to justice.

3. In saying this, I do not mean to discount the possibility that my interlocutors' worldviews have over time been shaped by understandings of personhood, sociality, and accountability that have generationally been passed down through Islamic religious discourse, praxis, or institutions, and social milieus that have been shaped by Islam as a dynamic discursive tradition (Asad 1986). However, this did not emerge in any explicitly identifiable way, but one should leave room for the possibility that it may have a role to play in shaping their interpretations of their lived experience.

4. In her ethnography of the forensic mediation of sexual violence in Baltimore, Maryland, Sameena Mulla (2014) discusses the various imaginaries of the home that subtend biopolitical regimes of governance. The home is a site of intimacy and stability but always potential risk and danger: "Although popular imaginaries regard and construct home as a location of intimacy and stability, the indexing of a range of behaviors and events within continually evolving discourses of 'home invasion' or 'domestic violence' demonstrate the institutionalization of statistical patterns of harm in or near the home" (2014, 178).

5. While for my interlocutors, the domestic space did map on to the space of the home, it is important to point out that this is not always the case. The domestic differs from the conceptualization of it in policy reports because: a) The domestic is, for many migrants, a liminal space and does not map on to the domicile or an owned piece of property. For migrants, the domestic can also mean the broader collective of people in their everyday lives that, while locally situated, is also geographically disbursed; b) For migrants, domesticity does not necessarily map on to the private sphere. The community relations that make up what we might call domestic life are nurturing, coercive, and deeply shaped by everyday structural conditions.

6. In *The Pastoral Clinic*, Angela García (2010) explores how family and community, while enabling each other's drug use, would provide each other with basic needs and tend to each other's illness. The alternative was the threat of imprisonment and constant policing via drug rehabilitation programs intertwined with the criminal justice system. For García, "care is not a life-affirming gesture reserved only for humanitarians toward the destitute, the healthy toward the sick, those who supposedly 'have' a life toward those who don't. Rather, care is *threaded through* the very practices (such as doing heroin) that may ultimately kill you" (2010, 179).

7. By carceral, I do not refer only to the use of the prison system to penalize perpetrators. The carceral refers to a whole array of technologies, structures, and tactics used and sanctioned by the state to contain and isolate the perpetrator from everyday social relations. These include temporary and long-term forms of imprisonment, but also detention centers and immigration holding facilities. According to Ruby Tapia, "The carceral state encompasses the formal institutions and operations and economies of the criminal justice system proper, but it also encompasses logics, ideologies, practices, and structures, that invest in tangible and sometimes intangible ways in punitive orientations to difference, to poverty, to struggles to social justice and to the crossers of constructed borders of all kind" (Tapia 2020).

8. Adelman (2004, 132–133) writes, "Scholarly revelation of the normative rather than of the deviant nature of domestic violence thus may undermine the original intent of such research to provide locally specific remedies. At the same time, rather than

resulting in the excuse or protection of such practices, culturalizing domestic violence may result in the demonization of culture." She has also written about the dangers of culturalizing certain practices from a scholarly perspective. She writes that viewing such norms as resulting from culture may lead to not only condoning violent practices but ignoring what people are doing locally to address them.

9. It is important to note, however, that Layla does mobilize orientalist stereotypes of certain countries in the region as antithetical to "freedom" because of symbols like the headscarf. Her remarks also create a dichotomy between Australia as a site of freedom and the Middle East as a site of oppression.

10. In this case, Wool is talking about Daniel, who has recently returned from serving a military tour in Iraq and is managing his relationship with Sam through a heteronormative conjugal lens. However, I find the idea that one sees obligations to others as an entry point into solidifying intimate relations resonant with my interlocutors' experiences.

11. Concerns with what happens when migrants return from an overseas marriage were discussed at various forums toward the latter part of my fieldwork. At the attorney-general's workshop on forced marriage in downtown Melbourne, a practitioner from an anti-trafficking and antislavery organization noted that schools were the primary sites where reporting of forced marriages occurred. She mentioned an example of an Afghan girl in Sydney who was married in Afghanistan. However, upon living together in Australia, the girl left her husband and the practitioner mentioned that her community held her up as an example of what could happen when a girl leaves her husband. Being ostracized from the community was seen as just as bad as, if not worse than, the marriage itself. The marriage was seen to lead to a host of other violences, including marital rape and physical and emotional abuse. It was not necessarily marriage itself that predicted such violences. While it is difficult to say what the statistical correlation is between coercion into marriage and these attendant forms of violence, the following is implied: a) When one does consent to marriage, one is immune or less at risk from such violences; and b) Community ostracism needs to be an object of legal intervention by the state, raising the question of which communities become subject to such forms of intervention and why. These forms of ostracism occurred in marriages entered into with full and free consent.

12. It is important to note that, in Sitara and Gulnaz's stories, the presence of their mothers and other female extended family members is not discussed. The fact that these are omissions in their responses is telling—it could be the case that they were not part of these conversations on marriage; or that they were, and my interlocutors chose not to discuss what role they did or did not play. These omissions reflect how women are subject to patriarchal logics but also overdetermined by them. This chapter was an attempt to find a middle ground in analyzing how familial coercion plays out and affects how people conceive of themselves as agentive beings.

REFERENCES

Abu-Lughod, Lila. 1991. "Writing against Culture." In *Recapturing Anthropology: Working in the Present*, edited by Richard Fox, 137–162. Santa Fe: School of American Research Press.

———. 2002. "Do Muslim Women Really Need Saving? Anthropological Reflections on Cultural Relativism and Its Others." *American Anthropologist* 104, no. 3 (September): 783–790.

———. 2011. "Seductions of the 'Honour Crime.'" *differences: A Journal of Feminist Cultural Studies* 22, no. 1 (May): 17–63.

———. 2013. *Do Muslim Women Need Saving?* Cambridge, MA: Harvard University Press.

Adelman, Madelaine. 2004. "Domestic Violence and Difference." *American Ethnologist* 31, no. 1 (February): 131–141.

Adey, Peter. 2009. "Facing Airport Security: Affect, Biopolitics, and the Preemptive Securitization of the Mobile Body." *Environment and Planning D: Society and Space* 27, no. 1 (January): 274–295.

Ahmad, Fauzia, and Sara Sheriff. 2001. "Muslim Women of Europe: Welfare Needs and Responses." *Social Work in Europe* 8, no. 1 (January): 2–10.

Alamri, Abeer Ahmed. 2013. "Participation of Muslim Female Students in Sporting Activities in Australian Public High Schools: The Impact of Religion." *Journal of Muslim Minority Affairs* 33, no. 3 (November): 418–429.

Alcorn, Gay, and Mike Bowers. 2018. "Morwell: A Powerhouse in the Grip of Coal Transition." *Guardian*, October 28, 2018. https://www.theguardian.com/australia-news/ng-interactive/2018/oct/28/victorian-election-2018-on-the-ground-in-morwell-part-one.

Almarhoun, Safa, and Hala Nasr. 2013. "'The Choice is Yours!' Forced Marriage: Beyond Criminalisation." *The Victorian Immigrant and Refugee Women's Coalition*. Paper Presented at the UNAA Status of Women Network's Roundtable, August 8, 2013.

Althusser, Louis. 1970. "Ideology and Ideological State Apparatuses (Notes Towards an Investigation)." In *The Anthropology of the State: A Reader*, edited by Aradhana Sharma and Akhil Gupta, 86–98. Oxford: Blackwell Publishing.

Al-Yaman, Fadwa, Mieke Van Doeland, and Michelle Wallis. 2006. *Family Violence among Aboriginal and Torres Strait Islander Peoples*. Canberra: Australian Institute of Health and Welfare.

Amoore, Louise. 2006. "Biometric Borders: Governing Mobilities in the War on Terror." *Political Geography* 25, no. 3 (March): 336–351.

Andersson, Ruben. 2014. "Time and the Migrant Other: European Border Controls and the Temporal Economics of Illegality." *American Anthropologist* 116, no. 4 (November): 795–809.

———. 2018. "The Price of Impact: Reflections on Academic Outreach amid the 'Refugee Crisis.'" *Social Anthropology* 26, no. 2 (December): 222–237.

Anitha, Sundari, and Aisha K. Gill. 2009. "Coercion, Consent, and the Forced Marriage Debate in the UK." *Feminist Legal Studies* 17: 165–184.

Anti-Discrimination Act 1977 (NSW). http://classic.austlii.edu.au/au/legis/nsw/consol_act/aa1977204/.

Appiah, Kwame Anthony. 1994. "Identity, Authenticity, Survival: Multicultural Societies and Social Reproduction." In *Multiculturalism: Examining the Politics of Recognition*, edited by Amy Guttmann, 149–164. Princeton: Princeton University Press.

———. 2016. "There Is No Such Thing as Western Civilisation." *Guardian*, November 9, 2016. https://www.theguardian.com/world/2016/nov/09/western-civilisation-appiah-reith-lecture.

Archambault, Caroline S. 2011. "Ethnographic Empathy and the Social Context of Rights: 'Rescuing' Maasai Girls from Early Marriage." *American Anthropologist* 113, no. 4 (November): 632–643.

Arendt, Hannah. 1958. *The Human Condition*. Chicago: University of Chicago Press.

Asad, Talal. 1986. "The Idea of an Anthropology of Islam." Occasional Papers Series. Washington, DC: Center for Contemporary Arab Studies, Georgetown University.

———. 2003. *Formations of the Secular: Christianity, Islam, Modernity*. Stanford: Stanford University Press.

Askola, Heli. 2018. "Responding to Vulnerability? Forced Marriage and the Law." *University of New South Wales Law Journal* 41, no. 3 (September): 977–1003.

Attorney-General's Department. 2018. *Religious Freedom Review: Report of the Expert Panel*. May 18, 2018. https://www.ag.gov.au/sites/default/files/2020-03/religious-freedom-review-expert-panel-report-2018.pdf.

———. n.d. *Forced Marriage Overview*. https://www.ag.gov.au/crime/people-smuggling-and-human-trafficking/forced-marriage.

Australian Bureau of Statistics. 2016. "Morwell (Eastern Victoria): 2016 Census All Persons QuickStats." https://www.abs.gov.au/census/find-census-data/quickstats/2016/SED25402.

Australian Catholic Religious against Human Trafficking. 2020. "My Rights—My Future: Forced Marriage: A Kit of Learning and Teaching Materials and Support Documents for Australian Secondary Schools." Updated June 2020. https://acrath.org.au/wp-content/uploads/2020/07/My-Rights-My-Future-forced-marriage-Kit-updated-June-2020.pdf.

Australian Department of Home Affairs. 2017. *Forced Marriage Information Sheet*. https://www.homeaffairs.gov.au/criminal-justice/files/forced-marriage-info-sheet.pdf.

Australian Federal Police (AFP). 2021a. "AFP Helping to Keep Afghan Arrivals Safe." December 17, 2021. https://www.afp.gov.au/news-media/media-extranet/afp-helping-keep-afghan-arrivals-safe.

———. 2021b. "Parliamentary Joint Committee on Law Enforcement: Inquiry into Law Enforcement Capabilities in Relation to Child Exploitation." August 25, 2021.

Australian Human Rights Commission. 2015. "Crimes Legislation Amendment (Powers, Offences and Other Measures) Bill 2015 (Cth)." https://humanrights.gov.au/our-work/legal/submission/crimes-legislation-amendment-powers-offences-and-other-measures-bill-2015.

———. 2018. "Face the Facts: Gender Equality in 2018." https://humanrights.gov.au/our-work/education/face-facts-gender-equality-2018.

Australian Institute of Health and Welfare. 2022. "Family, Domestic and Sexual Violence." https://www.aihw.gov.au/reports-data/behaviours-risk-factors/domestic-violence/data.

Australian Red Cross. 2019. "Forced Marriage: Community Voices, Stories and Strategies: Consultation with Community." Accessed December 1, 2019. https://www.redcross.org.au/getmedia/ad745e1b-c62f-4831-b8c3-a389b3037c34/Forced-Marriage-Community-Voices-Stories-and-Strategies-Australian-Red-Cross.pdf.aspx.

Aziz, Sahar F. 2014. "Coercive Assimilationism: The Perils of Muslim Women's Identity Performance in the Workplace." *Michigan Journal of Race and Law* 20, no. 1: 1–61.

———. 2015. "Coercing Assimilation: The Case of Muslim Women of Color." *Journal of Gender, Race, and Justice* 18: 389–398.
Baker, Emily. 2018. "Report Details Abuse of Forced Marriage Victims Living in Australia." *Canberra Times*, June 30, 2018. https://www.canberratimes.com.au/story/6015486/report-details-abuse-of-forced-marriage-victims-living-in-australia/.
Ballestero, Andrea S. 2012. "Transparency Short-Circuited: Laughter and Numbers in Costa Rican Water Politics." *PoLAR: Political and Legal Anthropology Review* 35, no. 2 (November): 223–241.
Banasiak, Dorota. 2016. "Migrant Women at Risk of Domestic Violence: SBS's Multilingual Report." *SBS News*, May 15, 2016. https://www.sbs.com.au/radio/explainer/migrant-women-risk-domestic-violence-sbss-multilingual-report.
Barker, K. 2012. "Influenza Preparedness and the Bureaucratic Reflex: Anticipating and Generating the 2009 H1N1 Event." *Health Place* 18, no. 4 (July): 701–709.
Barlas, Asma. 2002. *"Believing Women" in Islam: Unreading Patriarchal Interpretations of the Qur'an*. Austin: University of Texas Press.
Barrowclough, Anne. 2014. "It Is the Young Flesh They Want." *New Age Islam*, June 14, 2014. https://www.newageislam.com/islam-women-feminism/anne-barrowclough/it-young-flesh-they-want/d/87622
Basu, Srimati. 2015. *The Trouble with Marriage: Feminists Confront Law and Violence in India*. Berkeley: University of California Press.
Baudrillard, Jean. 1994. *Simulacra and Simulation*. Ann Arbor: University of Michigan Press.
Bell, Colleen. 2006. "Subject to Exception: Security Certificates, National Security and Canada's Role in the 'War on Terror.'" *Canadian Journal of Law and Society* 21, no. 1 (July): 63–83.
Berlant, Lauren. 1991. *The Anatomy of National Fantasy: Hawthorne, Utopia, and Everyday Life*. Chicago: University of Chicago Press.
———. 1998. "Intimacy: A Special Issue." *Critical Inquiry* 24, no. 2 (Winter): 281–288.
Berlant, Lauren, and Michael Warner. 1998. "Sex in Public." *Critical Inquiry* 24, no. 2 (Winter): 547–566.
Bernard, H. Russell. 2006. *Research Methods in Anthropology: Qualitative and Quantitative Approaches*. 4th ed. Lanham, MD: AltaMira Press.
———. 2012. *Social Research Methods: Qualitative and Quantitative Approaches*. 2nd ed. Los Angeles: SAGE Publications.
Bernstein, Elizabeth. 2010. "Militarized Humanitarianism Meets Carceral Feminism: The Politics of Sex, Rights, and Freedom in Contemporary Antitrafficking Campaigns." *Signs: Journal of Women in Culture and Society* 36, no. 1 (Autumn): 45–71.
Beydoun, Khaled A. 2018. *American Islamophobia: Understanding the Roots and Rise of Fear*. Berkeley: University of California Press.
Bloemraad, Irene, Anna Korteweg, and Gökçe Yurdakul. 2008. "Citizenship and Immigration: Multiculturalism, Assimilation, and Challenges to the Nation-State." *Annual Review of Sociology* 34: 153–179.
Borneman, John. 2001. "Caring and Being Cared For: Displacing Marriage, Kinship, Gender, and Sexuality." In *The Ethics of Kinship: Ethnographic Inquiries*, edited by James D. Faubion, 25–43. Lanham, MD: Rowman & Littlefield.
———. 2005. "Marriage Today." *American Ethnologist* 32, no. 1 (February): 30–33.
Boyle, Kaitlin M., and Kimberly B. Rogers. 2020. "Beyond the Rape 'Victim'-'Survivor' Binary: How Race, Gender, and Identity Processes Interact to Shape Distress." *Sociological Forum* 35, no. 2 (February): 323–345.
Bredal, Anja. 2011. "Border Control to Prevent Forced Marriage: Choosing Between Protecting Women and Protecting the Nation." In *Forced Marriage: Introducing a Social Justice and*

Human Rights Perspective, edited by Aisha K. Gill and Anitha Sundari, 90–111. New York: Zed Books.

Briskman, Linda. 2016. "Decolonizing Social Work in Australia: Prospect or Illusion." In *Indigenous Social Work around the World: Towards Culturally Relevant Education and Practice*, edited by Mel Gray, John Coates, and Michael Yellow Bird, 83–96. London: Routledge.

Brown, Jessica. 2016. "Human Rights, Gay Rights, or Both: International Human Rights Law and Same-Sex Marriage." *Florida Journal of International Law* 28, no. 217 (January): 218–239.

Brown, Wendy. 1995. *States of Injury: Power and Freedom in Late Modernity*. Princeton: Princeton University Press.

Brueggemann, Ingar, and Karen Newman. 1998. "For Better, for Worse." *Health and Human Rights* 3, no. 2: 54–64.

Bryant, Colleen, and Matthew Willis. 2008. *Risk Factors in Indigenous Violent Victimisation*. January 5, 2008. Australian Institute of Criminology.

Burke, Liz. 2016. "The Slave Trade in Our Own Backyard." *News.com.au*, December 2, 2016. https://www.news.com.au/lifestyle/real-life/news-life/the-slave-trade-in-our-own-backyard/news-story/a11b95d95f4e3e37ec1b444e59eb02e1.

Burn, Jennifer. 2013. "Putting an End to Forced Marriage in Australia." *Conversation*, October 19, 2013. https://theconversation.com/putting-an-end-to-forced-marriage-in-australia-17827.

Burn, Jennifer, and Frances Simmons. 2014. "Without Consent: Forced Marriage in Australia." *Melbourne University Law Review* 36, no. 3: 970–1008.

Cabot, Heath. 2019. "The Business of Anthropology and the European Refugee Regime." *American Ethnologist* 46, no. 3 (August): 261–275.

Caduff, Carlo. 2014. "On the Verge of Death: Visions of Biological Vulnerability." *Annual Review of Anthropology* 43: 105–21.

Calma, Tom. 2006. "What Does Australia Need to Do for Cultural Competence to Flourish?" Speech at the Cultural Competencies Conference, Australian Human Rights Commission, December 8, 2006. https://humanrights.gov.au/about/news/speeches/cultural-competencies-conference.

Campbell, R., S. M. Wasco, C. E. Ahrens, T. Sefl, and H. E. Barnes. 2001. "Preventing the 'Second Rape': Rape Survivors' Experiences with Community Service Providers." *Journal of Interpersonal Violence* 16, no. 12: 1239–1259.

Canaday, Margot. 2009. *The Straight State: Sexuality and Citizenship in Twentieth-Century America*. Princeton: Princeton University Press.

Carey, Jane, and Claire McLisky, eds. 2009. *Creating White Australia*. Sydney: Sydney University Press.

Carpi, Estella. 2017. "'Muslim Women' and Gender Inequality in Australia's Assimilationist-Undocumented Migration, Health Care and Public Policy in Germany Multicultural Policies. Participation in Sport as a Case Study." *About Gender-International Journal of Gender Studies* 6, no. 11: 324–353.

Carsten, Janet. 2003. *After Kinship*. Cambridge: Cambridge University Press.

Castañeda, Claudia. 2002. *Figurations: Child, Bodies, Worlds*. Durham, NC: Duke University Press.

Castañeda, Heide. 2008. "Undocumented Migration, Health Care and Public Policy in Germany." *Anthropology News*, May 2008.

———. 2012. "'Over-Foreignization' or 'Unused Potential'? A Critical Review of Migrant Health in Germany and Responses toward Unauthorized Migration." *Social Science & Medicine* 74, no. 6 (March): 830–838.

Centre for Multicultural Youth. 2016. "I Don't: A Forum Addressing Forced Marriage in Victoria: Report." Accessed October 6, 2016. https://www.cmy.net.au/sites/default/files/publication-documents/Final%20Report_Forced%20Marriage%20Forum.pdf.

REFERENCES

Cheers, Brian, Margaret Binell, Heather Coleman, Ian Gentle, Grace Miller, Judy Taylor, and Colin Weetra. 2006. "Family Violence: An Australian Indigenous Community Tells Its Story." *International Social Work* 49, no. 1 (January): 51–63.

Chen, Nancy N., and Leslie A. Sharp, eds. 2014. *Bioinsecurity and Vulnerability*. New Mexico: SAR Press.

Chouliaraki, Lilie, and Rafal Zaborowski. 2017. "Voice and Community in the 2015 Refugee Crisis: A Content Analysis of News Coverage in Eight European Countries." *International Communication Gazette* 79, no. 6–7 (September): 613–635.

Clifford, James. 1986. "Introduction: Partial Truths." In *Writing Culture: The Poetics and Politics of Ethnography*, edited by James Clifford and George Marcus. Berkeley: University of California Press.

Clifford, James, and George E. Marcus, eds. 1986. *Writing Culture: The Poetics and Politics of Ethnography*. Berkeley: University of California Press.

Collier, Jane F., Bill Maurer, and Liliana Suárez-Návaz. 1995. "Sanctioned Identities: Legal Constructions of Modern Personhood." *Identities* 21, no. 1–2 (May): 1–27.

Collier, Stephen J., and Andrew Lakoff. 2008a. "On Regimes of Living." In *Global Assemblages: Technology, Politics, and Ethics as Anthropological Problems*, edited by Aihwa Ong and Stephen J. Collier, 22–39. Oxford: Blackwell Publishing.

———. 2008b. "The Problem of Securing Health." In *Biosecurity Interventions*, edited by Stephen J. Collier and Andrew Lakoff, 7–32. New York: Columbia University Press.

Constable Nicole. 2009. "Sexuality and Discipline among Filipina Domestic Workers in Hong Kong." In *Gender in Cross-Cultural Perspective*, edited by C. Brettell and Carolyn Sargent, 545–564. Upper Saddle River, NJ: Pearson Prentice Hall.

cooke, miriam. 2007. "The Muslimwoman." *Contemporary Islam* 1: 139–154.

Cooper, Lesley, and Mary Morris. 2005. *Sustainable Tenancy for Indigenous Families: What Services and Policy Supports Are Needed?* Australian Housing and Urban Research Institute Final Report No. 81. Melbourne, Victoria.

Coutin, Susan B. 2000. "Denationalization, Inclusion, and Exclusion: Negotiating the Boundaries of Belonging." *Indiana Journal of Global Legal Studies* 7, no. 2 (Spring): 585–593.

Crimes Legislation Amendment (Slavery, Slavery-Like Conditions and People Trafficking) Act 2013 (Cth) S. 270.7A. 2013. https://www.ato.gov.au/law/view/pdf/acts/20130006.pdf

Das, Veena. 2006. *Life and Words: Violence and the Descent into the Ordinary*. Berkeley: University of California Press.

———. 2008. "Violence, Gender, and Subjectivity." *Annual Review of Anthropology* 37 (October): 283–299.

———. 2013. "Violence, Crisis, and the Everyday." *International Journal of Middle East Studies* 45, no. 4 (November): 798–800.

Das, Veena, Jonathan M. Ellen, and Lori Leonard. 2008. "On the Modalities of the Domestic." *Home Cultures* 5, no. 3 (April): 348–372.

Das, Veena, Arthur Kleinman, Mamphela Ramphele, and Pamela Reynolds, eds. 2001. *Violence and Subjectivity*. Berkeley: University of California Press.

Das, Veena, and Deborah Poole. 2004. "Anthropology in the Margins of the State." *PoLAR: Political and Legal Anthropology Review* 30, no. 1: 140–144.

Dastyari, Azadeh, and Asher Hirsch. 2019. "The Ring of Steel: Extraterritorial Migration Controls in Indonesia and Libya and the Complicity of Australia and Italy." *Human Rights Law Review* 19, no. 3: 435–465.

Dastyari, Azadeh, and Maria O'Sullivan. 2016. "Not for Export: The Failure of Australia's Extraterritorial Processing Regime in Papua New Guinea and the Decision of the PNG Supreme Court in 'Namah.'" *Monash University Law Review* 42, no. 2 (August): 308–338.

Dauvergne, Catherine, and Jennifer Millbank. 2010. "Forced Marriage and the Exoticization of Gendered Harms in United States Asylum Law." *Columbia Journal of Gender & Law* 19, no. 4 (February): 898–964.

Debenport, Erin. 2015. *Fixing the Books: Secrecy, Literacy, and Perfectibility in Indigenous New Mexico*. Santa Fe: SAR Press.

Deery, Shannon. 2017. "Experts Warn Child Bride Cases 'Tip of the Iceberg.'" *Herald Sun*, May 1, 2017. https://www.heraldsun.com.au/news/law-order/experts-warn-child-bride-cases-tip-of-the-iceberg/news-story/01c84b898173902056e8d86f84a52874&memtype=anonymous.

De Genova, Nicholas P. 2002. "Migrant 'Illegality' and Deportability in Everyday Life." *Annual Review of Anthropology* 31: 419–447.

———. 2017. "Introduction: The Borders of Europe and the European Question." In *The Borders of "Europe": Autonomy of Migration, Tactics of Bordering*, edited by Nicholas P. De Genova, 1–36. Durham, NC: Duke University Press.

De Jong, Ferdinand. 2007. *Masquerades of Modernity: Power and Secrecy in Casamance, Senegal*. Edinburgh: Edinburgh University Press.

De La Cadena, Marisol. 2010. "Indigenous Cosmopolitics in the Andes: Conceptual Reflections Beyond 'Politics'" *Cultural Anthropology* 24, no. 2 (April): 334–370.

De La Concha, Ángeles. 2017. "Erasing Female Victimhood: The Debate over Trauma and Truth." In *Victimhood and Vulnerability in 21st Century Fiction*, edited by Jean-Michel Ganteau and Susana Onega, 71–89. London: Routledge.

Delaney, David, and Helga Leitner. 1997. "The Political Construction of Scale." *Political Geography* 16, no. 2 (February): 93–97.

Department of Foreign Affairs and Trade. 2020. "Australian Government Response to the Human Rights Sub-committee of the Joint Standing Committee on Foreign Affairs, Defence and Trade Report: Advocating for the Elimination of Child and Forced Marriage." https://www.dfat.gov.au/sites/default/files/government-response-advocating-for-the-elimination-of-child-and-forced-marriage.pdf.

Department of Home Affairs. 2015. *National Action Plan to Combat Human Trafficking and Slavery: 2015–2019*. https://www.homeaffairs.gov.au/criminal-justice/files/trafficking-national-action-plan-combat-human-trafficking-slavery-2015-19.pdf.

Department of Social Services. 2016. *Third Action Plan of the National Plan to Reduce Violence against Women and Their Children 2016–2019*. https://www.dss.gov.au/sites/default/files/documents/10_2016/third_action_plan.pdf.

———. 2019a. *Forced and Early Marriage Fact Sheet*. March 7, 2019. https://www.dss.gov.au/women/publications-articles/reducing-violence/forced-and-early-marriage.

———. 2019b. *Fourth Action Plan of the National Plan to Reduce Violence against Women and Their Children (2019–2022)*. October 17, 2019. https://www.dss.gov.au/women-publications-articles-reducing-violence/fourth-action-plan.

———. n.d. *The National Plan to Reduce Violence against Women and Their Children 2010–2022*. https://www.dss.gov.au/women/programs-services/reducing-violence/the-national-plan-to-reduce-violence-against-women-and-their-children-2010-2022.

Dhingra, Reva, Mitchell Kilborn, and Olivia Woldemikael. 2021. "Immigration Policies and Access to the Justice System: The Effect of Enforcement Escalations on Undocumented Immigrants and Their Communities." *Political Behavior* 44: 1–29.

Dillon, Michael, and Luis Lobo-Guerrero. 2008. "Biopolitics of Security in the 21st Century." *The Review of International Studies* 34, no. 2 (April): 265–292.

Direction No. 90: Migration Act 1958 (Cth). March 8, 2021. https://immi.homeaffairs.gov.au/support-subsite/files/ministerial-direction-no-90.pdf.

Dittfeld, Tanja. 2020. "Seeing White: Turning the Postcolonial Lens on Social Work in Australia." *Social Work and Policy Studies: Social Justice, Practice, and Theory* 3, no.1: 1–21.

Douglas, Mary, and Aaron Wildavsky. 1982. *Risk and Culture: An Essay on the Selection of Technological and Environmental Dangers.* Berkeley: University of California Press.

Dreher, Melanie, and Neil MacNaughton. 2002. "Cultural Competence in Nursing: Foundation or Fallacy?" *Nursing Outlook* 50, no. 5 (September–October): 181–186.

Duncan, Sam, and Max Margan. 2017. "More than 50 Australian Girls as Young as Nine Married Off as Child Brides to Older Men—Often Leaving the Country before Police Can Stop Them." *Daily Mail*, September 12, 2017. https://www.dailymail.co.uk/news/article-4878544/Child-brides-Underage-girls-forced-marry-Australia.html.

Dunn, Kevin, and Jacqueline K. Nelson. 2011. "Challenging the Public Denial of Racism for a Deeper Multiculturalism." *Journal of Intercultural Studies* 32, no. 6 (November): 587–602.

Dziedzic, Stephen, and Henry Belot. 2017. "Australian Citizenship Law Changes Mean Migrants Will Face Tougher Tests." *ABC News*, April 20, 2017. https://www.abc.net.au/news/2017-04-20/migrants-to-face-tougher-tests-for-australian-citizenship/8456392.

Edgar, Iain R., and Andrew Russell. 1998. "Research and Practice in the Anthropology of Welfare." In *The Anthropology of Welfare*, edited by Andrew Russell and Iain R. Edgar. London: Routledge.

Eid, Paul. 2015. "Balancing Agency, Gender and Race: How Do Muslim Female Teenagers in Quebec Negotiate the Social Meanings Embedded in the Hijab?" *Ethnic and Racial Studies* 38, no. 11 (February): 1902–1917.

Elder, Catriona. 2016. "The Proposition: Imagining Race, Family, and Violence on the Nineteenth-Century Australian Frontier." *Ilha do Desterro* 69, no. 2: 165–176.

Ellinghaus, Katherine. 2003. "Absorbing the 'Aboriginal Problem': Controlling Interracial Marriage in Australia in the Late 19th and Early 20th Centuries." *Aboriginal History* 27: 183–207.

El-Tayeb, Fatima. 2013. "Time Travelers and Queer Heterotopias: Narratives from the Muslim Underground." *The Germanic Review: Literature, Culture, Theory* 88, no. 3 (September): 305–319.

Evason, Nina. 2023. "Afghans in Australia." *Cultural Atlas SBS*. https://culturalatlas.sbs.com.au/afghan-culture/afghan-culture-afghans-in-australia.

Everingham, Sara. 2017. "Northern Territory Emergency Response: Views on 'Intervention' Differ 10 Years On." *ABC News*, June 20, 2017. https://www.abc.net.au/news/2017-06-21/northern-territory-intervention-flawed-indigenous-nt-scullion/8637034.

Fabian, Johannes. 1986. *Time and the Other: How Anthropology Makes Its Object.* New York: Columbia University Press.

Family Violence Protection Act 2008 (Vic). 2008. https://www.legislation.vic.gov.au/in-force/acts/family-violence-protection-act-2008/053.

Fassin, Didier. 2012. *Humanitarian Reason: A Moral History of the Present.* Berkeley: University of California Press.

Fassin, Didier, and Estelle D'Halluin. 2005. "The Truth from the Body: Medical Certificates as Ultimate Evidence for Asylum Seekers." *American Anthropologist* 107, no. 4 (December): 597–608.

Fassin, Didier, and Richard Rechtman. 2009. *The Empire of Trauma: An Inquiry into the Condition of Victimhood.* Princeton: Princeton University Press.

Faubion, James D. 2001. "Introduction: Toward an Anthropology of the Ethics of Kinship." In *The Ethics of Kinship: Ethnographic Inquiries*, edited by James D. Faubion, 1–28. New York: Rowman & Littlefield.

———. 2018. "On Parabiopolitical Reason." *Anthropological Theory* 19, no. 2 (May): 1–19.

Fekete, Liz. 2016. "Anti-Muslim Racism and the European Security State." *Institute of Race Relations* 46, no. 1 (July).

Fernando, Mayanthi. 2014. *The Republic Unsettled: Muslim French and the Contradictions of Secularism.* Durham, NC: Duke University Press.

Fitz-Gibbon, Kate, and Silke Meyer. 2021. "Two Experts on How Much the $1.1 Billion for Women's Safety Can Achieve." *Conversation*, May 12, 2021. https://theconversation.com/two-experts-on-how-much-the-1-1-billion-for-womens-safety-can-achieve-160764.

"Forced Marriage Cases Increasing: AFP." 2017. *SBS News*, May 1, 2017. https://www.sbs.com.au/news/article/forced-marriage-cases-increasing-afp/20tqlr3hf.

"Forced Marriages in Australia a Bigger Problem Than We Think." 2020. *Women's Forum: Australia*, November 17, 2020. https://www.womensforumaustralia.org/forced_marriages_in_australia_a_bigger_problem_than_we_think.

Forrest, James, Garth Lean, and Kevin Dunn. 2016. "Challenging Racism through Schools: Teacher Attitudes to Cultural Diversity and Multicultural Education in Sydney, Australia." *Race Ethnicity and Education* 19, no. 3 (November): 618–638.

Foucault, Michel. 1976. *The Will to Knowledge: The History of Sexuality*. Translated by R. Hurley. New York: Penguin.

———. 1977a. "Nietzsche, Genealogy, History." In *Language: Counter-Memory, Practice: Selected Essays and Interviews*, edited by D. F. Bouchard, 143–164. Ithaca: Cornell University Press.

———. 1977b. *Security, Territory, Population: Lectures at the Collège de France 1977–1978*, edited by Michel Senellart. Translated by Graham Burchell. New York: Picador.

Fozdar, F. 2014. "They Want to Turn to Their Religion. But They Should Turn to Be Australians": Everyday Discourses about Why Muslims Don't Belong in Australia." In *Muslim Citizens in the West: Spaces and Agents of Inclusion and Exclusion*, edited by Samina Yasmeen and Nina Markovic. Farnham, U.K.: Ashgate Publishing.

Franklin S., and S. McKinnon. 2001. *Relative Values: Reconfiguring Kinship Studies*. Durham, NC: Duke University Press.

Friedman, Sara. 2010. "Determining "Truth" at the Border: Immigration Interviews, Chinese Marital Migrants, and Taiwan's Sovereignty Dilemmas." *Citizenship Studies* 14, no. 2 (April): 167–183.

———. 2015. *Exceptional States: Chinese Immigrants and Taiwanese Sovereignty*. Berkeley: University of California Press.

Friedman, Sara L., and Yi-Chien Chen. 2021. "Will Marriage Rights Bring Family Equality? Law, Lesbian Co-mothers, and Strategies of Recognition in Taiwan." *Positions* 29, no. 3: 551–579.

Funston, L. 2013. "Aboriginal and Torres Strait Islander Worldviews and Cultural Safety Transforming Sexual Assault Service Provision for Children and Young People." *International Journal of Environmental Research and Public Health* 10, no. 9 (September): 3818–3833.

Gaffney-Rhys, Ruth. 2011. "International Law as an Instrument to Combat Child Marriage." *The International Journal of Human Rights* 15, no. 3 (July): 359–373.

Gangoli, Geetanjali, and Melanie McCarry. 2008. "Criminalising Forced Marriage." *Criminal Justice Matters* 74, no. 1 (August): 44–46.

García, Angela. 2010. *The Pastoral Clinic: Addiction and Dispossession along the Rio Grande*. Berkeley: University of California Press.

Gerard, Alison, and Sharon Pickering. 2014. "Gender, Securitization and Transit: Refugee Women and the Journey to the EU." *Journal of Refugee Studies* 27, no. 3 (October): 338–359.

Gerber, Paula, Kristine Tay, and Adiva Sifris. 2017. "Marriage: A Human Right for All?" *Sydney Law Review* 36, no. 4: 643–668.

Gill, Aisha K. 2011. "Exploring the Viability of Creating a Specific Offence for Forced Marriage in England and Wales: Report on Findings." University of Roehampton. http://www.endthefear.co.uk/wp-content/uploads/2010/06/Forced-Marriage-Legislation_Report-of-Findings.pdf.

Gill, Aisha K., and Avtar Brah. 2013. "Interrogating Cultural Narratives about 'Honour'-Based Violence." *European Journal of Women's Studies* 2, no. 1 (November): 72–86.

Gill, Aisha K., and Trishima Mitra-Kahn. 2012. "Modernising the Other: Assessing the Ideological Underpinnings of the Policy Discourse on Forced Marriage in the UK." *Policy & Politics* 40, no. 1 (January): 104–119.

Giordano, Cristina. 2014. *Migrants in Translation: Caring and the Logics of Difference in Contemporary Italy*. Berkeley: University of California Press.

Girls Not Brides. 2022. "About Child Marriage." https://www.girlsnotbrides.org/about-child-marriage/.

Goldfarb, Kathryn E. 2021. "Parental Rights and the Temporality of Attachment: Law, Kinship, and Child Welfare in Japan." *Positions* 29, no. 3 (August): 469–493.

Goodmark, Leigh. 2018. *Decriminalizing Domestic Violence: A Balanced Policy Approach to Intimate Partner Violence*. Berkeley: University of California Press.

———. 2023. "Criminalizing Survival." *Inquest: A Decarceral Brainstorm*, February 2, 2023. https://inquest.org/criminalizing-survival/.

Good Shepherd Australia/New Zealand. 2018. "Statement on Child, Early and Forced Marriage: Australia Commission on the Status of Women (CSW62)." Accessed December 10, 2019, https://www.goodshep.org.au/media/2046/forced-marriage-intl-advocacy-csw-statement-for-gs-geneva-final-20180223.pdf.

Gorrey, Meghan. 2017. "Sabah Al-Mdwali's Murder Laid Bare Domestic Violence Struggles for Migrant Women." *Sydney Morning Herald*, September 1, 2017. https://www.smh.com.au/national/act/sabah-almdwalis-murder-laid-bare-domestic-violence-struggles-for-migrant-women-20170818-gxznh7.html.

Gouda, Frances. 2008. "Immigration and Identity Politics in a Postcolonial World: Review of Recalling the Indies: Colonial Culture & Postcolonial Identities." *The Asia Pacific Journal of Anthropology* 9, no. 4 (December): 363–371.

Green, V. 1972. "Comments on Charles Valentine, "Racism and Recent Anthropology of U.S. Blacks." *Human Organization* 31, no. 1 (Spring): 99–102.

Grewal, Inderpal. 2013. "Outsourcing Patriarchy: Feminist Encounters, Transnational Mediations, and the Crime of 'Honour Killings.'" *International Feminist Journal of Politics* 15, no. 1 (March): 1–19.

Gribaldo, Alessandra. 2014. "The Paradoxical Victim: Intimate Violence Narratives on Trial in Italy." *American Ethnologist* 41, no. 4 (November): 743–756.

Grosz, Elizabeth. 1994. *Volatile Bodies: Toward a Corporeal Feminism*. Bloomington: Indiana University Press.

Gupta, Akhil. 2012. *Red Tape: Bureaucracy, Structural Violence, and Poverty in India*. Durham, NC: Duke University Press.

Gusciute, Egle, Peter Mühlau, and Richard Layte. 2020. "All Welcome Here? Attitudes Towards Muslim Migrants in Europe." *Ethnic and Racial Studies* 37, no. 13 (December): 149–165.

Gusterson, Hugh. 1997. "Studying up Revisited." *PoLAR: Political and Legal Anthropology Review* 20, no. 1 (May): 114–119.

Gutmann, Amy. 1994. "Introduction." In *Multiculturalism: Examining the Politics of Recognition*, edited by Amy Gutmann, 3–24. Princeton: Princeton University Press.

Hage, Ghassan. 2000. *White Nation: Fantasies of White Supremacy in a Multicultural Society*. Annandale (NSW) Australia: Routledge.

———. 2011. "Multiculturalism and the Ungovernable Muslim." In *Essays on Muslims & Multiculturalism*, edited by Raymond Gaita, 155–186. Melbourne: Text Publishing.

Hale, Charles R. 2002. "Does Multiculturalism Menace? Governance, Cultural Rights and the Politics of Identity in Guatemala." *Journal of Latin American Studies* 34, no. 3: 485–524.

———. 2008. *Engaging Contradictions: Theory, Politics, and Methods of Activist Scholarship*. Berkeley: University of California Press.

Hamzeh, Manal. 2017. "FIFA's Double Hijabophobia: A Colonialist and Islamist Alliance Racializing Muslim Women Soccer Players." *Women's Studies International Forum* 63: 11–16.

Harrison, Jill Lindsey, and Sarah E. Lloyd. 2012. "Illegality at Work: Deportability and the Productive New Era of Immigration Enforcement." *Antipode* 44, no. 2 (February): 365–385.

Herzfeld, Michael. 1992. *The Social Production of Indifference: Exploring the Symbolic Roots of Western Bureaucracy*. London: Routledge.

Hildebrandt, Carla. 2022. "Federal Police Fear Hike in Child Forced Marriage as Overseas Travel Restrictions Lift." *ABC News*, September 3, 2022. https://www.abc.net.au/news/2022-09-04/nsw-forced-marriage-police-fear-spike-as-travel-resumes-/101317834.

Hirsch, Asher Lazarus. 2017. "The Borders Beyond the Border: Australia's Extraterritorial Migration Controls." *Refugee Survey Quarterly* 36, no. 3 (September): 48–80.

Ho, Engseng. 2006. *The Graves of Tarim: Genealogy and Mobility across the Indian Ocean*. Berkeley: University of California Press.

Hodžić, Saida. 2009. "Unsettling Power: Domestic Violence, Gender Politics, and Struggles over Sovereignty in Ghana." *Ethnos* 74, no. 3 (December): 331–360.

———. 2013. "Ascertaining Deadly Harms: Aesthetics and Politics of Global Evidence." *Cultural Anthropology* 28, no. 1 (February): 89–103.

Holland, Dorothy, William Lachiotte Jr., Debra Skinner, and Carole Cain. 1998. *Identity and Agency in Cultural Worlds*. Cambridge, MA: Harvard University Press.

Hollinsworth, David. 2012. "Decolonizing Indigenous Disability in Australia." *Disability & Society* 28, no. 5: 601–615.

Howard-Wagner, Deirdre. 2013. "From Denial to Emergency: Governing Indigenous Communities in Australia." In *Contemporary States of Emergency: The Politics of Military and Humanitarian Interventions*, edited by Didier Fassin and Mariella Pandolfi, 217–240. New York: Zone Books.

Howe, Cymene. 2013. *Intimate Activism: The Struggle for Sexual Rights in Postrevolutionary Nicaragua*. Durham, NC: Duke University Press.

Hull, Matthew S. 2012. *Government of Paper: The Materiality of Bureaucracy in Urban Pakistan*. Berkeley: University of California Press.

Husain, Fatima, and M. O'Brien. 1999. "Muslim Families in Europe: Social Existence and Social Care." Report for The European Commission Directorate General. University of North London.

Hussein, Shakira. 2016. *From Victims to Suspects: Muslim Women since 9/11*. New Haven: Yale University Press.

———. 2017. "How We Can Really Help Women and Girls Escape Forced Marriages." *Crikey*, January 16, 2017. https://www.crikey.com.au/2017/01/17/islamophobia-will-not-help-end-forced-marriages/.

Hussein, Shakira, and Alia Imtoual. 2009. "A Fraught Search for Common Political Ground: Muslim Communities and Alliance-Building in Post-9/11 Australia." *Borderlands* 8, no. 1: 1–18.

Inda, Jonathan Xavier, and Julie A. Dowling. 2013. "Introduction: Governing Migrant Illegality." In *Governing Immigration Through Crime: A Reader*, edited by Julie A. Dowling and Jonathan Xavier Inda, 1–36. Palo Alto: Stanford University Press.

"International Covenant on Civil and Political Rights." 1966. United Nations Human Rights Office of the High Commissioner, December 16, 1966. https://www.ohchr.org/en/instruments-mechanisms/instruments/international-covenant-civil-and-political-rights#:~:text=Every%20child%20shall%20have%2C%20without,family%2C%20society%20and%20the%20State.

Ivy, Marilyn. 1995. *Discourses of the Vanishing: Modernity, Phantasm, Japan*. Chicago: University of Chicago Press.

Jabour, Bridie. 2014. "Women from Ethnic Minorities Ignored by Domestic Violence Strategy." *Guardian*, October 15, 2014. https://www.theguardian.com/australia-news/2014/oct/15/australian-women-from-ethnic-minorities-ignored-by-domestic-violence-strategy.

Jaffe-Walter, Reva. 2015. *Coercive Concern: Nationalism, Liberalism, and the Schooling of Muslim Youth*. Stanford: Stanford University Press.

———. 2019. "Speculative Policing." *Public Culture* 31, no. 3 (January): 447–468.

Jenks, Angela. 2011. "From 'List of Traits' to 'Open-Mindedness': Emerging Issues in Cultural Competence Education." *Culture, Medicine, and Psychiatry* 35, no. 2 (May): 209–235.

Johnson, Yvonne M., and Shari Munch. 2009. "Fundamental Contradictions in Cultural Competence." *Social Work* 54, no. 3 (July): 220–231.

Juanola, Marta Pascual. 2021. "'I Don't Want to Do This': Forced into Marriage, Ruqia Haidari Was Dead Two Months Later." *WAtoday*, August 9, 2021. https://www.watoday.com.au/national/western-australia/i-don-t-want-to-do-this-forced-into-marriage-ruqia-haidari-was-dead-two-months-later-20210803-p58fed.html.

Jupp, James. 2007. *From White Australia to Woomera: The Story of Australian Immigration*. Cambridge: Cambridge University Press.

Kabir, Nahid Afrose. 2015. "The Cronulla Riots: Muslims' Place in the White Imaginary Spatiality." *Contemporary Islam* 9, no. 3 (October): 271–290.

Kampmark, Binoy. 2017. "Securitization, Refugees, and Australia's Turn Back the Boats Policy, 2013–2015." *Antipodes* 31, no. 1 (June): 61–75.

Karim, Lamia. 2001. "A Kinship of One's Own." In *The Ethics of Kinship: Ethnographic Inquiries*, edited by James D. Faubion, 98–124. Lanham, MD: Rowman & Littlefield.

Karlsen, Elibritt. 2016. "Refugee Resettlement to Australia: What Are the Facts?" Parliament of Australia. https://www.aph.gov.au/about_parliament/parliamentary_departments/parliamentary_library/pubs/rp/rp1617/refugeeresettlement.

Karp, Paul. 2017. "Australian Government to Replace 457 Temporary Work Visa." *Guardian*, April 28, 2017. https://www.theguardian.com/australia-news/2017/apr/18/australian-government-abolish-457-temporary-work-visa.

Keck, Frédéric, and Andrew Lakoff. 2013. "Preface: Sentinel Devices." *Limn* 3. https://limn.it/articles/preface-sentinel-devices-2/.

Khan, Shahnaz. 1998. "Muslim Women: Negotiations in the Third Space." *Signs: Journal of Women in Culture and Society* 23, no. 2 (Winter): 463–494.

Khatun, Samia. 2017. "The Book of Marriage: Histories of Muslim Women in Twentieth-Century Australia." *Gender & History* 29, no. 1 (October): 8–30.

———. 2019. *Australianama: The South Asian Odyssey in Australia*. Oxford: Oxford University Press.

Khosravi, Shahram. 2017. *Precarious Lives: Waiting and Hope in Iran*. Philadelphia: University of Pennsylvania Press.

Kim, Mimi E. 2018. "From Carceral Feminism to Transformative Justice: Women-of-Color Feminism and Alternatives to Incarceration." *Journal of Ethnic and Cultural Diversity in Social Work* 27, no. 3 (May): 219–233.

Kim, Seung-kyung, and Sara L. Friedman. 2021. "Productive Encounters: Kinship, Gender, and Family Laws in East Asia." *Positions* 29, no. 3 (August): 453–468.

Korteweg, Anna C., and Triadafilos Triadafilopoulos. 2013. "Gender, Religion, and Ethnicity: Intersections and Boundaries in Immigrant Integration Policy Making." *Social Politics* 20, no. 1 (Spring): 109–136.

Kowal, Emma. 2008. "The Politics of the Gap: Indigenous Australians and the End of the Self-Determination Era." *American Anthropologist* 110, no. 3 (August): 338–348.

———. 2015. *Trapped in the Gap: Doing Good in Indigenous Australia*. New York: Berghahn Books.

Koziol, Michael. 2018. "Labour Vows to Crack Down on Child Brides and Forced Marriages." *Sydney Morning Herald*, June 7, 2018. https://www.smh.com.au/politics/federal/labor-vows-to-crack-down-on-child-brides-and-forced-marriages-20180606-p4zjv1.html.

Kreet v. Sampir. 2011. FamCA 22. Accessed October 1, 2017. http://www.austlii.edu.au/cgi-bin/sinodisp/au/cases/cth/FamCA/2011/22.html?stem=0&synonyms=0&query=kreet.

Laborde, Cecile. 2008. *Critical Republicanism: The Hijab Controversy and Political Philosophy*. Oxford: Oxford University Press.

Laird, Siobhan E., and Prospera Tedam. 2019. *Cultural Diversity in Child Protection: Cultural Competence in Practice*. London: Bloomsbury Publishing.

Lakoff, Andrew. 2008. "The Generic Biothreat, or, How We Became Unprepared." *Cultural Anthropology* 23, no. 3 (July): 399–428.

Larance, Lisa Young, Margaret Kertesz, Cathy Humphreys, Leigh Goodmark, and Heather Douglas. 2022. "Beyond the Victim-Offender Binary: Legal and Anti-violence Intervention Considerations with Women Who Have Used Force in the US and Australia." *Affilia* 37, no. 3: 466–486.

Lazzari, Alex. 2003. "Indigenous Struggles and Contested Identities in Argentina." *The Journal of Latin American Anthropology* 8, no. 3: 59–83.

Lea, Tess. 2020. *Wild Policy: Indigeneity and the Unruly Logics of Intervention*. Palo Alto: Stanford University Press.

Lenneis, Verena, and Sine Agergaard. 2018. "Enacting and Resisting the Politics of Belonging through Leisure. The Debate about Gender-Segregated Swimming Sessions Targeting Muslim Women in Denmark." In *Leisure, Racism, and National Populist Politics*, edited by Aarti Ratna, Erica Rand, and Daniel Burdsey, 59–73. London: Routledge.

Lévi-Strauss, Claude. 1949. *The Elementary Structures of Kinship*. Boston: Beacon Press.

Lewin, Ellen. 2004. "Does Marriage Have a Future?" *Journal of Marriage and the Family* 66, no. 4 (November): 1000–1006.

Lloyd, Jane. 2014. "Violent and Tragic Events: The Nature of Domestic Violence-Related Homicide Cases in Central Australia." *Australian Aboriginal Studies* 1: 99–110.

Madigan, Lee, and Nancy Gamble. 1991. *The Second Rape: Society's Continued Betrayal of the Victim*. New York: Lexington Books.

Madley v. Madley. 2011. FMCAfam 1007. Accessed October 1, 2017. http://www.austlii.edu.au/cgi-bin/sinodisp/au/cases/cth/FMCAfam/2011/1007.html?stem=0&synonyms=0&query=madley.

Maguire, Magdalena. 2014. "The Right to Refuse: Examining Forced Marriage in Australia." Good Shepherd-Australia/New Zealand. https://goodshep.org.au/wp-content/uploads/2020/12/right-to-refuse_final-report_v2.pdf.

Mahdavi, Pardis. 2016. *Crossing the Gulf: Love and Family in Migrant Lives*. Stanford: Stanford University Press.

Mahmood, Saba. 2005. *Politics of Piety: The Islamic Revival and the Feminist Subject*. Princeton: Princeton University Press.

Mai, Nicola, P. G. Macioti, Calum Bennachie, Anne E. Fehrenbacher, Calogero Giametta, Heidi Hoefinger, and Jennifer Musto. 2021. "Migration, Sex Work and Trafficking: The Racialized Bordering Politics of Sexual Humanitarianism." *Ethnic and Racial Studies* 44, no. 9 (March): 1607–1628.

Maira, Sunaina Marr. 2009. *Missing: Youth, Citizenship, and Empire after 9/11*. Durham, NC: Duke University Press.

Malkki, Liisa. 2010. "Children, Humanity, and the Infantilization of Peace." In *In the Name of Humanity: The Government of Threat and Care*, edited by Miriam Ticktin and Ilana Feldman, 58–85. Durham, NC: Duke University Press.

Mamdani, Mahmood. 2002. "Good Muslim, Bad Muslim: A Political Perspective on Culture and Terrorism." *American Anthropologist* 104, no. 3 (September): 766–775.

REFERENCES

Marcus, George E. 1995. "Ethnography in/of the World System: The Emergence of Multi-Sited Ethnography." *Annual Review of Anthropology* 24, no. 1: 95–117.

Masco, Joseph. 2014. *The Theater of Operations: National Security Affect from the Cold War to the War on Terror*. Durham, NC: Duke University Press.

Massumi, Brian. 2016. *Ontopower: War, Powers, and the State of Perception*. Durham, NC: Duke University Press.

Mehta, Uday S. 1990. "Liberal Strategies of Exclusion." *Politics & Society* 18, no. 4 (December): 427–454.

Menjívar, Cecilia, and Daniel Kanstroom, eds. 2013. *Constructing Immigrant 'Illegality': Critiques, Experiences, and Responses*. Cambridge: Cambridge University Press.

Merry, Sally Engle. 2016. *The Seductions of Quantification: Measuring Human Rights, Gender Violence, and Sex Trafficking*. Chicago: University of Chicago Press.

Miles, Matthew B., and A. Michael Huberman. 1994. *Qualitative Data Analysis: An Expanded Sourcebook*. 2nd ed. Thousand Oaks, CA: SAGE Publications.

Mitchell, Timothy. 2009. "Society, Economy, and the State Effect." In *The Anthropology of the State: A Reader*, edited by Aradhana Sharma and Akhil Gupta. Malden, MA: Blackwell Publishing.

Mitropoulos, Angela. 2015. "Interview with Matthew Kiem: Cross-Border Operations." *New Inquiry*, November 18, 2015. https://thenewinquiry.com/cross-border-operations/.

Mohanty, Chandra Talpade. 1988. "Under Western Eyes: Feminist Scholarship and Colonial Discourses." *Feminist Review* 30: 61–88.

Motta, Sara C. 2016. "Decolonizing Australia's Body Politics: Contesting the Coloniality of Violence of Child Removal." *Journal of Resistance Studies* 2, no. 2: 100–133.

Mottram, Linda. 2019. "AFP to Launch Forced Marriage Awareness Campaign at Transit Points." *ABC News*, October 14, 2019. https://www.abc.net.au/radio/programs/pm/afp-to-roll-out-forced-marriage-awareness-campaign/11604952.

Mountz, Alison. 2011. "The Enforcement Archipelago: Detention, Haunting, and Asylum on Islands." *Political Geography* 30, no. 3 (March): 118–128.

———. 2015. "In/visibility and the Securitization of Migration: Shaping Publics through Border Enforcement on Islands." *Cultural Politics* 11, no. 2 (July): 184–200.

Mouzos, J., and T. Makkai. 2004. *Women's Experience of Male Violence: Findings from the Australian Component of the International Violence against Women Survey*. Canberra: Australian Institute of Criminology.

Mulla, Sameena. 2014. *The Violence of Care: Rape Victims, Forensic Nurses and Sexual Assault Intervention*. New York: NYU Press.

Murray, Suellen. 2007. "'Why Doesn't She Just Leave?': Belonging, Disruption, and Domestic Violence." *Women's Studies International Forum* 31: 65–72.

Naber, Nadine. 2012. *Arab America: Gender, Cultural Politics, and Activism*. New York: New York University Press.

Nader, Laura. 1972. "Up the Anthropologist: Perspectives from Studying Up." In *Reinventing Anthropology*, edited by Dell Hymes, 284–311. New York: Vintage.

National Children's and Youth Law Centre (NCYLC). 2013. *End Child Marriage in Australia: Research Report on the Forced Marriage of Children in Australia*. Sydney, University of New South Wales.

Neave, Marcia, Patricia Faulkner, and Tony Nicholson. 2016. *Royal Commission into Family Violence Recommendations*. Victorian Government Printer, March 2016. http://rcfv.archive.royalcommission.vic.gov.au/MediaLibraries/RCFamilyViolence/Reports/Final/RCFV-Summary.pdf.

Nelson, Diane M. 2001. "Phantom Limbs and Invisible Hands: Bodies, Prosthetics, and Late Capitalist Identifications." *American Anthropologist* 16, no. 3 (August): 303–313.

Ochs, Elinor, and Lisa Capps. 1996. "Narrating the Self." *Annual Review of Anthropology* 25, no. 1: 19–43.

Olszewska, Zuzanna. 2015. *The Pearl of Dari: Poetry and Personhood among Young Afghans in Iran.* Bloomington: Indiana University Press.

Ong, Aihwa. 1995. "Making the Biopolitical Subject: Cambodian Immigrants, Refugee Medicine, and Cultural Citizenship in California." *Social Science and Medicine* 40, no. 9 (May): 1243–1257.

Oxford English Dictionary. n.d. "Sequester." https://www.oxfordlearnersdictionaries.com/definition/english/sequester.

Pardy, Maree. 2012. "Responsible Judgement: Forced Marriage, Culture and Feminist Responsibility." In *Responsibility*, edited by Ghassan Hage and Robyn Eckersley, 141–56. Melbourne: University of Melbourne Press.

Park, Lisa Sun-Hee. 2011. *Entitled to Nothing*. New York: NYU Press.

Park, Lisa Sun-Hee, Rhonda Sarnoff, Catherine Bender, and Carol Korenbrot. 2000. "Impact of Recent Welfare and Immigration Reforms on Use of Medicaid for Prenatal Care by Immigrants in California." *Journal of Immigrant Health* 2: 5–22.

Parliamentary Debates. 2012. House of Representatives. "Crimes Legislation Amendment (Slavery, Slavery-Like Conditions and People Trafficking) Bill." May 30, 2012. https://parlinfo.aph.gov.au/parlInfo/search/display/display.w3p;query=Id:%22chamber/hansardr/4a17e30d-c43b-48b9-83ed-4280fc00314c/0000%22.

Parreñas, Rhacel. 2001. *Servants of Globalization: Women, Migration and Domestic Work*. Stanford: Stanford University Press.

Patton, Chloe. 2018. "Racialising Domestic Violence: Islamophobia and the Australian Forced Marriage Debate." *Race & Class* 60, no. 2 (August): 21–39.

Pedraza, Franciso I., Vanessa Cruz Nichols, and Alana M. W. LeBrón. 2017. "Cautious Citizenship: The Deterring Effect of Immigration Issue Salience on Health Care Use and Bureaucratic Interactions among Latino US Citizens." *Journal of Health, Politics, Policy and Law* 42, no. 5 (June): 925–960.

Perera, Suvendrini. 2009. *Australia and the Insular Imagination: Beaches, Borders, Boats, and Bodies*. New York: Palgrave Macmillan.

Peterson, Kristin. 2009. "Phantom Epistemologies." In *Fieldwork Is Not What It Used to Be: Learning Anthropology's Method in a Time of Transition*, edited by James D. Faubion and George E. Marcus, 37–51. Ithaca: Cornell University Press.

Phillips, Anne, and Dustin Moira. 2004. "UK Initiatives on Forced Marriage: Regulation Dialogue and Exit." *Political Studies* 52: 531–537.

Phillips, Richard. 2009. "Settler Colonialism and the Nuclear Family." *The Canadian Geographer* 53, no. 2 (June): 239–252.

Pickering, Sharon, and Caroline Lambert. 2002. "Deterrence: Australia's Refugee Policy." *Current Issues in Criminal Justice* 14, no. 1 (December): 65–86.

Pickering, Sharon, and Leanne Weber. 2014. "New Deterrence Scripts in Australia's Rejuvenated Offshore Detention Regime for Asylum Seekers." *Law & Social Inquiry* 39, no. 4 (Fall): 1006–1026.

Porter, Libby. 2006. "Planning in (Post)Colonial Settings: Challenges for Theory and Practice." *Planning Theory & Practice* 7, no. 4 (March): 383–396.

Potaka, Elise, and Marcus Costello. 2017. "It Happens Here: Underage Forced Marriage in Suburban Australia." *SBS News*, August 1, 2017. https://www.sbs.com.au/news/the-feed/article/it-happens-here-underage-forced-marriage-in-suburban-australia/mcjmigom1.

Povinelli, Elizabeth A. 2002. *The Cunning of Recognition: Indigenous Alterities and the Making of Australian Multiculturalism*. Durham, NC: Duke University Press.

———. 2006. *The Empire of Love: Toward a Theory of Intimacy, Genealogy, and Carnality*. Durham, NC: Duke University Press.

———. 2011. *Economies of Abandonment: Social Belonging and Endurance in Late Liberalism*. Durham, NC: Duke University Press.

Povinelli, Elizabeth A., and Kim Turcot DiFruscia. 2012. "A Conversation with Elizabeth A. Povinelli." *Trans-Scripts* 2: 76–90.

Poynting, Scott, and Linda Briskman. 2018. "Islamophobia in Australia: From Far-Right Deplorables to Respectable Liberals." *Social Sciences* 7, no. 11 (October): 1–17.

Prattis, Georgia and Joumanah El Matrah. 2017. "Marrying Young: An Exploratory Study of Young Muslim Women's Decision-Making around Early Marriage." Australian Muslim Women's Centre for Human Rights.

Prentice, Kathy, Barbara Blair, and Cathy O'Mullan. 2016. "Sexual and Family Violence: Overcoming Barriers to Service Access for Aboriginal and Torres Strait Islander Clients." *Australian Social Work* 70, no. 2 (July): 241–252.

Quek, Kaye. 2012. "A Civil Rather Than Criminal Offence? Forced Marriage, Harm and the Politics of Multiculturalism in the UK." *The British Journal of Politics & International Relations* 15, no. 4: 626–646.

Quinn, Naomi. 1982. "'Commitment' in American Marriage: A Cultural Analysis." *American Ethnologist* 9, no. 4 (November): 775–798.

Qureshi, K., K. Charsley, and A. Shaw. 2012. "Marital Instability among British Pakistanis: Transnationality, Conjugalities and Islam." *Ethnic and Racial Studies* 37, no. 2 (September): 261–79.

Rachwani, Mostafa. 2020. "The New Australian Citizenship Test: What Is it and What Has Changed?" *Guardian*, September 17, 2020. https://www.theguardian.com/australia-news/2020/sep/18/the-new-australian-citizenship-test-what-is-it-and-what-has-changed.

Racial Discrimination Act 1975 (Cth) S. 9. 1975. https://www.legislation.gov.au/Details/C2016C00089.

Radford, Jynnah, and Phillip Connor. 2019. "Canada Now Leads the World in Refugee Resettlement, Surpassing the U.S." Pew Research Center, June 19, 2019. https://www.pewresearch.org/fact-tank/2019/06/19/canada-now-leads-the-world-in-refugee-resettlement-surpassing-the-u-s/.

Raheja, Natasha. 2022. "Governing by Proximity: State Performance and Migrant Citizenship on the India-Pakistan Border." *Cultural Anthropology* 37, no. 3: 513–548.

Ramsay, Janet. 2007. "Policy Activism on a 'Wicked Issue': The Building of Australian Feminist Policy on Domestic Violence in the 1970s." *Australian Feminist Studies* 22, no. 53 (June): 247–318.

Rana, Junaid. 2007. "Controlling Diaspora: Illegality, 9/11, and Pakistani Labor Migration." *Pakistani Diasporas, Culture, Conflict, and Change*: 51–74.

———. 2011. *Terrifying Muslims: Race and Labor in the South Asian Diaspora*. Durham, NC: Duke University Press.

Raphael, Angie. 2021. "Husband Murdered Bride then Told Her Brother to 'Come and Get the Dead Body.'" News.com.au, August 2, 2021. https://www.news.com.au/national/courts-law/husband-murdered-bride-then-told-her-brother-to-come-and-get-the-dead-body/news-story/c6840514d315d6a3778b4d79b35af0d7.

Rappert, Brian. 2010. "Making Silence Matter: The Place of the Absences in Ethnography" (Proceedings from the Ethnographic Praxis in Industry Conference), 260–273.

Razack, Sherene H. 1995. "Domestic Violence as Gender Persecution: Policing the Borders of Nation, Race and Gender." *Canadian Journal of Women and the Law/Revue Femmes et Droit* 8, no. 1: 45–88.

———. 2004. "Imperilled Muslim Women, Dangerous Muslim Men and Civilised Europeans: Legal and Social Responses to Forced Marriages." *Feminist Legal Studies* 12, no. 2 (October): 129–174.

———. 2008. *Casting Out: The Eviction of Muslims from Western Law and Politics*. Toronto: University of Toronto Press.

Refugee Council of Australia. 2022a. "Global Resettlement Statistics." Last modified October 31, 2022. https://www.refugeecouncil.org.au/global-resettlement-statistics/6/.

———. 2022b. "How Many Refugees Have Come to Australia?" Last modified October 31, 2022. https://www.refugeecouncil.org.au/how-many-refugees-have-come/2/.

———. 2022c. "Statistics on Boat Arrivals and Boat Turnbacks." Accessed October 2, 2022. https://www.refugeecouncil.org.au/asylum-boats-statistics/.

Remeikis, Amy. 2017. "Pauline Hanson Says Islam is a Disease Australia Needs to 'Vaccinate.'" *Sydney Morning Herald*, March 24, 2017. https://www.smh.com.au/politics/federal/pauline-hanson-says-islam-is-a-disease-australia-needs-to-vaccinate-20170324-gv5w7z.html.

Riles, Annelise. 2006. "Anthropology, Human Rights, and Legal Knowledge: Culture in the Iron Cage." *American Anthropologist* 108, no. 1 (March): 52–65.

Robbins, Joel. 2013. "Beyond the Suffering Subject: Toward an Anthropology of the Good." *Journal of the Royal Anthropological Institute* 1, no. 3 (September): 447–462.

Rose, Nikolas. 1998. "Governing Risky Individuals: The Role of Psychiatry in Regimes of Control." *Psychiatry, Psychology and the Law* 5, no. 2 (September): 177–195.

Rostami-Povey, Elaheh. 2007. *Afghan Women: Identity and Invasion*. New York: Zed Books.

Rowse, Tim. 1990. "Are We All Blow Ins?" *Oceania* 6, no. 12: 185–191.

———. 1998. *White Flour, White Power: From Rations to Citizenship in Central Australia*. Cambridge: Cambridge University Press.

Rubin, Gayle. 1981. "The Traffic in Women: Notes on the 'Political Economy' of Sex." In *Toward an Anthropology of Women*, edited by Rayna R. Reiter, 157–210. New York: Monthly Review Press.

Rytter, Mikkel, and Marianne Holm Pedersen. 2013. "A Decade of Suspicion: Islam and Muslims in Denmark after 9/11." *Ethnic and Racial Studies* 37, no. 13 (August): 2303–2321.

Saggers, S., and D. Gray, eds. 1991. *Aboriginal Health and Society: The Traditional and Contemporary Aboriginal Struggle for Better Health*. Sydney: Allen & Urwin.

Samar, Vincent J. 2007. "Throwing Down the International Gauntlet: Same-Sex Marriage as a Human Right." *Cardozo Public Law, Policy, and Ethics Journal* 6: 2–43.

Samet, Robert. 2019. "The Subject of Wrongs: Crime, Populism, and Venezuela's Punitive Turn." *Cultural Anthropology* 34, no. 2: 272–298.

Samimian-Darash, Limor. 2016. "Practicing Uncertainty: Scenario-Based Preparedness Exercises in Israel." *Cultural Anthropology* 31, no. 3: 359–386.

———. 2022. *Uncertainty by Design: Preparing for the Future with Scenario Technology*. Ithaca: Cornell University Press.

Santiago-Irizarry, V. 2001. *Medicalizing Ethnicity: The Construction of Latino Identity in Psychiatric Settings*. Ithaca, NY: Cornell University Press.

Sawrikar, P., and Katz, I. 2009. "Enhancing Family and Relationship Service Accessibility and Delivery in Culturally and Linguistically Diverse Families in Australia." *Australian Family Relationships Clearinghouse* 1, no. 3. http://www.aifs.gov.au/afrc/pubs/issues/issues3.html.

Sawyer, Suzana. 2001. "Fictions of Sovereignty: Of Prosthetic Petro-Capitalism, Neoliberal States, and Phantom-Like Citizens in Ecuador." *The Journal of Latin American Anthropology* 6, no. 1 (March): 156–197.

Scheel, Stephan. 2017. "'The Secret Is to Look Good on Paper': Appropriating Mobility within and against a Machine of Illegalization." In *The Borders of Europe: Autonomy of Migration and Bordering Tactics*, edited by Nicholas De Genova, 37–63. Durham, NC: Duke University Press.

———. 2018. "Recuperation through Crisis Talk: Apprehending the European Border Regime as a Parasitic Apparatus of Capture." *South Atlantic Quarterly* 117, no. 2 (January): 267–289.

Selby, Jennifer A. 2009. "Marriage-Partner Preference among Muslims in France: Reproducing Tradition in the Maghrebian Diaspora." *Journal of the Society for the Anthropology of Europe* 9, no. 2 (May): 4–16.

Service for the Treatment and Rehabilitation of Torture and Trauma Survivors (STARTTS). 2015. "Cultural Competence in Working with People from Refugee Backgrounds." Professional Development Workshop. https://scoa.org.au/wp-content/uploads/2018/05/Participant-Booklet_STARTTS-Cultural-Competence-Workshop_May2018.pdf.

Shariff, Fauzia. 2012. "Towards a Transformative Paradigm in the UK Response to Forced Marriage: Excavating Community Engagement and Subjectivising Agency." *Social and Legal Studies* 21, no. 4 (August): 549–565.

Sharma, Aradhana, and Akhil Gupta. 2009. "Introduction: Rethinking Theories of the State in an Age of Globalization." In *The Anthropology of the State: A Reader*, edited by Aradhana Sharma and Akhil Gupta. Malden, MA: Blackwell Publishing.

Shaw, S. J. 2005. "The Politics of Recognition in Culturally Appropriate Care." *Medical Anthropology Quarterly* 19: 290–309.

Shehabuddin, Elora. 2014. "Gender and the Figure of the 'Moderate Muslim': Feminism in the Twenty-First Century." In *The Question of Gender: Joan W. Scott's Critical Feminism*, edited by Judith Butler and Elizabeth Weed, 102–142. Bloomington: Indiana University Press.

Sherwin, Richard K. 1994. "Law Frames: Historical Truth and Narrative Necessity in a Criminal Case." *Stanford Law Review* 47, no. 1: 39–83.

———. 2017. "Law Frames: Historical Truth and Narrative Necessity in a Criminal Case." In *Popular Culture and Law*, edited by Richard Sherwin, 177–221. London: Routledge.

Shore, Cris, and Susan Wright, eds. 1997. *Policy Worlds: Anthropology and the Analysis of Contemporary Power*. New York: Routledge.

———, eds. 2003. *Anthropology of Policy: Perspectives on Governance and Power*. London: Routledge.

Siagian, Sandra. 2018. "Why Victims Aren't Coming Forward about Forced Marriages." *ABC News*, June 18, 2018. https://www.abc.net.au/news/2018-06-18/why-arent-victims-coming-forward-about-forced-marriages/9881834?smid=abcnews-Twitter_Organic&WT.tsrc=Twitter_Organic&sf192100163=1.

Simpson, Audra. 2017. "The Ruse of Consent and the Anatomy of 'Refusal': Cases from Indigenous North America and Australia." *Postcolonial Studies* 20, no. 1 (June): 18–33.

Sinclair, Hannah. 2019. "Airline Passengers Targeted in New AFP Forced Marriage Awareness Campaign." *SBS News*, October 15, 2019. https://www.sbs.com.au/news/article/airline-passengers-targeted-in-new-afp-forced-marriage-awareness-campaign/yssc2im3g.

Soto Bermant, Laia. 2017. "The Mediterranean Question." In *The Borders of "Europe": Autonomy of Migration Tactics of Bordering*, edited by Nicholas De Genova, 121–140. Durham, NC: Duke University Press.

Southall Black Sisters. n.d. "The Forced Marriage Campaign." https://southallblacksisters.org.uk/campaigns/forced-marriage-campaign/.

Sowey, Helen. 2014. "From an Emic Perspective: Exploring Consent in Forced Marriage Law." *Australian and New Zealand Journal of Criminology* 51, no. 2 (April): 58–74.

Special Taskforce on Domestic and Family Violence in Queensland. 2015. *Not Now, Not Ever: Putting an End to Domestic and Family Violence in Queensland*. https://www.justice.qld.gov.au/initiatives/end-domestic-family-violence/about/not-now-not-ever-report.

Spene, David B., and Paula Murray. 1999. "The Law, Economics, and the Politics of Federal Preemption. Jurisprudence: A Quantitative Analysis." *California Law Review* 87: 1125.

Stanley, Anna 2016. "Resilient Settler Colonialism: 'Responsible Resource Development,' 'Flow-Through' Financing and the Risk Management of Indigenous Sovereignty in Canada." *Environment and Planning A* 48, no. 12 (July): 2422–2442.

Stevenson, Lisa. 2014. *Life Beside Itself: Imagining Care in the Canadian Arctic*. Berkeley: University of California Press.
Stewart, Kathleen. 2007. *Ordinary Affects*. Durham, NC: Duke University Press.
Stoler, Ann Laura. 1995. *Race and the Education of Desire: Foucault's History of Sexuality and the Colonial Order of Things*. Durham, NC: Duke University Press.
———. 2010. *Along the Archival Grain: Epistemic Anxieties and Colonial Common Sense*. Princeton: Princeton University Press.
Stoler, Ann Laura, and Karen Strassler. 2000. "Castings for the Colonial: Memory Work in 'New Order' Java." *Comparative Studies in Society and History* 42, no. 1 (January): 4–48.
Strathern, Marilyn. 1991. *Partial Connections*. Walnut Creek, CA: AltaMira Press.
Sutton, P. 2009. *The Politics of Suffering: Indigenous Australia and the End of the Liberal Consensus*. Melbourne: Melbourne University Press.
Syrett, Nicholas L. 2016. *American Child Bride: A History of Minors and Marriage in the United States*. Chapel Hill: UNC Press Books.
Tahir, Madiha. 2019. "Violence Work and the Police Order." *Public Culture* 31, no. 3: 409–418.
Tahirih Justice Center. n.d. "Forced Marriage Policy." Accessed June 6, 2023. https://www.tahirih.org/what-we-do/policy-advocacy/forced-marriage-policy/.
Tapia, Ruby. 2020. "What Is the Carceral State?" Documenting Criminalization and Confinement: University of Michigan Carceral State Project. https://storymaps.arcgis.com/stories/7ab5f5c3fbca46c38f0b2496bcaa5ab0.
Tapia, Silvana Tapia. 2016. "Sumak Kawsay, Coloniality and the Criminalisation of Violence against Women in Ecuador." *Feminist Theory* 17, no. 2 (April): 141–156.
Taslitz, Andrew. 1999. *Rape and the Culture of the Courtroom*. New York: NYU Press.
Tate, Winifred. 2020. "Anthropology of Policy: Tensions, Temporalities, Possibilities." *Annual Review of Anthropology* 49: 83–99.
Tatz, Colin. 1972. "The Politics of Aboriginal Health." *Politics* 7, no. 2: 3–23.
Taussig, Michael T. 1999. *Defacement: Public Secrecy and the Labor of the Negative*. Palo Alto: Stanford University Press.
———. 2003. "Viscerality, Faith, and Skepticism." In *Magic and Modernity: Interfaces of Revelation and Concealment*, edited by Birgit Meyer and Peter Pels. Stanford: Stanford University Press.
Taylor, Chloë. 2018. "Anti-Carceral Feminism and Sexual Assault-A Defense: A Critique of the Critique of the Critique of Carceral Feminism." *Justice: Social, Criminal, Juvenile* 34: 29–49.
Taylor, Ian, Paul Walton, and Jock Young. 1973. *The New Criminology: For a Social Theory of Deviance*. New York: Harper Torchbooks.
Terrio, Susan J. 2010. *Judging Mohammad: Juvenile Delinquency, Immigration, and Exclusion at the Paris Palace of Justice*. Stanford: Stanford University Press.
Thai, H. C. 2008. *For Better or Worse: Vietnamese International Marriages in the New Global Economy*. New Brunswick, NJ: Rutgers University Press.
Theobald, Jacqualine Lee. 2011. "A History of the Victorian Women's Domestic Violence Services Movement: 1974–2005." PhD diss. RMIT University.
Throop, C. Jason. 2010. *Suffering and Sentiment: Exploring the Vicissitudes of Experience and Pain in Yap*. Berkeley: University of California Press.
Ticktin, Miriam. 2008. "Sexual Violence as the Language of Border Control: Where French Feminist and Anti-immigrant Rhetoric Meet." *Signs: Journal of Women in Culture and Society* 33, no. 4: 863–889.
———. 2011. *Casualties of Care: Immigration and the Politics of Humanitarianism in France*. Berkeley: University of California Press.
———. 2017. "A World without Innocence." *American Ethnologist* 44, no. 4: 577–590.
Tohidi, Nayereh E. 2007. "Muslim Feminism and Islamic Reformation: The Case of Iran." *Feminist Theologies*: 93–116.

Tonkinson, R. 2007. "Homo Anthropologicus in Aboriginal Australia: 'Secular Missionaries,' Christians, and Morality in the Field." In *The Anthropology of Morality in Melanesia and Beyond*, edited by J. Barker, 171–189. England: Ashgate Publishing.

Tsing, Anna Lowenhaupt. 2005. *Friction: An Ethnography of Global Connection*. Princeton: Princeton University Press.

Tuohy, Wendy. 2017. "Most Girls at Risk of Being Married against Their Will Are 'Falling through the Gaps." *Herald Sun*, January 21, 2017. https://www.heraldsun.com.au/news/victoria/most-girls-at-risk-of-being-married-against-their-will-are-falling-through-the-gaps/news-story/e714c49642b8a5f81d767de900fc6dda?memtype=anonymous&memtype=anonymous.

Uddin, Mohammad Shams. 2006. "Arranged Marriage: A Dilemma for Young British Asians." *Diversity in Health and Social Care* 3, no. 3: 211–219.

Unchained at Last. n.d. "Unchained at a Glance: Mission." Accessed June 6, 2023. https://www.unchainedatlast.org/unchained-at-a-glance/.

United Nations General Assembly. 1948. *Universal Declaration of Human Rights* (UDHR). 302.2: 14–25.

———. 1962. *Convention on Consent to Marriage, Minimum Age of Marriage and Registration of Marriages*. New York. November 7, 1962. https://treaties.un.org/doc/treaties/1964/12/19641223%2002-15%20am/ch_xvi_3p.pdf

———. 1979. *Convention on the Elimination of All Forms of Discrimination against Women*. New York. December 18, 1979. https://www.ohchr.org/en/instruments-mechanisms/instruments/convention-elimination-all-forms-discrimination-against-women.

United Nations High Commissioner for Refugees (UNHCR). 2022. *Global Trends: Forced Displacement in 2021*. June 16, 2022. https://www.unhcr.org/62a9d1494/global-trends-report-2021.

Victoria Museum of Immigration. 2017. "Immigration History from Afghanistan to Victoria." https://origins.museumsvictoria.com.au/countries/afghanistan/.

Victoria State Government. 2016. "Afghanistan-Born: Victorian Community Profiles: 2016 Census." https://www.vic.gov.au/sites/default/files/2019-08/Afghanistan-Community-Profile-2016-Census.pdf.

———. 2017. "Mandatory Reporting." Accessed June 1, 2017. https://providers.dffh.vic.gov.au/mandatory-reporting.

Vidal, Laura. 2016. "Forced Marriage Is Happening in Australia and We Need to Do Something about It." *Huffington Post*, August 3, 2016. https://www.huffingtonpost.com.au/lauravidalau/forced-marriage-is-happening-in-australia-and-we-need-to-do-something-about-it_b_9405022.html.

———. 2018. "Developing Innovative, Best Practice Solutions to Address Forced Marriage in Australia." *Report to the Winston Churchill Memorial Trust of Australia*. The Winston Churchill Memorial Trust.

———. 2020. "Rethinking Australia's Response to Forced Marriage Prevention." *Politics and Society-Monash University*. https://lens.monash.edu/@politics-society/2020/10/26/1381571/rethinking-australias-response-to-forced-marriage.

Vine, David, Cala Coffman, Katalina Khoury, Madison Lovasz, Helen Bush, Rachael Leduc, and Jennifer Walkup. 2020. "Creating Refugees: Displacement Caused by the United States' Post-9/11 Wars." Watson Institute for International and Public Affairs, Brown University. https://watson.brown.edu/costsofwar/files/cow/imce/papers/2020/Displacement_Vine%20et%20al_Costs%20of%20War%202020%2009%2008.pdf.

Volpp, Leti. 2011. "Framing Cultural Difference: Immigrant Women and Discourses of Tradition." *differences: A Journal of Feminist Cultural Studies* 22, no. 1: 90–110.

Walia, Harsha. 2021. *Border and Rule: Global Migration, Capitalism, and the Rise of Racist Nationalism*. London: Haymarket Books.

Wallach Scott, Joan. 2010. "Gender: Still a Useful Category of Analysis?" *Diogenes* 57, no. 1 (October): 7–14.

Watson, Irene. 2010. "In the Northern Territory Intervention: What Is Saved or Rescued and at What Cost?" In *Violence in France and Australia: Disorder in the Postcolonial Welfare State*, edited by Craig Browne and Justine McGill, 53–76. Sydney: Sydney University Press.

Weber, Leanne. 2006. "The Shifting Frontiers of Migration Control." In *Borders, Mobility and Technologies of Control*, edited by Sharon Pickering and Leanne Weber, 21–43. New York: Springer.

———. 2007. "Policing the Virtual Border: Punitive Preemption in Australian Offshore Migration Control." *Social Justice* 34, no. 2: 77–93.

Weber, Leanne, and Jude McCulloch. 2019. "Penal Power and Border Control: Which Thesis? Sovereignty, Governmentality, or the Pre-emptive State?" *Punishment & Society* 21, no. 4 (October): 496–514.

Wedel, Janine R., and Gregory Feldman. 2005. "Why an Anthropology of Public Policy?" *Anthropology Today* 21, no. 1: 1–2.

Wedel Janine R., Cris Shore, Gregory Feldman, and Stacy Lathrop. 2005. "Toward an Anthropology of Public Policy." *Annual Review of Anthropology* 600, no. 1 (July): 30–51.

Weissman, Deborah M. 2019. "The Politicization of Domestic Violence." In *The Politicization of Safety: Critical Perspectives on Domestic Violence Responses*, edited by Jane K. Stoever, 38–60. New York: NYU Press.

Wendt, Sarah. 2009. *Domestic Violence in Rural Australia*. Annandale, NSW: The Federation Press.

Wendt, Sarah, and Joanne Baker. 2013. "Aboriginal Women's Perceptions and Experiences of a Family Violence Transitional Accommodation Service." *Australian Social Work* 66, no. 4 (April): 511–527.

Weston, Kath. 1997. *Families We Choose: Lesbians, Gays, Kinship*. New York: Columbia University Press.

Wild, R., and P. Anderson 2007. *Ampe Akelyerneman Meke Mekarle: Little Children Are Sacred; Report of the Northern Territory Board of Inquiry into the Protection of Aboriginal Children from Sexual Abuse*. Darwin, NT: Northern Territory Government.

Wilson, Amrit. 2007. "The Forced Marriage Debate and the British State." *Race & Class* 49, no. 1 (July): 25–38.

Wilson, Dean, and Leanne Weber. 2008. "Surveillance, Risk and Preemption on the Australian Border." *Surveillance & Society* 5, no. 2: 124–141.

Wilton, Jo. 2015. "Forced Marriage Workshop Presentation to Community Workers." Anti-Slavery Australia.

Winter, Bronwyn. 2008. *Hijab and the Republic: Uncovering the French Headscarf Debate*. Syracuse, NY: Syracuse University Press.

"Without Consent." 2012. *ABC News*, March 28, 2012. https://www.abc.net.au/news/2012-03-29/without-consent/3933100.

Wool, Zoë. 2015. *After War: The Weight of Life at Walter Reed*. Durham, NC: Duke University Press.

Wool, Zoë, and Seth Messinger. 2012. "Labors of Love: The Transformation of Care in the Nonmedical Attendant Program at Walter Reed Medical Center." *Medical Anthropology Quarterly* 26, no. 1 (March): 26–48.

Woollacott, Angela. 2015. *Settler Society in the Australian Colonies: Self-Government and Imperial Cultures*. Oxford: Oxford University Press.

Worthing, Simone. 2020. "Setting the Captives Free." *Others*, September 25, 2020. https://others.org.au/features/setting-the-captives-free/.

Wundersitz, Joy. 2010. *Indigenous Perpetrators of Violence: Prevalence and Risk Factors for Offending*. Canberra: Australian Institute of Criminology.

Yanagisako, Sylvia J., and Collier, Jane F. 1987. "Toward a Unified Analysis of Gender and Kinship." In *Gender and Kinship: Essays Toward a Unified Analysis*, edited by Sylvia Yanagisako and Jane F. Collier, 14–50. Palo Alto: Stanford University Press.

Yasmeen, Samina. 2007. "Muslim Women as Citizens in Australia: Diverse Notions and Practices." *Australian Journal of Social Studies* 42, no. 1 (Autumn): 41–54.

Yeoh, Brenda S. A., Shirlena Huang, and Theodora Lam. 2005. "Transnationalizing the "Asian" Family: Imaginaries, Intimacies, and Strategic Intents." *Global Networks* 5 (October): 307–315.

Younis, Tarek, and Sushrut Jadhav. 2019. "Keeping Our Mouths Shut: The Fear and Racialized Self-Censorship of British Healthcare Professionals in PREVENT Training." *Culture, Medicine, and Psychiatry* 43 (April): 404–424.

Yurdakul, Gökçe, and Anna C. Korteweg. 2013. "Gender Equality and Immigrant Integration: Honor Killing and Forced Marriage Debates in the Netherlands, Germany, and Britain." *Women's Studies International Forum.* 41, no. 3 (November–December): 204–214.

———. 2020. "State Responsibility and Differential Inclusion: Addressing Honor-Based Violence in the Netherlands and Germany." *Social Politics* 27, no. 2: 187–211.

Zana, Famida. 2021. "Are Criminal Laws Enough to Protect Victims of Forced Marriage in Australia?" Right Now: Human Rights in Australia, July 23, 2021. https://rightnow.org.au/opinion/are-criminal-laws-enough-to-protect-victims-of-forced-marriage-in-australia/#:~:text=Despite%20the%20AFP's%20numerous%20attempts,have%20resulted%20from%20outside%20intervention.

Zeweri, Helena. 2017. "Encounters on the Shore: Geographies of Violence in Australia's Contemporary Border Regime." *Rejoinder.* https://irw.rutgers.edu/rejoinder-webjournal/borders-bodies-homes/294-encounters-on-the-shore-geographies-of-violence-in-australia-s-contemporary-border-regime.

Zeweri, Helena. 2020a. "Beyond Response and Representation: Muslim Australian Women Reimagining Anti-Islamophobia Politics." *Feminist Formations* 32, no. 2 (September): 111–135.

Zeweri, Helena. 2020b. "Managing Refugee Mobilities: Global Flows of Migration Deterrence Technologies." *Platypus: The CASTAC Blog*, June 17, 2020. https://blog.castac.org/2020/06/managing-refugee-mobilities-global-flows-of-migration-deterrence-technologies/.

Zeweri, Helena. 2023. "Configuring Arranged Marriage as a Foil to Forced Marriage in Multicultural Australia." In *Arranged Marriage: The Politics of Tradition, Resistance, and Change*, edited by Péter Berta. New Brunswick: Rutgers University Press.

Zeweri, Helena, and Sara Shinkfield. 2021. "Centring Migrant Community Voices in Forced Marriage Prevention Social Policy: A Proposed Reframing." *Australian Journal of Social issues* 56, no. 3 (February): 427–442.

INDEX

Pages in italics refer to illustrative matter.

Aboriginal Australians: displacement and assimilation of, 25–26, 53–54, 177n23; forced separation of, 58, 60, 176n17; Lloyd on trauma of, 62, 177n19; state policing of marriage and kinship of, 34, 57–58, 61–64, 176n15
Aboriginal Family Violence Prevention Legal Service, 64
Aboriginals Ordinance (1918), 58
Aboriginals Protection and Restriction of the Sale of Opium Act (1897), 58
Aborigines Protection Act (1886), 58
abuse, 58, 62, 63, 129–136, 176n18, 177n21. *See also* domestic violence framework; family violence prevention
Acts Interpretation Act (1901), 175n9
addiction narratives, 76, 120
Adelman, Madelaine, 127
Afghan immigrants and refugees, 8, 9, 82, 97, 102–103, 105–111, 113, 140–146, 157–158
Afghanistan, 15
Afghan-Soviet War (1979–1989), 9, 140. *See also* Taliban
AFP. *See* Australian Federal Police (AFP)
American Girl Bride (Syrett), 27
anthropology, as discipline, 17–18, 171n7. *See also* research methods
Anti-Discrimination Act (1977), 21
Anti-Slavery Australia (ASA), 46, 155
Anti-social Behaviour, Crime and Policing Act (2014), 40
Archambault, Caroline, 26–27
Arendt, Hannah, 178n5
arranged marriage *vs.* forced marriage, 171n6. *See also* forced marriage
assimilation, 23, 25–26, 53–54, 177n23, 179n1 (ch. 3). *See also* settler colonial state
Attorney-General Forced Marriage Information Pack for Community Organizations and Service Providers, *74–75*, 76
Australian Bureau of Statistics, 38
Australian Catholic Religious against the Trafficking of Humans (ACRATH), 46
Australian Citizenship Legislation Amendment, 94
Australian Criminal Code, 3, 12, 45

Australian Department of Families, Housing, Community Services and Indigenous Affairs, 46
Australian Federal Police (AFP): Counter-Terrorism, Trafficking, and Narcotics Unit, 46, 107; forced marriage cases and, 10, 105–111; scenario trainings of, 69, 94. *See also* policing and surveillance
Australian Immigrant and Refugee Women's Alliance, 45
Australian Institute for Health and Welfare, 38
Australian Institute of Criminology, 13
Australian Muslim Women's Centre for Human Rights (AMWCHR), 24, 45, 46, 180n9
Australian Red Cross, 46
Australia's National Research Organization for Women's Safety (ANROWS), 180n8
author's positionality, 17–18, 32–33

Baudrillard, Jean, 79–80
biopolitical project, 5, 102–105, 116–122, 123. *See also* forced marriage prevention
biosecurity, 14, 67–68. *See also* scenario trainings
border control, 10–12, 56, 57. *See also* Australian Federal Police (AFP); migration
Borneman, John, 27
Briskman, Linda, 53
British colonialism. *See* settler colonial state
Brown, Wendy, 155
bureaucratic rationality, 114
Burn, Jennifer, 43, 160

Caduff, Carlo, 67, 68
Calma, Tom, 20–21
Canada, 8
care regimes, 91–92, 123, 163
Castañeda, Claudia, 174n21
Castañeda, Heide, 99
Centre for Multicultural Youth, 48
child marriage prevention, 26–27, 41, 174nn2–3. *See also* forced marriage
child protection framework, 175n12. *See also* forced separation
Child Protective Services (CPS), 34–35, 73
child sexual abuse, 58, 62, 63, 176n18, 177n21

205

citizenship: coercion and "good," 18, 80; Indigenous peoples and, 62; institutional knowledge and, 25; kinship configurations and, 23, 24; legislation on, 94; marriage and benefits of, 26, 35; migrants and debates on, 115, 126, 154, 160; national values of, 33, 34, 52–53
clash of civilization theory, 39
Clifford, James, 171n7, 180n1
coercion, 162–163;—consent binary, 3–4, 10, 11; court cases on marriage, 42–43; into marriage, as term, 4. *See also* forced marriage; violence, overview
Commission on the Status of Women (CSW), 37
Commonwealth Department of Family and Community Services, 60
community empowerment trainings, 111–113
community ostracism, 182n11
confidentiality, 69, 102–104, 105, 112
consensus framework, 160–161
consent/coercion binary, 3–4, 10, 11. *See also* coercion
Convention on the Elimination of All Forms of Discrimination Against Women (CEDAW), 37–38, 174n2
Cook, James, 53
Coomaraswamy, Radhika, 38
Countering Religious Extremism initiative, 9
Counter-Terrorism, Trafficking, and Narcotics Unit (AFP), 46
CRAF (common risk assessment framework), 93
criminalization of forced marriage, 3, 12, 40
criminal justice system, 3, 6, 180n4, 181n7
Culturally and Linguistically Diverse (CALD), as term, 47–48
culturally competent social welfare, 2–3, 20–22, 47–52, 179n2 (ch. 3), 179n3 (ch. 4). *See also* social welfare system
cultural relativism, 16–18, 177n1
culture, framework of, 21, 125, 129, 135–136, 173n18

Dandenong, Australia, 1, 9, 23, 28, 77
Das, Veena, 5, 146, 150, 173n16
Debenport, Erin, 113
De Jong, Ferdinand, 104
demographics, 9–10
Denunciation Act, 99
Department of Foreign Affairs and Trade (DFAT), 10, 46
Department of Immigration and Border Protection, 46, 106, 107
detention, 8, 26, 45, 55, 95, 127, 132–133, 138, 148, 157
deviance, 13, 22–26, 154, 176n18
disclosure and vulnerability, 91–92, 97–101. *See also* risk
displaced persons, overview, 7–9, 25–26, 90. *See also names of specific nationalities*
dispositif, 6
domestic border control, 10–12
domestic space, construction of, 127–129, 140–146, 181nn4–5. *See also* familial relations

domestic violence framework, 38–39, 60–62, 181n8, 182n11. *See also* family violence prevention; violence against women framework
dress, 15, 147, 148, 149, 182n9
duress, 42–43, 124, 151. *See also* familial relations
Dustin, Moira, 43
Dutch East India Company, 53
Dutton, Peter, 52

Economic and Social Council (ECOSOC; UN), 37
economic insecurity, 27
educational systems and forced marriage, 27
Ellinghaus, Katherine, 176n14
The Empire of Love (Povinelli), 25
engaged universalism, 4
epistemologies: of storytelling, 123; of victimhood, 79, 80; of violence prevention, 3, 6, 7, 24, 79, 92, 100–101, 120, 122, 154
ethical dilemmas of forced marriage prevention work, 5, 7, 89–92, 96–101
European Union (EU) and forced marriage prevention, 40–41, 68

familial relations: construction of domestic space and, 127–129; deviance and, 22–26; love and, 84, 107, 140, 147, 149–150; Muslim women's opinions of, 124, 126; Sofia's struggle and reconciliation of, 140–146; transformation of, 129–136, 146–150; two sisters case and, 118–119. *See also* domestic space, construction of; duress; forced marriage
Family Law Act (1975), 43
family violence intervention order (FVIO), 76
family violence prevention: cultural competence in, 47–52; defined, 59–60; state intervention for, 61–62, 132–133, 177n22. *See also* abuse; domestic violence framework; forced marriage prevention
Family Violence Protection Act (2008; FVPA), 48, 175n11
Faubion, James, 68
federal funding for anti-trafficking programs, 46
feminist movements, 3, 33
figured identities, 78–79
forced marriage: *vs.* arranged marriage, 171n6; defined, 71; global discourses on, 37–39; as "hidden" problem, 13–15; information sheet on, 74–75, 76; Layla's understanding of, 129–136; in Massai community of Kenya, 26–27; as migration issue, 39–42, 52–53, 80–86, 158; as a "Muslim issue," 114, 172n9; as term, 3–4, 173n20. *See also* child marriage prevention; familial relations; marriage; violence, overview
Forced Marriage Educational Curriculum, 71
forced marriage prevention, 1–6, 12–13, 154–155; 2013 legislation on, 42–43; criminalization of, 3, 12, 40; ethical dilemmas of, 5, 7, 89–92, 96–101; legislative debates on, 43–47, 172nn9–10; reflections

on, 158–162; rescue logics and, 15–16, 57–58, 61–62; scenario trainings on, 68–80, 82–88; schools and, 89–91; sequestration in, 111–115; system construction of, 105–111; two sisters case of, 102–103, 105–111, 116–119, 180n5, 180n7; UN frameworks on, 37–38, 174nn2–3; update on, 155–158. *See also* biopolitical project; family violence prevention
Forced Marriage Unit (FMU; U.K.), 40–41
forced separation, 58, 60, 76, 129–130. *See also* child protection framework; sequestration
FORESIGHT program, 68
Foucault, Michel, 6, 24
Fourth Action Plan of the National Plan to Reduce Violence against Women and their Children, 50
Fourth World Conference on Women (1995; Beijing), 38

Gambaro, Teresa, 44
García, Angela, 120, 127, 181n6
Gill, Aisha, 161
global displacement, 7–9
Global War on Terror, 7–8, 14, 154
Goldfarb, Kathryn, 23
Goodmark, Leigh, 128
Grosz, Elizabeth, 116
Gupta, Akhil, 101

Hage, Ghassan, 91, 179n2 (ch. 3)
Haidari, Ruqia, 157–158, 172n12
Hale, Charles, 159
Halimi, Mohammad, 157
Harazi, Maged Al-, 50
Hawke, Alex, 94
Hazara Afghans, 9, 57, 77, 140. *See also* Afghan immigrants and refugees
Herzfeld, Michael, 92
"hidden" problem of forced marriage, 13–15. *See also* forced marriage
hijab, 15
Hinchey, John, 51
Hodžić, Saida, 125, 126
honor-based violence, 33, 38, 39, 50, 85, 110, 178n6. *See also* violence, overview
Howard administration, 58, 63
humanitarian reason, 18–19
human rights framework, 3, 37
Human Trafficking Investigative Team, 30
Huntington, Samuel, 39
Hussein, Shakira, 88

immigration policies, 7–9, 56. *See also names of specific legislation*
Indigenous peoples. *See* Aboriginal Australians
institutional knowledge, defined, 25
inter-cousin marriage, 71–72
International Covenant on Economic, Social, and Cultural Rights (ICESCR), 37
intimacy, 22–23, 25, 173n19
invisibility, 111, 115–116
Iran, 140
Iranian immigrants and refugees, 8

Iraq, 15
Iraqi immigrants and refugees, 8, 97, 129–136
ISIS (Islamic State), 172n9
Islamophobia, 15–16, 29
Istanbul Convention (2011), 40
Ivy, Marilyn, 116

Jadhav, Sushrut, 99
Jaffe-Walter, Reva, 7, 78
Jan, Sakina Mohammad, 157, 172n12
Journing, Rod, 12–13
Jupp, James, 53, 54

Kabir, Nahid, 15–16
Keating administration, 60
Keck, Frédéric, 86
Keenan, Michael, 43–44, 47
Kelly, Craig, 44
Kershaw, Reece, 176n12
kinship and deviance, 22–26
Kowal, Emma, 62, 99
Kreet v. Sampir, 42–43

Lakoff, Andrew, 86
Lebanese refugees, 76
Lewin, Ellen, 27
Lloyd, Jane, 60, 62
love in settler colonial states, 22, 25, 26, 44, 152
love marriage, 23, 27–28, 44, 152
Lughod, Lila Abu, 178n6

Mabo v. Queensland, 177n23
Madley v. Madley, 42–43
Manus detention center, Papua New Guinea, 8–9, 95
marriage: defined, 175n9; liberalism and, 26–28; settler colonial logics of, 24–25, 53–64; as social institution, 174n4; transformation and practices of, 146–150; UN on, 37, 174nn2–3. *See also* forced marriage
Marriage Act (1961), 41, 42, 43, 175n7
Masco, Joseph, 104
Massai community, Kenya, 26–27
Mdwali, Sabah Al-, 50
Messinger, Seth, 173n19
migration: anxieties on, 7–9, 56; forced marriage as specific problem of, 39–42, 52–53, 80–86, 158; punitive policies about, 7–9
Migration Act (1958), 94
Ministerial Council of Immigration and Multicultural Affairs (MCIMA), 47
miscegenation, 58–59, 176n15
Mitchell, Timothy, 101
modernization theory, 171n5
Morwell, Australia, 9, 28, 69–70, 73, 76, 79, 81
Mulla, Sameena, 92, 104, 181n4
Multicultural Centre Against Family Violence (MCAF), 48, 51
multiculturalism, as concept, 21–22, 47, 62, 91, 99, 125, 166, 171n6
Multicultural Liaison Officers (MCLOs), 10
Murray, Suellen, 59

Muslim migrant communities: honor-based violence rhetoric and, 85; rescue logic and, 15–16; state anxieties about, 3, 5, 90, 114, 172n9–10; Volpp on violence in, 178n2. *See also names of specific nationalities*
My Blue Sky (website), 156

narrative asymmetries, 113–114
Narre Warren, Australia, 9, 23, 28, 114, 140, 146, 148
National Action Plan to Combat Human Trafficking and Slavery, 46
National Action Plan to Combat Modern Slavery, 2020-2025, 46
National Children's and Youth Law Centre (NCYLC), 12, 175n8, 178n7
nationalist imaginary, 52–53, 55
National Plan to Reduce Violence against Women and Their Children 2010–2022, 60
national security threats, rhetoric of, 7–8
Nauru detention center, 8, 95, 148
Nelson, Diane, 116
Noble Park, Australia, 9, 28
nondisclosure, 100–101. *See also* disclosure and vulnerability
Non English Speaking Backgrounds (NESB) groups, 47
nonintervention, principles of, 96, 99–100
Northern Territory Intervention, 58
Not Now, Not Ever: Putting an End to Domestic and Family Violence in Queensland (report), 60

offshore detention centers, 8, 26, 55, 95, 138, 148, 157
offshore humanitarian program, 8
Ong, Aihwa, 90
onshore humanitarian program, 8
ostracism, 182n11

Pakistan: forced marriages and, 44, 102, 106–109, 117–118; refugees in, 76, 95, 137, 162
Papua New Guinea, 8
parabiopolitical sophiology, 68
Pardy, Maree, 17
parental love, 84, 107
penal convicts and Australian settler colonial state, 53–54
Perera, Suvendrini, 55
phantom-like figures, 111, 115–116, 180n10
Philip, Arthur, 53
Phillips, Anne, 43
Pickering, Sharon, 57
policing and surveillance, 9–10. *See also* Australian Federal Police (AFP)
policy, as term and concept, 153, 173n17
positionality of author, 17–18, 32–33
Povinelli, Elizabeth, 25, 26, 44, 152
Poynting, Scott, 53
pre-emptive logics, 14–15, 21, 55–56
present absences, 179n2 (ch. 4)
prevention work on forced marriage. *See* forced marriage prevention
prognosticators, 86

Project Respect, 46
Project Skywarp, 155–157
PTSD, 130–131

Quinn, Naomi, 27

Racial Discrimination Act (1975), 21
Rana, Junaid, 19
Rappert, Brian, 104
Razack, Sherene, 90
reapprehension of violence, 150–152
Reclaim Australia, 53
reconciliation of family, 140–146
refugee population statistics, 8, 28, 70, 172n8
refuge movement, 60
regimes of living, 173n15
Relationships Australia, 48
rescue logics, 15–16, 57–58, 61–62. *See also* family violence prevention; forced marriage prevention; victimhood, construction of
research methods, 1, 28–32, 102–103. *See also* anthropology, as discipline
Riles, Annelise, 105
risk, 69–78, 92–97. *See also* disclosure and vulnerability; scenario trainings
Roxburgh Park, Australia, 9, 28
Roxon, Nicola, 12, 44–45
Royal Commission into Family Violence, 50
Royal Commission on Human Relationships, 59
Rudd administration, 172n10

Safe Space, 51
Safe Steps, 48
Samet, Robert, 19
Samimian-Darash, Limor, 68
Saudi Arabia, 132
Sawyer, Suzana, 115
Scarlet Alliance, 46
scenario trainings, 65–80, 82–88
secrecy, 113, 141. *See also* nondisclosure
security logics, 67–69
Selby, Jennifer, 27
sentimental domesticity, 145
separation. *See* forced separation
sequestration, 111–115. *See also* forced separation
settler colonial state, 24–25, 34, 53–64, 154, 177n23. *See also* Whiteness
sexual abuse, 58, 62, 63, 176n18. *See also* abuse
Shakir, Mohammad, 175n7
Shariff, Fauzia, 160
Sharma, Aradhana, 101
Shepparton, Australia, 9, 28, 41, 114, 157
Sherwin, Richard, 180n11
Simmons, Frances, 43
Simpson, Audra, 25–26
simulacrum, 79–80
"Slavery, Slavery-Like Conditions and People Trafficking" section (Australian Criminal Code), 3, 45
social policy, 19–20

INDEX

social welfare system, 6; care regimes in, 91–92, 123, 163; culturally competent practices of, 2–3, 20–22, 47–52; security logics of, 67–69
Southall Black Sisters (SBS), 40
Southern Migrant Resource Centre, 48
Sowey, Helen, 161
spousal visas, 10–12, 42, 52, 95
Sri Lankan immigrants and refugees, 8
STARTTS (Service for the Treatment and Rehabilitation of Torture and Trauma Survivors), 21
Stevenson, Lisa, 91, 123, 173n14, 177n19
STPP (Support for Trafficked People Program), 46, 73, 103, 156, 179n1 (ch. 4)
suffering subject, 18–19, 86–88, 120. *See also* victimhood, construction of
Sunshine West, Australia, 9, 28
surveillance, 9–10. *See also* Australian Federal Police (AFP)
Sydney Morning Herald (publication), 51
Syrett, Nicholas, 27
Syrian immigrants and refugees, 97

Tahirih Justice Center, 41
Taliban, 9, 76, 95, 139, 140, 157–158. *See also* Afghanistan
Tapia, Silvana, 125, 181n2
Tate, Winifred, 65–66, 159
Taussig, Michael, 104
temporary work visa, 114–115
terra nullius, 177n23
terrorism, 39
Theobald, Jacqueline, 59
toleration politics, 171n6. *See also* multiculturalism, as concept
Torres Strait Islanders, 53–54
transnational border control, 10–12. *See also* Australian Federal Police (AFP); migration
trust, 97–101
truth regime, as concept, 6
Tsing, Anna, 4
Turnbull administration, 52, 53, 94, 114–115, 172n10
Tylor, E. B., 173n18

Unchained at Last organization, 41
UN Convention on Consent to Marriage, Minimum Age of Marriage and Registration of Marriages, 174n2
UNHCR (United Nations High Commissioner for Refugees), 8
UNHCR Global Trends: Forced Displacement in 2021 (publication), 8
United Kingdom, 40–41, 160
United Nations frameworks, 37–38, 174nn2–3, 175n6

United States, 8, 15; child marriage prevention in, 27, 41, 42; illegality and vulnerability in, 91–92
Universal Declaration of Human Rights (UDHR), 37, 174n1
U.S./NATO intervention, 9

Vamvakinou, Maria, 97
veiling, 15, 147, 148, 149, 182n9
victimhood, construction of, 65–67, 70, 79–80, 171n4. *See also* rescue logics; scenario trainings; suffering subject
Victoria Immigration Museum, 49
Victorian Forced Marriage Network (VFMN), 32, 33, 52, 103, 105–107, 109, 114, 115
Victorian Immigrant and Refugee Women's Coalition, 48
Victorian Immigrant and Refugee Women's Coalition (VIRWC), 45
Victorian Multicultural Commission, 50
Vidal, Laura, 12
Vietnam War, 8
violence, overview, 1–6, 137–140, 150–152. *See also* coercion; forced marriage; honor-based violence
violence against women framework, 33, 37–39, 85, 125, 175nn6–7. *See also* domestic violence framework; honor-based violence
visa reforms, 114–115
vulnerability: disclosure and, 97–101; of phantom-like figures, 111, 115–116; risk and, 69–78, 92–97. *See also* scenario trainings

wartime displacement, 7–9, 25–26, 90, 154. *See also names of specific nationalities*
Weber, Leanne, 57
Weissman, Deborah, 128
Wellness Springs, 48
Weston, Kath, 24
Whiteness: anti-racism and ambivalence to, 99; assimilation and, 23, 25–26, 53–54, 177n23, 179n1 (ch. 3); marriage conflicts and, 25, 27, 162, 178n2; state and social policies on, 47, 53–55, 57–58; violence and assumptions about, 62. *See also* settler colonial state
"Without Consent" (*ABC Four Corners* program), 44
Women's Information and Referral Exchange, 48
Wool, Zoë, 145, 173n19, 182n10
Woollacott, Angela, 54
World War I, 8

Yasmeen, Sameena, 16
Younis, Tarek, 99

ABOUT THE AUTHOR

HELENA ZEWERI is an assistant professor of anthropology at the University of British Columbia and faculty affiliate with the UBC Centre for Migration Studies. Prior to this appointment, she was an assistant professor of global studies at the University of Virginia from 2020 to 2022. Rooted in ethnographic methods and interdisciplinary critical theory, Helena's research focuses on migration, social welfare, and diasporic political life in imperial and settler colonial states. Her current project is an ethnographic and historical study of refugee rights advocacy in the Afghan diaspora, with a focus on Australia and the United States. She received her PhD in cultural anthropology from Rice University and MAs in Near Eastern studies from New York University and anthropology from The New School.

Available titles in The Politics of Marriage and Gender: Global Issues in Local Contexts series

Joanne Payton, *Honor and the Political Economy of Marriage: Violence against Women in the Kurdistan Region of Iraq*

Rama Srinivasan, *Courting Desire: Litigating for Love in North India*

Hui Liu, Corinne Reczek, and Lindsey Wilkinson, eds., *Marriage and Health: The Well-Being of Same-Sex Couples*

Sara Smith, *Intimate Geopolitics: Love, Territory, and the Future on India's Northern Threshold*

Rebecca Joubin, *Mediating the Uprising: Narratives of Gender and Marriage in Syrian Television Drama*

Raksha Pande, *Learning to Love: Arranged Marriages and the British Indian Diaspora*

Asha L. Abeyasekera, *Making the Right Choice: Narratives of Marriage in Sri Lanka*

Natasha Carver, *Marriage, Gender and Refugee Migration: Spousal Relationships among Somali Muslims in the United Kingdom*

Yafa Shanneik and Annelies Moors, eds., *Global Dynamics of Shi'a Marriages: Religion, Gender, and Belonging*

Anna-Maria Walter, *Intimate Connections: Love and Marriage in Pakistan's High Mountains*

Viktoriya Kim, Nelia G. Balgoa, and Beverley Anne Yamamoto, *The Politics of International Marriage in Japan*

Anne-Marie D'Aoust, ed., *Transnational Marriage and Partner Migration: Constellations of Security, Citizenship, and Rights*

Minjeong Kim and Hyeyoung Woo, eds., *Redefining Multicultural Families in South Korea: Reflections and Future Directions*

Erin E. Stiles and Ayang Utriza Yakin, eds., *Islamic Divorce in the Twenty-First Century: A Global Perspective*

Joanna Davidson and Dinah Hannaford, eds., *Opting Out: Women Messing with Marriage around the World*

Péter Berta, ed., *Arranged Marriage: The Politics of Tradition, Resistance, and Change*

Bruce Whitehouse, *Enduring Polygamy: Plural Marriage and Social Change in an African Metropolis*

Xiaoling Shu and Jingjing Chen, *Chinese Marriages in Transition: From Patriarchy to New Familism*

Helena Zeweri, *Between Care and Criminality: Marriage, Citizenship, and Family in Australian Social Welfare*